Romancing the Zombie

CONTRIBUTIONS TO ZOMBIE STUDIES

White Zombie: *Anatomy of a Horror Film*. Gary D. Rhodes. 2001

The Zombie Movie Encyclopedia. Peter Dendle. 2001

American Zombie Gothic: The Rise and Fall (and Rise) of the Walking Dead in Popular Culture. Kyle William Bishop. 2010

Back from the Dead: Remakes of the Romero Zombie Films as Markers of Their Times. Kevin J. Wetmore, Jr. 2011

Generation Zombie: Essays on the Living Dead in Modern Culture. Edited by Stephanie Boluk and Wylie Lenz. 2011

Race, Oppression and the Zombie: Essays on Cross-Cultural Appropriations of the Caribbean Tradition. Edited by Christopher M. Moreman and Cory James Rushton. 2011

Zombies Are Us: Essays on the Humanity of the Walking Dead. Edited by Christopher M. Moreman and Cory James Rushton. 2011

The Zombie Movie Encyclopedia, Volume 2: 2000–2010. Peter Dendle. 2012

Great Zombies in History. Edited by Joe Sergi. 2013 (graphic novel)

Unraveling Resident Evil*: Essays on the Complex Universe of the Games and Films*. Edited by Nadine Farghaly. 2014

"We're All Infected": Essays on AMC's The Walking Dead *and the Fate of the Human*. Edited by Dawn Keetley. 2014

Zombies and Sexuality: Essays on Desire and the Living Dead. Edited by Shaka McGlotten and Steve Jones. 2014

...But If a Zombie Apocalypse Did *Occur: Essays on Medical, Military, Governmental, Ethical, Economic and Other Implications*. Edited by Amy L. Thompson and Antonio S. Thompson. 2015

How Zombies Conquered Popular Culture: The Multifarious Walking Dead in the 21st Century. Kyle William Bishop. 2015

Zombifying a Nation: Race, Gender and the Haitian Loas on Screen. Toni Pressley-Sanon. 2016

Living with Zombies: Society in Apocalypse in Film, Literature and Other Media. Chase Pielak and Alexander H. Cohen. 2017

The Written Dead: Essays on the Literary Zombie. Edited by Kyle William Bishop and Angela Tenga. 2017

Romancing the Zombie: Essays on the Undead as Significant "Other." Edited by Ashley Szanter and Jessica K. Richards. 2017

Romancing the Zombie

Essays on the Undead as Significant "Other"

Edited by Ashley Szanter *and* Jessica K. Richards

Foreword by Kyle William Bishop

Contributions to Zombie Studies

McFarland & Company, Inc., Publishers
Jefferson, North Carolina

ISBN (print) 978-1-4766-6742-3
ISBN (ebook) 978-1-4766-3067-0

Library of Congress cataloguing data are available

British Library cataloguing data are available

Printed in the United States of America

McFarland & Company, Inc., Publishers
Box 611, Jefferson, North Carolina 28640
www.mcfarlandpub.com

From Ashley: To my mom, Barbara Soards Szanter, who may have thought me strange, but always thought me capable. You aren't here to see this, but this one's for you.

From Jessica: To Matthew, thanks for living with my sometimes zombie status.

To our families, for teaching us to love in a world that occasionally resembles a zombie apocalypse.

Table of Contents

Acknowledgments

Considering this was our first foray in the academic editing business, we certainly would not have gotten here without the immense support and encouragement from those around us. When we first started writing about sexy zombies and Millennials, we really only meant to get a short article into the *Chronicle of Higher Education*; we thank them for their rejection—without it, we would not have this book.

We would like to next thank Weber State University, our home institution, for their research resources as well as the smart, engaging individuals who work here. To Hal Crimmel, thank you for suggesting a collection of essays as we pursued the possibilities of where we could go with this idea. We thank our former professors and current colleagues who taught us to pursue these atypical research passions and to discover the ever-increasing borders of popular culture scholarship: Becky Jo Gesteland, Sally Shigley, and Julia Panko. Their mentorship during our graduate careers that transformed into the camaraderie we now share means the world to us. We thank Scott Rogers for creating courses like "Advanced Zombie Studies" that teach students and academia at large the inherent value in popular culture studies. We thank him for inspiring us to have serious, intellectual conversations about zombies, and to Weber State's English Department for encouraging professors to develop exciting, eye-catching courses for students who thought literary studies was only about Shakespeare. We believe that more universities should follow this example and take a chance on cutting edge courses that allow students to critically examine those cultural artifacts they love in order to become more invested critical thinkers. There is value in popular culture the same way there is value in our English canon, so we should encourage professors and departments alike to take those risks and broaden the scope of literary and textual studies beyond its current borders.

To our students, without whom we would not have noticed the generational shift in attitudes towards attractive zombies—you're kind of weird, but we like that about you. You are why we love to teach, and your ability to challenge our perceptions continues to be one of the reasons we walk into that classroom everyday. Most especially, we'd like to thank our fellow adjuncts in Elizabeth Hall 414 who very patiently listened to (what likely amounted to) hours of conversations about death, dead bodies, necrophilia, thanatophilia, zombie strippers, and other equally disconcerting topics: especially Patricia Eves Cieslak, Angie Kelson-Packer, and Logan Mickel.

Since a few essays of this book were written by contributors we met at the Southwest Popular/American Culture Association (SWPACA) conference, we want to make sure to thank those who continually work to organize one of the best regional conferences we've ever had the pleasure of attending. After transforming our short article into a full-fledged essay, we benefited from 2016's "Zombies and Sex" roundtable where we discussed these ideas with like-minded scholars fascinated by this growing trend.

The 2016 conference is also where we debuted our presentation "The Modern Zombie Makeover"—a crude version of our essay in this book. We want to thank all the people who attended the panel and helped create one of the most engaging conference Q&As we've ever witnessed, let alone been a part of. One of the individuals in that room, Kyle William Bishop, has been a great friend and supporter of our work (even though our opinions consistently differ when it comes to zombies). His body of scholarship, which we admit features in this text, opened the door for a new guard of zombie scholars—especially those in this volume who we hope to see more work from in the future.

We would like to take the time to thank all of our contributors who helped bring this volume to fruition. While we've only met a few of you in person, it has been a privilege to work with you throughout the creation of these essays and this text as a whole. You fully committed to the writing and revision process—making our job as editors more streamlined than we could have hoped. And a special thank you for being so diligent about responding to emails! We all know how spotty academics can be about emails. To Joshua White, your talent amazes us, and we thank you.

Though we took the opportunity to thank our families, we wanted to elaborate on their help, love, and support. Ashley would like to thank her sisters, Stephanie and Katy, who may mock her scholarly interests in the undead but still talk about their zombie-loving sister with endearing curiosity. You make my life better by just being in it, and your support means the world to me. To my aunt, Arline and my dad, Robert, thank you both for your support of my work.

Jessica would like to thank her family for helping her to live life appreciating all the small and significant details. If it was not for early morning car rides with her father analyzing rock'n'roll songs for their lyrical significance and her mother's love of reading (From *Cherry Ames: Student Nurse* to *Persuasion*), she probably would not have paid as much attention to the English language. I am so grateful for the lessons you taught me about the importance of the words on the page. To my siblings (Joseph, Laura, and Ethan), I love you more than I can say. Thank you for being amazing, smart, and engaging people who push me to learn something new every day. To Matt, I could not have done this without your support; you are such a wonderful partner. I am so glad I chose you.

Without the support of our families, the book you hold in your hands would not be possible.

Foreword

Kyle William Bishop

Zombies, man.

We used to know what they were, back when the world was a simpler place. The dead risen from their graves to relentlessly assault the living. Hungry for brains, but often for more, they pursued their human prey with myopic relentlessness, ignoring all else but the sweet, juicy promise of soft flesh and hot blood. Voracious eating machines, zombies served no purpose beyond their own instinctual, animal desires. An instinct to consume, to consume at all costs and without satisfaction.

Then the academics got involved.

Suddenly, the zombie was more than just the star of a host of B-reel movies and drive-in schlock. They became the oppressed masses, the remnants of a racist, domineering colonial ideology. The Haitian zombies were unburied, thrust into the light of day as the original walking dead terrors, tragic victims of curses, black magic, and, later, extraterrestrial science, forced to labor in the sugar fields or to act as the unwilling soldiers in racial or interplanetary warfare. These zombies were to be feared, yes, but only inasmuch as they were also to be pitied.

But at least we could all agree on one irrevocable, undebatable constant in the lore: zombies had no agency. Although their dress and sometimes mannerisms often marked them as individuals, as distinct cogs in a mighty zombie machine, those parts of the overwhelming horde were *not* subjects, did *not* possess individual consciousness. The zombie curse or plague or infection destroyed the higher, human brain functions, reducing the body to little more than an instinctual automaton, a machine operating on a kind of Darwinian autopilot that lacked any self-awareness or sense of self-preservation or subjective personality. These creatures, unlike their undead kin (particularly vampires), lost their individual minds, either upon death or reanimation, to become part of a hive mind, a collective, whether zombie or ghoul or somnambulist or Borg. That was one of the things that made zombies so frightening—you couldn't reason with zombies, you couldn't frighten zombies, you couldn't bribe zombies. They just came and came and came until you were dead, dismembered, or one of them.

Of course, Darwin's laws apply to fantastic species just as they do those in the biological world. The zombie, left untouched and unchanged for decades, was a doomed creature, one that would invariably die out and disappear from the dreamscape of the imagination were it not for evolution. Survival of the fittest in the horror genre is a concept often reserved for the beleaguered human protagonists, but that process must needs affect the monsters as well. As I have chronicled elsewhere,[1] the zombie, a creature that had begun to fade from popular view in the 1980s and '90s, was reborn in the twenty-first century, reanimated once again with new qualities, characteristics, and tendencies to make it relevant, timely, and frightening to a new generation and a new group of otherwise jaded horror fans. This evolved zombie was faster, more ferocious, and more durable than its prosaic kin, a creature born, more often than not, of science and human hubris. This super-zombie could exceed human endurance, break through flimsy fortifications, use rudimentary tools, organize as part of a purposeful collective, and even begin to think for itself.

With the inescapable tidal wave of the "zombie renaissance" crashing down on the cultural shore of the new century, the long-established protocols of the creature and its narrative subgenre have gone the way of a child's flimsy sandcastle. The one non-negotiable characteristic of the twentieth-century zombie, the lack of agency that bound the cursed zombie victim with the voracious zombie monster, has been washed out into the ocean of progress. The result is far more than just a Bub, *Day of the Dead*'s (1985) promising zombie ingénue, more than the tragic-comic zombies of *Return of the Living Dead* (1985). These new zombies are *agents*,[2] zombies that can think for themselves, can remember their human existence, can even begin to construct new (un)lives based on subjective wants and desires. And what does a newly risen monster want more than anything else? As Mary Shelley taught us so long ago—love.

Enter the romantic zombie. Zombies that want not only to taste the hot, juicy satisfaction of human flesh but also to know the carnal pleasures of that flesh. Zombies that long for human contact, for romance, for a personal connection. Or maybe just a date to the prom. These zombies, mostly male, have quickly become the perplexingly desirable objects of young girls' teenaged sex fantasies, the dreamy "bad boys" that top the list of "can't have" partners. The mysterious others that, despite their shambling walks and propensity to decompose, have suddenly become hotter paranormal romance commodities than the tried-and-true vampires. The zombie had already conquered the horror world of the twenty-first century, and they have now become the most eligible paranormal lotharios as well. And as with their older kin, there's nothing, apparently, we can do to stop them.

I have written extensively about the zombie cultural phenomenon, analyzing its development from Haiti to Hollywood to mainstream television. I have watched countless zombie movies (most of them bad), played disturbing video games, devoured graphically illustrated comic books, and even read zombie literature (a thing I once thought improbable at best). And in all of my research, scholarly pontifications, and rants on Twitter, I have consistently decried, criticized, and mocked the agentic zombie hero, claiming that "to depict a conscious zombie realistically in a serious narrative requires major alterations to the fundamental characteristics of the zombie" (*How Zombies Conquered Popular Culture* 14). Indeed, in my most recent book, I take particular delight in decrying the romantic zombie, devoting an entire chapter to my disdain for Jonathan Levine's 2013 film *Warm Bodies*,[3] a clever take on Shakespeare's *Romeo and Juliet* that nevertheless undermines the very essence of the zombie figure while also sending a very dangerous message to susceptible young women.[4] I have made it clear that I don't particularly enjoy stories about thinking "agent zombies," and I dislike romantic zombies even more. I was set in my ways. I had spoken. Fear my wrath.

And then Ashley Szanter and Jessica K. Richards came into my world. They brashly contradicted my outdated opinions, openly challenging my established thesis regarding the romantic zombie at the Southwest Popular and American Culture Association conference in Albuquerque in a session on the next generation of zombies, a session I was fortunate to attend. And then, amazingly, they asked *me* to help them further their research. They asked for *my* feedback on their paper. The paper in which they attacked *my* thesis. The nerve, I say!

Through their diligent efforts, Szanter and Richards gathered other, like-minded scholars and fans to assemble a collection of essays on agentic and romantic zombies, essays that challenge the approach of more traditional scholars, such as myself, with new ideas, insights, and arguments that engage more willingly with new, Millennial concerns. These theorists not only embrace the narratives of new zombie texts—such as *Warm Bodies*, the films *Fido* (2006) and *Life After Beth* (2014), the television serials *In the Flesh* (2013–14) and *iZombie* (2015–), and mash-up novels such as *Pride and Prejudice and Zombies* (2009)—but they also reexamine those treasured zombie tales of the past century. Their efforts have resulted in the volume of essays you now hold in your hands. New and timely essays presenting new and valuable scholarship on this new and dynamic kind of zombie. And here *I* am, slightly baffled, writing the foreword to that collection. In other words, Szanter and Richards are *right*.

This collection represents an important contribution to the growing body of zombie scholarship, demonstrating the value of taking sentient, agentic, and romantic zombie figures and narratives seriously and examining the kind of cultural work they are performing. While scholars such as myself might continue to kick against the pricks of these new developments in the zombie tradition, it remains, nonetheless, an essential and progressive part of the zombies' evolution as monstrous metaphors for twenty-first century living. In some ways, then, I must pass the torch of zombie studies to this new generation of Millennial scholars, enterprising academics who will push our understanding of the zombie and its cultural value through to the next phase of its development, production, and consumption. And maybe, just maybe, I'll come around and embrace the romantic zombie myself.

Notes

1. See my *American Zombie Gothic* (McFarland, 2010).
2. I use here Craig Derksen and Darren Hudson Hick's term for the sentient zombie (Derksen and Hick 15).
3. Based on the 2010 novel by Isaac Marion.
4. See *How Zombies Conquered Popular Culture* (McFarland, 2015), 163–179.

Works Cited

Bishop, Kyle William. *American Zombie Gothic: The Rise and Fall (and Rise) of the Walking Dead in Popular Culture*. McFarland, 2010.

_____. *How Zombies Conquered Popular Culture: The Multifarious Walking Dead in the 21st Century*. McFarland, 2015.

Derksen, Craig, and Darren Hudson Hick. "Your Zombie and You: Identity, Emotion, and the Undead." *Zombies Are Us: Essays on the Humanity of the Walking Dead*, edited by Christopher M. Moreman and Cory James Rushton. McFarland, 2011, pp. 11–23.

Introduction: Kissing Corpses and Significant "Others"

Facing Our Obsession with Apocalyptic Love

Ashley Szanter *and* Jessica K. Richards

Responding to the increased critical work in zombie studies, we stumbled upon this "deeply weird thing that freaked us right out" wherein the zombie became a desirable romantic partner. In a college writing section, a heated discussion broke out regarding the film *Warm Bodies* (2013). The film's use of necrophiliac themes was off-putting, as male protagonist and love interest R (Nicholas Hoult) is a zombie who exhibits clear signs of decomposition. One of the shocking points of discussion centered on R's and the female protagonist Julie's (Teresa Palmer) burgeoning relationship. He is, for all intents and purposes, a romanticized and, to some extent, sexualized corpse. Despite necrophilia being a nearly universal taboo, R's undeadness was not repulsive or even off-putting to these students. In fact, they rooted for the couple to overcome their odds and find love amidst the apocalypse. Floored by this discovery, we began our research into why there was such a disconnect between our revulsion and our students' attraction to love stories that incorporate blatant necrophilia. This research led to this collection of essays on zombies and romance.

Early in our research, we discovered other texts melding romantic narratives—including zombie/human, zombie/zombie, human/human—in apocalyptic settings. In 2009, Sony Pictures released *Zombieland,* a zombie romantic comedy, or zom-rom-com, in the vein of *Shaun of the Dead* (2004). While *Shaun* is fundamentally about experiencing the myriad responsibilities of adulthood as a sort of apocalypse, *Zombieland* adheres to tropes of the traditional romantic film. Instead of the typical obstacles facing archetypal romantic pairings in comedies (which inevitably lead to someone running desperately through an airport), the main characters of *Zombieland* learn to love again despite the dangers of the apocalypse. What is significant here is that much of the romantic formula remains the same despite the (hopefully for most) unromantic nature of the undead. Boy meets girl; their attraction to each other grows; and they fall in love. They face an insurmountable obstacle, which is miraculously surmounted. They achieve a happily ever after.

But happily ever afters do not usually occur in typical zombie films. Everyone dies, or is maimed, and we usually discover that human beings are worse than a horde of the undead. What results from a pairing of these two seemingly antithetical genres is a sort of cultural parody of both romance and zombies, an awkward amalgamation that does much to reveal how problematic their generic tropes are in modern culture. *Zombieland* is not the only work that subsumes these two genres to create a new hybrid. The zombie romance proliferates in a variety of zombie treatments, grappling varyingly with love and the undead—potentially in response to vocal critics of both the romance and zombie genres. This focus on romance places significant attention on individualization and identity, which is a new development within the zombie canon.

While intermingling love and the undead is not a new concept, it remains unstudied. Both the zombie and romance genres have largely gone without significant critical attention or consideration until relatively recently. This lack of interest seems to arise from several contributing factors: the romance and the zombie genres rely upon tropes to which the plots generally must adhere: a family member's inevitable turn into a zombie and the declaration of love at the end of the romance. Both genres have been accused of being cheaply made and mass-produced, and both have a propensity to appeal to the lowest common denominator in audiences. In other words, they are immensely popular. In the following section, we discuss the reasons for the critical dismissal of these disparate genres.

Zombily Ever After

It is, perhaps, important to discuss what, exactly, we mean by "romance." While romantic elements appear in a broad spectrum of literature, we are specifically discussing its contemporary treatments, and so for this collection, we think it is appropriate to explore this definition through the mediums that refer to themselves as romantic, the most significant of these being American romantic comedies and romance novels.

Traditionally, comedies contain a resolution in the form of a happy marriage. Romance typically honors the reader's contract, or expectation, of a happy ending. As Frantz and Selinger note in their introduction, the Romance Writers of America describe the essential components of a romance novel: "'Two basic elements comprise every romance novel' ... 'a central love story' and 'an emotionally satisfying and optimistic ending' in which 'the lovers who risk and struggle for each other are rewarded with emotional justice and unconditional love'" (3). These two ingredients are also responsible for another objection that prevents popular modern romance from attracting critical attention: the romance novel is generally seen as too fantastical to be considered serious literature. Injecting romance narratives with zombies (or, alternately, injecting zombie narratives with romance) allows the genre to combat accusations that romantic narratives are too idealistic or naive. Similarly, when zombie fiction appropriates the traditional comedic marriage resolution from romance, it infuses a much-needed levity into an often apocalyptic world.

Romance in the zombie genre is not new. The romantic subplot of Victor Halperin's 1932 film *White Zombie* set the stage for other quasi-romantic zombie films like William Beaudine's *Voodoo Man* (1942). Although romance takes a back seat in George A. Romero's *Night of the Living Dead* (1968), it remains an interesting part of John Rossi's *Return of the Living Dead* (1985–2005) series—particularly *Return of the Living Dead 3* (1993). While romance does appear in some of the more traditionally horrific zombie films, such as Danny Boyle's *28 Days Later* (2002) and Zac Snyder's *Dawn of the Dead* (2004) reboot, more deeply romantic subplots find their way into zombie comedies, like Edgar Wright's *Shaun*, Andrew Currie's *Fido* (2006) and Ruben Fleischer's *Zombieland*.[1] These evolutions of the zombie film veer away from the raw sexuality of *Otto; or, Up with Dead People* (2008) and *Zombies vs. Strippers* (2012). Instead, they begin to move towards showcasing romance, sometimes devoid of explicit sexuality, as a central concern in the zombie apocalypse space.

Digging Up Zombie Romance from Six Feet Under

The zombie genre emerges from rather humble origins. (In Hitchcockian fashion, George A. Romero famously used chocolate syrup as blood and roasted ham as the consumed flesh in *Night*.) Bad makeup, limited budgets, and poor special effects continue to plague the genre. Although canonical zombie works often transcend these limitations, it is hard to argue that cheesiness, kitsch, and an overreliance on buckets of blood do not pervade popular conceptions of the modern zombie movie.[2] A part of the much maligned horror genre, the "bad zombie film" remains part of a cultural expectation, and films, such as *Zoombies* (2016), in which animals at a safari park contract a disease which makes them undead (with the tagline "It's *Jurassic World* of the dead"), proudly uphold that tradition.

Because of such expectations, it has taken considerable effort to legitimize the cultural importance of the zombie in academic circles In *How Zombies Conquered Popular Culture* (2015), Kyle William Bishop declares "zombie scholars need no longer hide in the shadows or struggle to come up with legitimizing euphemisms for their chosen scholastic passions" (Bishop 1). Even the recent recognition of a "zombie renaissance," which includes innovative storytelling and high production values for "realistic" walking cadavers, as in the television version of *The Walking Dead* (2010–present), has not staved off questions about the cultural relevance of the zombie by the general public. We encounter this attitude frequently in our students and occasionally in our colleagues and peers. The early dismissal of these cultural products reverberates through the popular consciousness. At present, it is the task of contemporary academics to redeem the zombie genre through revealing its importance.

Because of the vast number of cultural products in both the zombie and romance categories, it is difficult to separate their popularity from the available texts. Perhaps the most logical bridge between these two genres is the paranormal romance, which branches off of the Gothic literary tradition.[3] While there is certainly a categorical difference between the romance present in the Gothic and modern romance narratives, which detail romantic relationships, there is some significant overlap worth mentioning here. Romantic relationships between people[4] in these stories often end with happy conclusions, the couple reunited, or some version of the marriage plot—a traditional Comedic[5] element.[6]

While scholars credit Horace Walpole's *Castle of Otranto* (1764) as being the first gothic novel, it is Anne Radcliffe who dominates the genre. Radcliffe is the mother of the "Female Gothic," Indeed, the Gothic was only rescued from critical obscurity because of its status as a women's genre (see *The Madwoman in the Attic* [1979]). This rescue is significant in the scope of this collection because of what it contributes to the growth of interiority and persistent self-examination within literature. This is not to say that strides were not made elsewhere, particularly by the Romantic poets who attempted to encapsulate the process of their minds experiencing nature, but that the origin of the gothic romance, which is tied to the growth of zombiism[7] (Bishop 13), is also an exploration of the self. As Jerrold E. Hogle argues, it is the image of the zombie horde's archaic and phantasmagoric nature that roots it within the gothic tradition; but, we argue that, contemporarily, it is also related to a desire for persistent self-examination.[8]

We see this tradition carried on today. While many malign zombie fiction's movement away from traditional representations of the zombie horde, calling the works which use zombie romance an insult to the genre, we view it as further exploring its generic roots. Just as the gothic uses weather and circumstance to externally illustrate character interiority, the physical expression of love and romance, for us, marks an exploration of the nature of being. The development of the agentic zombie is thus part of a natural progression, and so the use of romantic love is an extension of the exploration of the self and humanity.[9]

Many of our contemporary notions about the self, interiority, and self-actualization come to us from the history of various romantic traditions (i.e., Gothic romance, the Romantics, and romantic love). As inheritors of these traditions, we now alter our conceptions of romance as an act of pure interiority to include the sexualization inherent in 21st-century constructions of the romantic as both an emotional and physical act. Contemporary culture, particularly in the West, emphasizes sex as part and parcel of the romantic experience—a far cry from the sonnets of Petrarch. Because of this, we interpret the term "necrophilia" more widely; rather than simply the perverse act of sex with a corpse, we see "-philia" here broadened to include its original definition of "desire," thereby changing the term from "sex with corpses" to a "desire for the dead." This collection features several essays that deal very explicitly with sex and sexual desire. But, rather than taking us farther away from our goal to trace the evolution of zombie romance, we believe the discussions of sexuality in some essays function to physically illustrate the affection (perceived or real) between two characters instead of a base, detached expression of sexuality: romance and sex are one in the same.

While, on its own, modern fictional romance narratives represent a billion-dollar industry and are, by far, the most popularly consumed genre, and are generally ignored by both critics and academics (Regis). The romantic film shares the same fate as its fictive predecessor. Critics accuse these works of failing to thwart inherently patriarchal structures and fueling fantasies of a lifetime of domestic servitude. These concerns are not unfounded. *The Flame and Flower* (1972), which is widely regarded as one of the first popular romance novels, turns the rape of a young woman into an opportunity to achieve a form of domestic bliss. Despite these complaints, Sarah S.G. Frantz and Eric Murphy Selinger argue critics should take the opportunity to look beyond simply whether the modern romance is "good or bad for their readers" (5) and instead examine what these novels express as cultural products with a more comprehensive and intersectional approach (Frantz and Selinger). Clearly, popular romance has much to overcome if it is to be taken seriously within academic study.

Making Death and Dying Kinda … Hot?

Examined best in McGlotten and Jones's *Zombies and Sexuality: Essays on Desire and the Living Dead* (2014), popular culture's sexualization of the zombie retained a "bodies on bodies" appeal rather than one striking emotional connection and longevity. The sexualization of the zombie often hinges on the zombie as object. They are the ultimate form of objectification; there is nothing beyond the physical. While McGlotten and Jones's collection covered a much-needed gap in zombie scholarship, we wish to distinguish this collection from its predecessor. Rather than exploring the zombie as a purely sexualized body, this volume aims to explore the zombie as a consensual romantic partner, which necessitates personality, attraction, and, perhaps most importantly, agency. Modern romance requires consent in order to be acceptable to the public, and narratives deviating from this acceptability serve to critique cultural constructions of romantic love. Therefore, the traditional zombie monster no longer has a place when new narratives incorporate romance.

The essays in this volume are just the first attempt to grapple with how romance and zombies influence one another. Enmeshing these genres and their conventions produces works that engage viewers and prompt the creation of other, similar narratives. But we argue that this collection, while perhaps the first of its kind, should not be the last. As the romantic zombie evolves within our culture, we anticipate even more problematic and captivating stories that delve further into questions of identity, culture, and challenge how we engage with popular entertainment. As you read the essays in this collection, we invite you to consider how the romantic zombie speaks to our modern concerns as a culture and how academic investment in these two genres could transform the landscapes of both romance and zombie studies.

When romance becomes the defining factor of a zombie film, there are some necessary changes. Traditionally, the horde presents zombies as a faceless threat: one cog in a much larger machine of destruction. For romance to trump casual sexuality, there must be a non-negotiable presence of individual agency for both humans *and* zombies. The zombie must have choice and emotion in order to form the proper interpersonal connections underlying the modern romance genre. Jennifer Huss Basquiat's essay, "From Slavery to Sex: Commodifying Romance in the Zombie Film," presents the inherent connections between containment and romance when zombies cannot exercise agency—as those in *White Zombie* or *Fido*. The lack of zombie agency means humans can never truly engage in a consensual romantic relationship with the zombie creature. Instead, humans project their own emotion onto a being incapable of choice or reciprocation. This corruption of romantic expression results in zombie narratives that simultaneously subvert and reinforce cultural constructions of the ideal romantic partner. But that imagery cannot function appropriately in the romantic space.

As such, the zombie has undergone massive change on the individual level in order to facilitate the growing demand for zombie romance narratives. Scott Rogers presents an intriguing case of the attractive zombie love interest in his "Nobody Wants to be Un-Anything: *Pushing Daisies* and the Problem of a Kinder, Gentler Undead." Though not considered part of traditional zombie canon, Rogers argues that the show's careful avoidance of defining the "alive again" characters creates a problematic dynamic for viewers as it puts them in the uncomfortable position of rooting for necrophilia, or some strange iteration of romantic and sexual attraction to individuals who were, however briefly, dead. *Pushing Daisies* (2007–2009) creates a storyworld where the dead can be quirky and charismatic as well as physically attractive, which further complicates the viewer's desire to see the romantic leads live happily ever after.

Warm Bodies remains the seminal and *most* critically examined of recent zom-rom-coms. Paul Muhlhauser and Jack D. Arnal's essay, "Uncanny Valley Romance: *Warm Bodies, Her* and the Bits and Bytes of Affection," explores how the evolution of technological connection via social media compromises the formation of modern relationships. Through a comparative analysis of the films *Warm Bodies* and *Her* (2013), they argue that zombie romances present an alternative reality, devoid of the cyber connectedness of the modern age, which forces "meatspace" interactions. By removing the technical element, zombie romance narratives reinforce the importance of interpersonal, face-to-face connections in forming lasting romantic bonds. Muhlhauser and Arnal argue that, while *Her* reveals the dystopian horror of false romance in the age of artificial intelligence, *Warm Bodies* presents a preferable return to old fashioned (albeit heteronormative) courtship through meatspace interactions devoid of cyber distractions.

Adhering to traditional zom-rom-coms, much of the current zombie romance genre prioritizes heteronormative constructions of romantic love. In "'This place. It's never going to accept people like us. Never ever": (Queer) Horror, Hatred and Heteronormativity in *In the Flesh*," Connor Jackson approaches the cult television show through a queer lens to uncover how the new, individualized zombie contributes to the ongoing conversation of queer identity. While Jackson recognizes the show's attempts to combat homophobia and heterosexism, he argues that equating the queer community's struggles to those of the show's "Partially Deceased Syndrome Sufferers" is fundamentally flawed as it contributes to the further marginalization of the LGBTQ+ community's representation on screen.

Further challenging the complex influence of romance within highly patriarchal structures, Whitney Cox and Ashley Ruth Lierman explore a darker side of zombie/human romance in "The Idea of Love and the Reality of *Deadgirl*." *Deadgirl* (2008) chronicles two young men who stumble upon a Romeroesque female corpse restrained in an abandoned hospital. One of men, JT (Noah Segan), decides to use the "deadgirl" as a sex object—effectively raping her for the duration of the film. Cox and Lierman break down the film's deeply patriarchal and heteronormative narrative to expose the horror that lies beneath. Through an examination of sexual politics and the toxicity of Western masculinity, they investigate how romantic love can often present terrifying narratives addressing everything from culturally ingrained homophobia to the pervasiveness of rape culture.

Veering away from *Deadgirl*'s violence and aligning with more traditional rom-coms, both Joe Dante's *Burying the Ex* (2014), Jeff Baena's *Life After Beth* (2014), and Ben and Chris Blaine's *Nina Forever* (2015) present distinctly romantic narratives about zombie/human relationships. Fernando Gabriel Pagnoni Berns, Canela Ailen Rodriquez Fontao, and Patricia Vazquez provide an interesting angle on the evolution of romantic relationships in "Zombies Want Serious Commitment: The Dread of Liquid Modernity in *Life After Beth*, *Burying the Ex* and *Nina Forever*." Using the term "liquid modernity," they argue that modern relationships lack the stability of the past by relying on the mutability of contemporary bonds forged through social media. Zombie lovers, then, take on horrific significance by reinforcing the commitment behind eternal love bonds as they resist attempts at detachment by their partners. Fundamentally, the zombie's enduring presence harkens back to a time of stability and enduring bonds of love absent from the current landscape of romance for Millennials and their inheritors.

In the editors' essay, "The Sexy Millennial Reinvention of the Undead in *Warm Bodies* and *iZombie*," we explore the Millennial belief that we have been pushed to the fringes of our own culture: a belief which perpetuates the idea that we *are* the zombies. The zombie is our protagonist of choice. And, if we must see ourselves as zombies, zombies cannot be repulsive, decaying creatures; zombies must be desirable. Millennials are the first generation to not view the zombie monster as an "Other"—an obstacle to be faced and conquered. Rather, we view ourselves as the zombies facing a culture of humans who we do not recognize as our own.

While much of the generational analysis in this text focuses on Millennials, zombies also provide an outlet for the aging Baby Boomers. Simon Bacon, in "Memories of You: The Undying Love of the Zombie in *Harold's Going Stiff*," argues for the intergenerational importance of memory through romantic connections. Bacon's essay mirrors our own in his presentation of a film that places the protagonist, Harold (Stan Rowe), as representative of the Baby Boomer generation. The narrative connects his detachment to Millennials, portraying them as participants in the cybersphere but disconnected from the tangible world. Ultimately, Bacon argues that the film makes the case for love and romantic connection as the crux of remembrance and memory-making. Through emotional attachment, zombie and human characters regain lost memories and firmly anchor themselves to humanity.

Providing a darker approach to the zombie romance is Henry Hobson's *Maggie* (2015). Not your usual zombie film, *Maggie* chronicles the transformation of Midwestern teenager Maggie Vogel (Abigail Breslin) from human to zombie. In his essay, "The Zombie Apocalypse as Hospice Care: *Maggie* and the Zombie Turn as Cipher for Terminal Illness," William A. Lindenmuth investigates how *Maggie* expanded the zombie genre through an exploration of "the turn"—a common but largely unexplored trope in zombie studies. Lindenmuth argues that *Maggie* flips the common conflict of "kill (the infected) or be killed (by the infected)" on its head and instead suggests that those facing this transformation could enjoy the time they have left—including romantic love, which is best explored through Maggie's innocent relationship with the infected Trent (Bryce Romero).

Adopting a folksier and somewhat neo–Gothic tone, Burr Steers's *Pride and Prejudice and Zombies* (2016) remains the most recent filmic incarnation of the personalized zombie monster. Amy Carol Reeves's essay, "*La Petite Mort*: Death and Desire in *Pride and Prejudice and Zombies*," breaks down both the film and its novelized predecessor. Exploring how each sexualizes and fetishizes the young Bennet sisters, Reeves argues that the deadly skill of the sisters' violence, particularly Elizabeth (Lily James) and Jane (Bella Heathcote), mimics notions of death present in the etymological origins of "orgasm," thereby equating their combat expertise to sexual expression and fulfillment, while also juxtaposing how the novel and film play with the idea of violence and orgasm to sexualize Austen's original novel for a young adult audience. Furthermore, Steers's choice to transform the dashing George Wickham (Jack Huston) into a leader of the undead complicates the narrative's presentation of zombies as mindless, repulsive monsters in lieu of a more genteel, romantic alternative.

Because the zombie romance concept threads its way through the zombie genre from its inception to the present day, we question why the presence of romanticized and individualized zombies increased exponentially in post–9/11 zombie culture. George J. Sieg argues that the apocalyptic settings throughout the zombie genre not only heighten the stakes for human survivors but also allow audiences to participate in "disaster euphoria." Rather than encouraging savagery and violence, human responses to disaster often elicit altruism and camaraderie—a suspension of materialism which encourages community support and outreach. In "Disaster Utopia and Survival Euphoria: (A)Sexuality in the Zombie (Post)Apocalypse," Sieg asserts that several traditionally horrific zombie narratives best demonstrate this euphoric experience through classic romance and the cultivation of interpersonal affection.

Operating within this post-apocalyptic space, the reigning narrative in zombie studies is AMC's *The Walking Dead*. The show's dark and often nihilistic storyworld presents viewers with an original take on the zombie narrative. In creator Robert Kirkman's words, "the idea behind *The Walking Dead* is to stay with the character, in this case, Rick Grimes for as long as is humanly possible.... *The Walking Dead* will be the zombie movie that never ends" (Kirkman, *The Walking Dead Vol. 1: Days Gone Bye*). Whereas most zombie stories chronicle a finite period, Kirkman and AMC reimagined the genre by giving themselves infinite time to explore and develop the zombie space. As such, much of *The Walking Dead* focuses on interpersonal, often romantic, relationships between surviving characters. In Amanda Taylor's essay, "Love and Marriage in the Time of *The Walking Dead*," she explains, using psychological analysis, how stable romantic relationships have a positive impact on larger groups, which is particularly important when considering the dire circumstances of Rick's group of zombie apocalypse survivors. Looking at the dynamics of the show's most significant and long-lasting relationships, she uses both attachment and triangle/triangulation theory to assert that *The Walking Dead* argues that the development of romantic/love based relationships aids in everyone's survival, while privileging heteronormative monogamous relationships within vacillating gender roles.

It is undeniable that *The Walking Dead* put zombie television on the proverbial map. While some shows, like the relatively unknown *Zombie Hunters: City of the Dead* (2007–2014), predate AMC's series, the proliferation of the zombie on television resulted from *The Walking Dead*'s success. One of the newer and more popular zombie shows is the CW's *iZombie* (2015–present), an adaptation of Vertigo Comics's *iZOMBIE* (2010–2012). *iZombie* transforms the zombie genre by introducing viewers to a spectrum of zombification. When the zombie goes without brains for an extended period of time, they "turn" and become traditional, Romeroesque corpses: decaying, unstoppable monsters.

Deviating even further from traditional zombie characteristics, the refined zombies of *iZombie* prepare their brains as they would human meals. Most episodes incorporate a montage where the protagonist prepares a variety of brain-meals from sushi to lasagna. Through a food studies framework, Jennifer Rachel Dutch takes on *iZombie* by critiquing the show's gratuitous incorporation of brain cuisine in "Braaaiiinnnsss: The Recipe for Love in *iZombie*." Challenging typical presentations of the zombie's relationship with its food, Dutch argues that *iZombie* takes great pains to present restaurant quality preparations of brain matter as a means of anchoring the zombie characters to their human pasts. This new approach to brain preparation encourages romantic bonds through shared meals and cultural conformity.

While those in some popular circles remain hesitant to accept these romanticized zombies, we believe these newest iterations of the zombie monster provide audiences with fresh perspectives on an old creature. The zombie always represents some cultural anxiety, and romantic zombies suggest concerns about defined social roles, binaries, romantic connections, and the struggle to craft and perform identity. These authors grapple with romance's historical influence on the zombie as well as its evolved forms. While this collection opens a specific conversation about why romance is revolutionizing the zombie genre (or vice versa), we hope to open new avenues of zombie scholarship that acknowledge evolutions within available and upcoming zombie texts.

Notes

1. There are other films, like *Zombie Honeymoon* (2005), which embody horror without the horde and romance without the comedy's happy ending.

2. We recognize the artistry of much of the work being done in the genre, but many people categorize the zombie genre as tacky or cheap, and there are particular films that support the public's conclusions.

3. Bram Stoker's *Dracula* incorporates a hyper-sexualized, though not exactly attractive, monster. He gets a more attractive treatment in 1931's *Dracula*. Then we get the Anne Rice's *Interview the Vampire*, Joss Whedon's *Buffy the Vampire Slayer*, and Stephenie Meyer's *Twilight* that all result from these gothic roots.

4. We are of course aware that romance, and the courtly, the chivalric, and comedic predate the gothic novel, but we find that tracing the trajectory of paranormal romance contextualizes the significance of the zombie as a modern romantic partner.

5. We mean Aristotelian Comedy here.

6. See Ann Radcliffe's works, Jane Austen's gothic parody *Northanger Abbey*, Charlotte Brontë's *Jane Eyre*, and Bram Stoker's *Dracula*.

7. See Bishop's *American Zombie Gothic: The Rise and Fall (and Rise) of the Walking Dead in Popular Culture* (McFarland, 2010).

8. Elizabeth Moers argues in *Literary Women* (1976) that "nothing separates female experience from male experience more sharply, and more early in life, than the compulsion to visualize the self." She argues this working and reworking of identity lends the gothic much of its horror.

9. Although not a zombie narrative, the creature's education and his birth of self in *Frankenstein* illuminates this mirroring and exploration of identity so prevalent in the gothic. While we are not trying to prefigure Frankenstein as a sort of proto-zombie, as has been discussed at great length elsewhere, it is nonetheless true that he is reanimated flesh trying to understand what it means to be human, and he demands a partner to love.

Works Cited

Bishop, Kyle William. *How Zombies Conquered Popular Culture: The Multifarious Walking Dead in the 21st Century*. McFarland, 2015.

Frantz, Sarah S.G., and Eric Murphy Selinger, eds. *New Approaches to Popular Romance Fiction: Critical Essays*. McFarland, 2012.

Kirkman, Robert, and Tony Moore. *The Walking Dead, Vol. 1: Days Gone Bye*. Image, 2013.

From Slavery to Sex

Commodifying Romance in the Zombie Film

Jennifer Huss Basquiat

> You are what you consume, and as an organism and consciousness, you in fact become [both] a commodity and predator yourself—McGill 56

The theme of containment, in one form or another, threads itself through virtually every contemporary zombie film and/or television program. Most of these films assume some sort of apocalyptic event, explained or otherwise, and rightly focus on the management of the undead. However, as the trope of the zombie claims true staying power in our angst ridden 21st century, filmmakers are pushing the boundaries of onscreen human/zombie interaction. Instead of portraying zombies as thoroughly unattractive mounds of decaying and shuffling flesh, recent entries into the zombie genre such as *Warm Bodies* (2013) and *iZombie* (2015–present) have deftly suggested zombies as romantic partners, despite the obvious challenges of decomposition and the strong cultural taboo of necrophilia. "R," (Nicholas Hoult) the remarkably well-preserved and attractive zombie in *Warm Bodies,* leads a horde of his brethren who, "warmed by love, regain their ability to speak and feel" (Patrick 151). Liv Moore (Rose McIver), the plucky and appealing zombie protagonist of *iZombie,* makes a "conscious choice to be a force for good in the human world. All in all, a fine role model for our young people" (Genzlinger). In both of these cases (and discussed in greater length elsewhere), zombies regain their humanity through love and human interaction, despite their consumption of human brains. Rather than presented as undead creatures with no redeemable qualities, these 21st century "monsters have been transformed into misunderstood romantic heroes" (Buckley 215).

As appealing as these representations may be, romance and the necessary containment a zombie requires do not make agreeable bedfellows. Despite the fabricated appeal of the matinee-ready zombie, modern day, flesh-craving zombies require external restraint and control to ensure the survival of their human love interests. Moreover (and notwithstanding their romantic appeal in these films), these zombies are never understood to be fully realized individuals; rather, they are commodities to be controlled, idealized romantic partners waiting for the stroke of their master's brush to fully come into being. Whether lacking free will, craving flesh, or a combination of both, the reality for these films is the same: zombies, as objects of romantic affection, are not truly conscious. They are incapable of consent. They are cast only as objects, mirroring our collective desire to mold them into our own submissive sexual partners.

The suggestion that zombies lack free will is hardly revolutionary. However, many fans (and scholars, alike) often overlook the folkloric roots of the genre that inextricably tie slavery and commodification to the zombie figure. The very term, "zombie" derives from the Haitian Kreyòl *zonbi* by way of West Africa:

> In the West African language called Kikongo, the word *nsambi* means "god" or "spirit." … In Haiti, this word—generally rendered *zombie* [French] or *zonbi* [Kreyòl] and spelled *zombie* in English—persisted as a designation of spirit and in particular, of a certain kind of spirit: the spirit of a person who has been "captured" by a magician to force it to perform his bidding [Tann 71].

In Haiti, the process of zombification is generally understood to be the result of ingesting biological pharmaceuticals, which cause its victims to fall into a deep coma resembling death. While only *houngans* or *bokors* (Vodou priests) hold the secrets to the particular process, virtually no one in Haiti believes zombies are actually reanimated corpses. Rather, Haitian zombies are generally recognizable by their vague look and glassy eyes which places them in "that misty zone which divides life from death" (Métraux 282).

It is also worth noting that the Haitian zombie, with its seemingly aimless shuffle and complete disinterest in flesh, hardly resembles modern day zombies seen on screen since Romero's *Night of the Living Dead* (1968). Rather, Haitian zombies have been stripped of their free will, of their individual character and personality. Haitians generally believe that the human soul is divided into two parts: the *gros-bon-ange* (big good angel) and the *ti-bon-ange* (little good angel). While the *gros-bon-ange* is understood to control base biological functions, the *ti-bon-ange* is "that psychic element in the self that makes it possible to detach from the pressures of the world in order to make morally upright and responsible decisions. The ti-bon-ange is the conscience" (Desmangles 67). It is this *ti-bon-ange* that is harnessed by a Vodou priest, making the physical body a macabre puppet for whomever controls the strings.

Zombies in Haiti, therefore, are eternal slaves. For Haitian citizens, former slaves who won their independence from France by defeating Napoleon's army in 1804, the figure of the *zonbi* is more than a movie monster; it is the horrifying reality of undying and never-ending bondage. Nothing could evoke "as much horror as the idea that some unknown individual could cause you to die and then be reborn as a slave, not even capable of desire because your very soul had been stolen" (Tann 72). Laroche more pointedly argues that "It is not by chance that there exists in Haiti the myth of the zombi, that is, of the living-dead, the man [sic] whose mind and soul have been stolen and who has been left only the ability to work. The history of colonization is the process of man's [sic] general zombification" (47).

Curiously, within Haitian culture, it is explicitly illegal to "make" a zombie. Article 246 of the Haitian Penal Code reads: "Also shall be qualified as attempted murder the use against any person of substances that, without causing actual death, produce a more or less prolonged lethargic coma. If after the administering of such substances, the person has been buried, the act shall be considered murder no matter what result follows" (ANH). Given Haiti's history of enslavement as a French colony, it is hardly surprising that the forbidden nature of the *zonbi* has been codified into law. But how did such peculiar and context-specific folklore find its way into American popular culture?

In 1929, William Seabrook's sensationalistic travelogue, *The Magic Island*, was released in the United States. That Seabrook, himself a white American, had traveled to Haiti to "uncover" Vodou secrets of the exoticized Other was endemic of the day. Fueled, in part, by the American Marines' occupation of Haiti from 1915 to 1934, foreigners "became active in the business of representing Haitian culture, especially from the 1920s onward" (Largey 199). Most of these tales purported to be the result of "eye-witness" accounts (stopping short of ethnographic methodology), when, in fact, they fed the most egregious and racist stereotypes designed to impress gullible foreigners. Noted Haitian writer, Jean Price-Mars, remarks, "Thus, when foreign writers arrive in our country ... they do nothing but draw out absurd beliefs, the most abracadabraish remarks and put them into the mouths of authentic personalities to give their stories a veneer of truth" (155). Seabrook's tome also introduced the Haitian Kreyòl term *zonbi* into English for the very first time, "The *zombie*, they say, is a soulless human corpse, still dead, but taken from the grave and endowed by sorcery with a mechanical semblance of life—it is a dead body which is made to talk and act and move as if it were alive" (93). Eh, voilà, the zombie was born in America.

However, it was not just the introduction of the term, *zombie*, which struck fear into the hearts of white America. As Haitian sociologist, Laënnec Hurbon remarks,

> What Seabrook's *Magic Isle* presented to the American imagination for the first time was the theme of zombies—those apparently dead and buried, but then brought back to a semi-conscious state and put to work in the fields of sugar cane [sic]. This theme was to enjoy an extraordinary good fortune, but at the same time, it would end up being indissolubly linked with Vodou. The horror film was born in the United States, exploiting the theme of zombification, a practice that was forever after spelled Haitian "Voodoo" [sic] [188].

And so it was that the zombie entered the American landscape, not only with the aura of Vodou surrounding it, but entrenched in the dehumanization and commodification of the West African slave trade employed by French colonial powers.

Capitalizing on the popularity of *The Magic Island* and eager to profit from a burgeoning fascination with Vodou, *White Zombie* was released in 1932. This film,

> the first [zombie] horror film, found its scenario in Seabrook's 1929 publication. Madeleine, a white woman, debarks in Haiti and falls under the power of a magician, a great planter who possesses many zombies who are dedicated to work night and day in the sugarcane fields. Madeleine, transformed into a zombie by the planter who lusts after her, introduces the Western public to the horror of the Vodou system.... After the release of *White Zombie*, there was to be no truce in the production of the image of Vodou as the ultimate place of zombification [Hurbon 192].

On its face, *White Zombie* is also replete with various cultural critiques. Given its release in 1932, an allegory to The Great Depression cannot be overlooked. Skal writes, "The shuffling spectacle of the walking dead in films like *White Zombie* was is many ways a nightmare vision of a breadline.... Millions already knew that they were no longer completely in control of their lives; the economic strings were being pulled by faceless frightening forces" (168). Kee suggests that zombies in this film "represent a very real fear of the colonial master [while offering] a critique of both slavery and the abuse of the worker under the capitalist system," but the larger, implicit fear exposed by the popularity of *White Zombie* indicates a darker force is at work: the specter of race.

The very title of the film, itself, *White Zombie*, exposes cultural and racial anxieties. As Phillips so aptly argues, "zombies are one thing, but a white zombie is a sign of horror.... The source of horror is the fear, for whites, of a loss of sovereign physical and mental autonomy and/or fear of 'unnatural' servitude" (28). The real threat to white, American society becomes the fear that the tables may actually turn, that whites, through an exoticized and othered sorcery, will be forced to adopt the submissive, captive position of the African slave. The political and social realities of the time only compounded these fears. The previously mentioned (and lengthy) occupation of the United States Marines in Haiti from 1915 to 1934 provided a very specific backdrop to contextualize racial anxieties. More to the point, "voodoo [sic] zombie stories articulated White U.S. fears that an independent Haiti might threaten the U.S.'s economic, political, and sexual dominance over Blacks" (Hamako 108). Given Haiti's emergence as a sovereign nation through a Vodou-infused and successful slave rebellion, this fear carries particularly sharp teeth as it reinforces "both fear of Haiti as a black country and as a country with a non–Christian, African culture" (Tann 74).

Yet, within this racially and culturally charged context, romance (both its loss and attempted acquisition) emerges as a major plot point of *White Zombie*. Driving the action of the film, "Madeleine, the young protagonist of this precedent-setting tale, a fresh arrival to the phantasmagoric tropical island where walking cadavers roam the roads, is blissfully in love with a freshly scrubbed young man she met on board the ship that brought her from the United States. Enraptured by her newly found love, she is deaf to the entreaties of a rich planter who covets her" (Paravisini-Gebert 43). Seeking to marry her new love, Neil (John Harron), she drinks a potion concocted by "Murder" Legendre (Bela Lugosi) at the behest of Monsieur Beaumont (Robert Frazer), the owner of the Haitian plantation where the wedding is to take place. Wanting to claim her for himself, Beaumont is unsuccessful at wooing her away from her young man and thus, turns to Legendre (a captivating Bela Lugosi) to bewitch her. Madeleine (Madge Bellamy) drinks the zombie poison, "falls into a death swoon at the altar, and is buried in her wedding gown" (Paravisini-Gebert 43). As the film progresses, it becomes clear that Legendre has no intention of allowing Beaumont to keep the young girl; she is for his purposes only.

The other male characters, American Neil (Madeleine's fiancé) and Haitian plantation owner Beaumont, fare no better in their treatment of Madeleine; she exists only to fulfill their respective desires. As Kyle William Bishop summarizes, "the rest of the plot unfolds quite rapidly. Beaumont has a change of heart, finding no comfort in the reanimated Madeleine's beauty when there are no sparks of a soul in her eyes. He begs Legendre to restore her to life, but the sinister voodoo [sic] master double crosses the Frenchman, administering him a dose of zombie powder so Legendre can have the 'white zombie' all to himself" (*American Zombie Gothic* 75). Romance in *White Zombie* cannot escape the legacy of slavery and commodification. Madeleine is only something to be possessed, and possession (for two of the main characters) only comes at the hand of zombification. Moreover, "the wedding-night motif, with its promise of carnal fulfillment, emphasizes the erotic quality of her deathlike vulnerability, as does the flimsy shroud (wedding dress) in which she is buried and in which she will spend most of the movie" (Paravisini-Gebert 43). As such, Madeleine emerges not as a fully realized heroine seeking romance through willful engagement, but rather, as she is "zombified to become, implicitly at least, a sex slave" (Phillips 28).

But what of Madeleine's faithful and distraught fiancé? While Beaumont and Legendre clearly treat her as a commodity, a mere object to be owned, certainly Neil envisions his wife to be an autonomous figure. Unfortunately, he does not. When rumors begin to circulate that Madeleine is not, in fact, dead, that she exists as the victim of a coma-inducing poison, Neil is horrified. Rather than expressing relief that his beloved is still alive, he openly shudders and delivers a particularly telling line: "You don't think she's alive—in the hands of natives? Better dead than that!" (*White Zombie*). While much scholarship discusses a clear racial component to this exchange, something else is occurring as well. Certainly (and quite peculiar to the time), implied miscegenation emerges as a threat to the myth of racial purity; Madeleine, as the white heroine, carries with her all of the baggage associated with the implied violation of a white woman at the hands of a strong, black native. However, there is more at work here than the tired trope of race-mixing.

Madeleine, in the lexicon of contemporary purity language, is 'damaged' goods. As Neil implies with his outburst, she is an object that has lost some of its luster, a commodity that does not carry the same value once tainted by native influence and/or sexuality. That Neil would rather see his beloved dead than recovered from Legendre's spell lays bare the cultural anxieties and expectations thrust upon women. Madeleine, as Neil's fiancée, embodies cultural standards of purity. Further, Madeleine, as a zombie created by both Beaumont and Legendre, is the ultimate romantic prize: stripped of her autonomy and free will. *White Zombie* not only emerges as the first zombie film to infect American popular culture, it also becomes the first zombie film to insert the guise of romance as a major plot point. Madeleine, through the targeted use of Haitian Vodou (and the legacy of colonialism and slavery that accompanies it), becomes nothing more than chattel.

Voodoo Man (1944) continues this theme as a man attempts to transfer the spirits of young, beautiful, and unwilling zombies to the body of his dead wife. In this film, "Voodoo" is no longer contained by Haiti; it has infiltrated Middle America. The film opens with a young, white woman seeking directions to Twin Falls. While nothing else is provided to pinpoint the location of events, several characters reference the main, male character as "that sap from Hollywood … working for a fancy studio" implying an "us vs. them" mentality that serves to frame the rest of the characters as "regular" Americans (*Voodoo Man*). The story, itself, is nothing groundbreaking. Near the town of Twin Falls, single women are disappearing without a trace. One such woman, Stella (Louise Currie), is in town as the maid of honor for her cousin's wedding. Her cousin, Betty (Wanda McKay), is marrying the Hollywood sap, Ralph (Tod Andrews). While travelling together, Stella is abducted as Ralph seeks help after indeterminable car trouble. She is kidnapped by the underlings of Dr. Richard Marlowe (Bela Lugosi), who have been tipped off to her presence by the gas station attendant.

This somewhat convoluted and conspiratorial plot point casts Dr. Marlowe as the "Voodoo Man" of the title, using a combination of "Voodoo" rites and hypnotic magic to claim the souls of his victims. But to what end? Again, love/romance emerges as the agent of action. Dr. Marlowe is grieving the death of his beloved wife, Evelyn (Ellen Hall), somehow dead, yet remarkably preserved for the past twenty-two years. She, herself, is in a zombified state. Dr. Marlowe is abducting young, beautiful women in an attempt to transfer their souls to the body of his dead wife. The number of zombies he "owns" reflects the number of his failed attempts. He, quite literally, possesses a stable of zombified women (each with her own compartment) that he keeps hidden in the basement. These women are not seen as individuals and (aside from the aforementioned Stella) are not named in the film. In perhaps the most flagrant way possible (and alarming even in its day), *Voodoo Man* serves to "objectify women more than offer any legitimate scares" (Vuckovic 43).

Despite the transplanted location, and at least one assertion that "Haiti has dropped entirely from the context" of this film, the shadowy menace of Haitian Vodou is still present (Luckhurst 87). Dr. Marlowe dresses all of his zombies in flowing white gowns reminiscent of the white clothing worn by Vodou initiates in Haiti (*Divine Horsemen*). Further, he relies on the sorcery of his accomplice (adorned in a ridiculous mockery of "native" vestments more appropriate for *Scooby-Doo*) to cast the necessary spells that will accompany the doctor's own hypnotic gaze. Finally, the attempted zombie transfer occurs according to a native drumbeat, the true hallmark of Haitian Vodou, as noted in Seabrook's sensationalized travelogue and something the American audience would have been well acquainted with at this point: "The wailing chant, the throbbing drums, the miraculous aliveness of their own belief in wonders to be manifested" (36–37).

Much as in *White Zombie*, the application of Haitian Vodou, of Haitian *zonbis*, brings the legacy of bondage, slavery, containment, and commodification to *Voodoo Man*. Fueled by a desire to be reunited with his love, Dr. Marlowe systematically commodifies each young woman he chooses to abduct. These women are not willing participants; they have not consented to their roles in his zombified game of reanimation. They are mere objects, designed solely as pawns for his romantic amusement. Moreover, and perhaps more problematic, his deceased wife, Evelyn, has not given willful consent for her role, either. We only know that she has died and that her grieving husband has kept her alive for twenty-two years. At no point does he explain that he is fulfilling her wishes, or that they concocted this plan together before her death. No, we only see a man so torn by the loss of his wife, he seeks to reanimate her body with any stolen soul that seems a good fit. As well intended as he may be, he does not view these women (including his wife) as true partners; rather, they exist only as objects to be possessed, utilized, and ultimately, discarded.

As the zombie genre moved into the postmodern era, it appeared to leave its foundational roots of Haitian Vodou behind. Zombies truly became reanimated figures without a soul of any kind; there seemed to be nothing left behind for a *houngan* or *bokor* to harness. Moreover (and discussed in greater length elsewhere), the entry of George A. Romero's *Night of the Living Dead* into the public domain (through distributor copyright error) essentially rewrote the "rules" of the zombie game (Heffernan). Exposed over and over to these same tropes and characterizations, the American public began to shift their understanding of the zombie as movie monster. Gone were the representations of beautiful, young women claimed as zombie victims. Gone were the powerful men intent on possessing their supple flesh. Gone were what Romero, himself, has called the "blue collar zombies," slave laborers meant to work eternally in their physically controlled bodies (Inguanzo 16). Left in their place, contemporary representations began to reign supreme as the decaying, flesh or brain-eating ghouls we so easily recognize today.

Driving this perception was the American public, who quickly reclassified Romero's ghouls as zombies, despite his "divergence from traditional zombie lore, and not one reference or mention of the word 'zombie' in the film" (Inguanzo 78). Moreover, this new breed of zombie brought something new to the game: the threat of contagion. Instead of a latent fear of soul possession and the ensuing slavery, humans could now be turned into zombies by mere biology. Whether by bite, blood product, viral infection, or other, it did not take the targeted use of Haitian Vodou to ensnare, just the reality of being alive. Not surprisingly, tropes of the zombie as romantic figure began to wane. But as we find ourselves deeply buried in a zombie renaissance of sorts (and with no discernible end in sight), zombies begin to occupy (once again) the most unlikely of representations, the romantic hero.

One such film to tackle the difficulty of portraying zombies as sympathetic, romantic figures is *Fido*. Released in 2006, *Fido* appears to be set in 1950s America, soon after an alien invasion and subsequent radiation have caused the dead to reanimate. The resulting 'zombie wars,' wherein "mankind [was] pitted against legions of the undead" (and taking place through quick voiceover work), have been won and the world is now safe thanks to Zomcon, the subsidiary tasked with protection (*Fido*). In this new reality, zombies are utilized as domestic help (ironically not far removed from Haitian zombies as slave laborers) and interact regularly with the humans in their care. Yet, *Fido* still exists in a universe of containment and commodification. In order to interact safely with non-zombies, the undead must wear "domestication collars." A spokesperson for Zomcon explains:

> And then a breakthrough—the domestication collar. With the collar in place, a red light comes on telling us that the zombie's desire for human flesh has been contained, making the zombie as gentle as a household pet. But if the collar light goes out, call Zomcon, or push the nearest safety button, and we'll be there to handle any zombie problem, large or small.... So thank you, Zomcon, for winning the Zombie Wars, and building a company for tomorrow that gives us a safer future today. Zomcon. A better life through containment [*Fido*].

As sweet as the titular character may seem to be and described as he is as a "sentient being with thoughts, feelings, and laudable goals in life," he still needs a containment device to avoid eating the neighbors (Manning 161). Even under the stylistic glow of 1950s era optimism, *Fido* cannot escape the harsh reality that accompanies romantic suggestion and necessary zombie regulation. Containment has already arrived; commodification cannot be far behind.

Having set the scene in postwar, suburban America, *Fido* unfolds in short order. With the zombie wars successfully won, American suburbia, personified through the sterile town of Willard, is relatively safe from the gnawing jaws of the undead. Zombies are now widely utilized as servants, thanks to the success of domestication collars. More to the point, zombies have become domestic slaves with no free will. They are externally controlled by Zomcon's hardware and enslaved by their individual owners. Bishop writes, "Currie's zombies are abused and misused slaves, making them sympathetic victims as well as murderous monsters" (*American Zombie Gothic* 205). Murderous monsters they may be, but in the world of *Fido*, zombie slaves are also sought after status symbols. As Helen (Carrie-Anne Moss), later to emerge as Fido's love interest, bemoans, "I'm going to take this apple pie over to the Johnson's and see if they actually own all of those zombies" (*Fido*). This need to 'keep up with the Joneses' and project prosperity and wealth prompts Helen to acquire a zombie of her very own for assistance with her household duties. As she introduces her new acquisition to her husband, she gleefully exclaims, "Isn't it wonderful! Now we're not the only ones on the street without one" (*Fido*). As Fido (Billy Connelly) makes his first appearance onscreen, "the white gloves of the butler zombie clearly identify [him] as a servant, but unlike human servants, this zombie is property. As a commodity, the zombie is a status symbol" (Braun 166). For Timmy (K'Sun Ray), Helen's son, their new zombie also becomes a pet and trusted companion.

Timmy warms to human/zombie interaction quite quickly. After his zombie scares away some neighborhood bullies, Timmy plainly states, "We should get a name for you before Mom does. I know! How about Fido?" (*Fido*). Fido gives a zombie groan of agreement as Timmy smiles, throws the ball, and says, "Good catch, Fido!" (Fido). Several significant things happen in this exchange. Timmy is establishing his relationship with Fido as one of ownership. The right to name (and the subsequent naming) also exposes a power dynamic. In addition, choosing the name, "Fido," reinforces the zombie's role as pet, a plaything for Timmy's amusement. Fido may be part of the family now, but clear boundaries and expectations have been set.

Despite being a more mainstream zombie movie, in *Fido* "all the elements of the apocalyptic Romero narrative are present, including a fortified zone, zombies wandering the perimeters, disaster capitalists, and intimate conflicts raging within surviving families" (Ahmad 132). A substantial part of the conflict raging within the Robinson household is Helen's dissatisfaction with her emotionally distant husband, Bill (Dylan Baker). Bill believes that human emotional connection is a spectacularly bad idea in a post-apocalyptic, zombie world. Human emotions are messy and only complicate the inevitable: the need to destroy loved ones when they turn. His killing of his own father (briefly explained in flashbacks) underscores this point. Consequently, Bill fails on the romantic front in a plethora of ways, most noticeably his emotional unavailability and his obtuse ignorance regarding his wife's pregnancy. Yet, Fido, with his surprisingly appealing zombie charm and appreciative attention, has time to listen to her complaints, to see her as she wishes to be seen. As Bill becomes wary of Helen's increased affection for Fido, she wearily says "Lighten up, Bill," before seductively dancing with Fido after her husband's refusal to do so (*Fido*). As Bill leaves the room, we plainly hear the lyrics of Helen and Fido's intimate dance number: "Say, every time I turn it loose you cats. Come down and cook my goose. When I start I just can't stop. But if you keep this up you're gonna blow your top! Put a lid on it. Too late this time. Put a lid on it. I've got to get what's mine" (Squirrel Nut Zippers). Helen is clearly using Fido as a prop to both elicit a response from her husband as well as pursue her own happiness. As likable and tempting as Fido may be (and indeed, the viewer is rooting for him), he is still treated as a commodity. He is the object through which Helen creates the reality she desires. He is not a completely willing or equal partner in her romantic game.

And yet, it is Fido with whom Helen builds a future. As tensions between the zombie domestic help and the corporate Zomcon brew, anarchy prevails (albeit it briefly) and zombies breach the safety perimeter, endangering Timmy who ventured to Zomcon headquarters to save his beloved Fido. Fido had been removed from the Robinson household because as Mr. Bottoms, the head of Zomcon, clearly tells Timmy, "You made friends with a zombie.... Yes, sir. These little problems are all about containment" (*Fido*, Currie). Removed from the rampant human emotions displayed by both Helen and Timmy, Fido has been relegated to factory work in the basement of Zomcon.

Timmy, with the help of his neighbor, Mr. Theopolis, sneak into Zomcon, attempt to free Fido, and purposely invite mayhem by releasing a zombie from his domestication collar as a diversion. Watching his carefully cultivated illusion of security crumble, Mr. Bottoms drags Timmy out to the perimeter fence and plainly states, "Out there is chaos, in here is safety. People who don't understand that, end up on the wrong side of the fence" (*Fido*). He then opens the gate, throws Timmy into the unprotected "wild zone," and secures the perimeter.

As Timmy's fear builds and the wild zombies approach, Bill and Fido arrive to save the day. Bill demands that his son be allowed back into the protected zone and rushes Mr. Bottoms. The two men engage in an armed scuffle, each jockeying for control of the gun. Bill loses this battle and is subsequently shot and killed. Distraught by his father's death and angry at the man who caused it, Timmy releases Fido from his collar, points him in the direction of Mr. Bottoms, and enthusiastically says, "Get him, boy!" (*Fido*, Currie). Defying the mythology of this story, Fido targets his attack. Despite being surrounded by humans, Fido only eats the Zomcon executive, leaving Timmy (and his late-arriving mother) alone. In short order, civilization is restored through military force, Timmy's dad is buried in his dream of a "head coffin" (which prevents complete zombification), and Fido adopts the father figure role in the Robinson household. The film ends with a pleasant suburban barbeque where Fido and Timmy play catch, Fido plays with Helen's newborn baby, and Fido and Helen look adoringly into each other's eyes. However, theirs is still a romance that is built on required containment (Fido is again wearing his domestication collar) and the ensuing objectification that occurs.

As much as Helen and Fido illustrate the romantic tension that can exist between human and zombie, Helen's neighbor, Mr. Theopolis (Tim Blake Nelson) has taken zombie commodification to the next level. Mr. Theopolis is a former Zomcon employee who quit the company and kept both zombie hardware and repair material as part of his severance package. His own zombie, Tammy (Sonja Bennett), is remarkably well preserved: young, blond, beautiful, and wearing clothing of a 1950's pin-up girl. Timmy notices that she looks different than most zombies, and he and Mr. Theopolis share this exchange:

> TIMMY: She looks good for a zombie.
>
> MR. THEOPOLIS: Same as the day I met her. She was shopping in the grocery store for candy corn with her mom, had some kind of a brain aneurism. They slapped a collar on her before she even hit the floor, got her before there was any decomposition [*Fido*].

Throughout the film, Mr. Theopolis treats Tammy as his personal sex slave. He kisses her squarely and passionately on the mouth, slaps her bottom when she is performing household chores, and dresses her in provocative clothing designed to accentuate her figure. In one telling scene, Mr. Theopolis and Tammy are seen engaging in some sort of sexual bondage play. Tammy is secured by arm shackles, domestication collar removed, while her lover teases her with the possibility of a bite as he moves in toward her. Mr. Theopolis has constructed a relationship of power and dominance, purely for his own pleasure. Tammy was chosen for her youth, beauty, and most importantly, her well preserved flesh. Armstrong suggests that "from the point of view of Capital, a zombie is an ideal worker ... the promise of restored integrity renders the commoditization of the body possible" (98). In this case, Tammy is a sex worker who has not consented to her role. Consequently, "the flesh of the body is divorced from the humanity of the human body so that the zombie body is just flesh that performs a function in the same way a mechanical device like a robot might" (Braun 166). As promising as the zombies in *Fido* might appear on screen, it cannot be forgotten that they are enslaved and commodified objects, specifically, commodified objects that reflect their own subjugation as well as the desires of their oppressors.

As Braun so aptly suggests in her essay, this clear subjugation muddies our understanding of what zombies are and how zombies are thought to behave:

> ... the zombie is powerless like the slave, however the zombie's powerlessness in the face of their instinct to eat human flesh seems to justify their control (and subsequent loss of power) by those humans who are still living. [Yet] Fido's ability to override his instinct to eat Timmy and Helen when his collar is turned off ... suggests [he] is a unique specimen whose status as an object is misassigned.... Fido might not be so unique and the rationale for subjugating zombies because they are powerless to control their urges might be an illegitimate reason for controlling their every move (168).

Do Fido and Tammy adopt "civilized" behaviors because they are fighting their natural urges? Or do they adopt these same refined behaviors because they are treated differently by their captors? Is the zombie's desire for flesh within the confines of Willard a (rightful) product of wrongful enslavement? Regardless of the myriad ways in which zombies are portrayed as possible romantic partners, their mere presence exposes the dark underbelly of privilege and manipulation.

As softly as Fido presents its satire of both the zombie genre and the lure of suburbia, it is still a film with bite. Christie notes that the tame zombies presented in *Fido*, who have been "zombified as a cheap and malleable labor source ... resurrect some of the folkloric origins of the Caribbean 'zonbi' and many of its racist and imperialist implications" (64). Wrapping such history up in romance should not soften its blow. Calling out to the foundational folklore of the Haitian *zonbi* only serves to revive the dominating themes of slavery, containment, and commodification, themes that are essential to the zombie film. Zombies are not, nor can they ever be, truly willing romantic partners. In their current place in most film canon, they are incapable of giving consent.

And yet, the suggestion that zombies can make appealing romantic partners continues to gather steam in American popular culture. In reality (if there is such a thing when discussing the zombie apocalypse), zombies only become what we project onto them. The very nature of their mythology relegates them to the realities of the containment that comes with slavery and the commodification that is sure to follow. Zombies act as blank canvases on which humans paint their fears as well as their desires:

> Feelings of any kind are not known to the walking dead. Every form of psychological warfare, from attempts at enraging the undead to provoking pity have all met with disaster. Joy, sadness, confidence, anxiety, love, hatred, fear—all of these feelings and thousands more that make up the human "heart" are as useless to the living dead as the organ of the same name. Who knows if this is humanity's greatest weakness or strength? The debate continues, and probably will forever [Brooks 15].

This debate will certainly not be settled here. Whether or not this very human tendency to inject "heart" into the zombie narrative is humanity's greatest strength or greatest weakness remains to be seen. The larger (and more significant question) is what our proclivity to project these feelings onto the zombie, as if the zombie is capable of reciprocity, says about our comfort level with privilege and the disharmonious ways in which power is reflected in the choices we make. As clearly outlined above, zombie mythology does not lend itself to the emotional depth required of contemporary romantic relationships. Zombies are mere repositories for our cultural angst and our most base desires. They are not able-bodied and willing participants in the romantic conventions that have recently been thrust upon them. Zombies, real or imagined, must be seen for what/who they are, not repositioned as what/who we wish them to be.

Works Cited

Ahmad, Aalya. "Gray Is the New Black: Race, Class, and Zombies." *Generation Zombie: Essays on the Living Dead in Modern Culture*, edited by Stephanie Boluk and Wylie Lenz. McFarland, 2011, pp. 130–46.

ANH (Archives Nationales d'Haïti). *Code Pénal*. Official documents of state. Port-au-Prince, Haiti.

Armstrong, Timothy. *Modernism, Technology, and the Body: A Cultural Study*. Cambridge University Press, 1998.

Bishop, Kyle William. *American Zombie Gothic: The Rise and Fall (and Rise) of the Walking Dead in Popular Culture*. McFarland, 2010.

Braun, Michele. "It's So Hard to Get Good Help These Days." *Race, Oppression, and the Zombie*, edited by Christopher M. Moreman and Cory James Rushton. McFarland, 2011, pp. 162–73.

Brooks, Max. *The Zombie Survival Guide: Complete Protection from the Living Dead.* Broadway Books, 2003.
Buckley, Catherine. "The Heart-Throb Zombie: Teen Movies and Summit Entertainment's Construction of Warm Bodies." *Thinking Dead: What the Zombie Apocalypse Means*, edited by Murali Balaji. Lexington Books, 2013, pp. 215–26.
Christie, Deborah. "And the Dead Shall Walk." *Better Off Dead: The Evolution of the Zombie as Post-Human*, edited by Deborah Christie and Sarah Juliet Lauro. Fordham University Press, 2011, pp. 61–65.
Desmangles, Leslie G. *The Faces of the Gods: Vodou and Roman Catholicism in Haiti.* University of North Carolina Press, 1992.
Divine Horseman: Living Gods of Haiti. Dir. Maya Deren, Microcinema International, 1985.
Fido. Directed by Andrew Currie. Lionsgate/Anagram, 2006.
Genzlinger, Neil. "Review: 'iZombie,' the Undead as a Force for Good." *New York Times*, 16 Mar. 2015. www.nytimes.com/2015/03/16/arts/television/review-izombie-the-undead-as-a-force-for-good.html
Hamako, Eric. "Zombie Orientals Ate My Brain!" *Race, Oppression, and the Zombie*, edited by Christopher M. Moreman and Cory James Rushton. McFarland, 2011, pp. 107–23.
Heffernan, Kevin. "Inner-City Exhibition and the Genre Film: Distributing Night of the Living Dead (1968)." *Cinema Journal*, vol. 41, no. 3, 2002, pp. 59–77.
Hurbon, Laënnec. "American Fantasy and Haitian Vodou." *Sacred Arts of Haitian Vodou*, edited by Donald Cosentino. UCLA Fowler Museum of Cultural History, 1995, pp. 181–197.
Inguanzo, Ozzy. *Zombies on Film: The Definitive Story of Undead Cinema.* Rizzoli Universe, 2016.
Kee, Chera. "'They are not men … they are dead bodies!': From Cannibal to Zombie and Back Again." *Better Off Dead: The Evolution of the Zombie as Post-Human*, edited by Deborah Christie and Sarah Juliet Lauro. Fordham University Press, 2011, pp. 9–23.
Largey, Michael. *Vodou Nation.* University of Chicago Press, 2006.
Laroche, Maximilien. "The Myth of the Zombi." *Exile and Tradition: Studies in African and Caribbean Literature*, edited by Rowland Smith. Longman, 1976, pp. 44–61.
Luckhurst, Roger. *Zombies: A Cultural History.* Reaktion Books, 2015.
Manning, Paul. "Zombies, Zomedies, Digital Fan Cultures and the Politics of Taste." *The Zombie Renaissance*, edited by Laura Hubner, Marcus Leaning, and Paul Manning. Palgrave Macmillan, 2015, pp. 160–73.
McGill, Bryant. *Voice of Reason: Speaking to the Great and Good Spirit of Revolution of Mind.* Paper Lyon Publishing, 2012.
Métraux, Alfred. *Voodoo in Haiti.* Schoken Books, 1972.
Moreman, Christopher M., and Cory James Rushton, eds. *Zombies Are Us: Essays on the Humanity of the Walking Dead.* McFarland, 2011.
Night of the Living Dead. Directed by George A. Romero, Image Ten, 1968.
Paravisini-Gebert, Lizabeth. "Eroticism and Exoticism if the Representation of the Woman as Zombie." *Sacred Possessions: Vodou, Santeria, Obeah, and the Caribbean*, edited by Margarite Fernandez Olmos and Lizabeth Paravisini-Gebert. Rutgers University Press, 2000, pp. 37–58.
Patrick, Brian Anse. *Zombology.* Arkos Media LTD, 2014.
Phillips, Gyllian. "White Zombie and the Creole: William Seabrook's The Magic Island and American Imperialism in Haiti." *Generation Zombie: Essays of the Living Dead in Modern Culture*, edited by Stephanie Boluk and Wylie Lenz. McFarland, 2011, pp. 27–40.
"Pilot." *iZombie.* Written by Rob Thomas and Diane Ruggiero-Wright. Directed by Rob Thomas. The CW, 17 Mar. 2015.
Price-Mars, Jean. *Une étape de l'évolution haïtienne.* Imprimerie La Presse, 1929.
Scooby Doo on Zombie Island. Directed by Jim Stenstrum. Turner Home Entertainment, 2005.
Skal, David J. *The Monster Show.* Faber and Faber, 2001.
Seabrook, William. *The Magic Island.* Harcourt, Brace and Company, 1929.
Squirrel Nut Zippers. "Put a lid on it." *Hot.* Mammoth, Hollywood, Polygram, 1996.
Tann, Mambo Chita. *Haitian Vodou.* Llewellyn Publications, 2012.

Voodoo Man. Directed by William Beaudine. Banner Productions, 1944.
Vuckovic, Jovanka. *Zombies! An Illustrated History of the Undead.* St. Martin's Griffin, 2011.
Warm Bodies. Directed by Jonathan Levine. Summit Entertainment, 2013.
White Zombie. Directed by Victor Halperin. Victor and Edward Halperin Productions, 1932.

Nobody Wants to Be Un-Anything

Pushing Daisies *and the Problem of a Kinder, Gentler Undead*

SCOTT ROGERS

Representations of zombies on film and screen have changed radically since Romero's *Night of the Living Dead* in 1968—now including fast zombies, a general movement toward zombies-as-infecteds, and semi-sentient zombies. Even more, since at least 2013, there has been an effort to render zombies as aesthetically pleasing—or, at least, as no longer visually repulsive. Films such as *Warm Bodies* (2013) and series such as *iZombie* (2015) present viewers with zombies who are more or less physically intact. This is important, for zombies have traditionally inhabited a relatively safe position in the uncanny valley; they look somewhat like humans, but their physical decay marks them as distinctly not human. *Warm Bodies* and *iZombie* complicate this zombie/human dynamic by presenting us with zombie protagonists who are aesthetically mostly human-seeming—their skin might be pale and their eyes might be an inhuman color, but they are physically whole and are not decaying.

Kyle William Bishop provides a useful discussion of traditional zombie characteristics in *American Zombie Gothic* (2010). Bishop explains that zombies are "corpses raised from the dead" who "pursue the living humans with relentless, tireless dedication and kill people mercilessly by eating them alive" (Bishop 20). Zombies are "in an active state of decay" (21) and, unlike vampires, "never transcend their essential identity as dead, decaying bodies" (21). Bishop goes on to draw an important distinction between the dead and the undead:

> Because zombies are technically "dead" rather than the more romantic "undead" (i.e., vampires)—thus occupying a separate place in the continuum of monsters [...]—they

> possess only a rotting brain and have no real emotional capacity. To that end, zombies cannot be reasoned with, appealed to, or dissuaded by logical discourse—or repelled by superstitions such as garlic or crosses, for that matter. The other supernatural foes devised by authors and other Hollywood filmmakers are generally conscious and thinking figures, at least somewhat [20].

This distinction between the dead and the undead is an important one, since zombies occupy a peculiar position on Bishop's scale of dead-to-alive (21). Because they are an animated, dead, decaying body, they are closer to a corpse or a mummy than they are to a vampire. But Bishop admits, both in *American Zombie Gothic* and in *How Zombies Conquered Popular Culture* (2015), that the location of zombies on this continuum is changing. He notes that "...in recent years, traditional supernatural monsters have become sympathetic protagonists and misunderstood heroes" (20) but acknowledges that "[w]ithout dramatic alterations to the zombie's essential identity, such a re-casting of the walking dead seems to remain an illogical impossibility for creators of zombie tales and films" (20). In this essay, I want to explore the ways this "re-casting" has been experimented with in other representations of the reanimated dead.

We can find one such example of this transformation in Bryan Fuller's series, *Pushing Daisies* (2007–09). There is little dispute over the novelty of the show. Despite his work garnering both critical and fan acclaim, Fuller has struggled in television; his shows—*Dead Like Me* (2003–04), *Wonderfalls* (2004), *Pushing Daisies*, *Hannibal* (2013–15)—have typically pulled in low ratings, and thus his networks have canceled every show he has created. *Pushing Daisies*, which early advertisements described as a "forensic fairy tale" ("*Pushing Daisies* First Look") is a mixture of magical realism (reminiscent of Fuller's earlier, also-canceled series, *Wonderfalls*), crime drama, film noir, camp, verbal dexterity, and sweetness.

The premise of the series is relatively simple. Ned, the protagonist and pie-maker, learns as a child that he has the ability to raise the dead simply by touching a dead thing. If Ned touches them again, they go back to being dead. We do not know why Ned has this ability, and all we are told is that "this touch was a gift given to him, but not by anyone in particular. There was no box, no instructions, no manufacturer's warranty. It just was. If Ned does not touch them within a minute, something else has to die to balance out the life returned. The terms of use weren't immediately clear, nor were they of immediate concern" ("Pie-Lette"). As an adult, Ned opens a pie-shop, revives rotten fruit for his pies, and solves crimes with private detective Emerson Cod ("murders are much easier to solve when you can ask the victim who killed them" ["Pie-Lette"]). Their business plan is straightforward: Ned touches murder victims and asks them how they died; Emerson solves the crime, and they collect the reward.

Ned's life is further complicated by Charlotte Charles (nicknamed "Chuck"), his childhood love, who is murdered while on a cruise. Ned raises her from the dead but cannot bring himself to return her to the dead, and so *Pushing Daisies* is, at its core, a love story about a pair of lovers who can never touch. They kiss through cling wrap. They hold hands either through gloves (Ned even has a divider in his car with a glove attached, *a la* an incubator). They hug themselves while they look longingly at one another. This touching by proxy that Ned and Chuck engage in certainly adds to the unabashed sweetness of the series, for it prohibits the series from allowing its protagonists to act on their carnal desires and forces them to express their love in distinctly non-sexual ways. Indeed, even after Ned and Chuck move in together, the prohibition forces them to engage in elaborately choreographed dances simply to navigate his apartment without accidentally touching. The sweetness of their relationship—amplified by their necessary abstinence—is troubled, though, by its eventual sexualization. In one scene, Chuck enters Ned's apartment wearing only a comforter, stands before him, and drops it to stand naked in front of him. While this scene is most certainly endearing insofar as it is as close as Chuck and Ned will ever get to a sex act, the viewer's response is important, for such sexualization—sweet as it may be—raises a series of problems at the heart of the show about the difficulties associated with representing physical attraction involving the reanimated dead. It is not my intention here to suggest that *Pushing Daisies* is a part of such a movement aimed at transforming the representation of the zombie. Instead, I contend, what we are seeing in *Pushing Daisies*, *Warm Bodies*, and *iZombie* is in many ways the same transformation of the re-animated dead that we have witnessed with vampires since the 1931 *Dracula* represented Dracula as essentially human—a significant departure from the monstrous representation in the 1922 film *Nosferatu*. Indeed, this representational trajectory seems relatively consistent: iconic monsters become increasingly aesthetically acceptable and eventually sexualized.

Pushing Daisies tends to distract attention from its necrophiliac dimension by relying on its cleverness and sweetness to direct the viewer's attention away from the sexual elements of Ned and Chuck's relationship. Indeed, the show's clever dialogue, super-saturated color scheme, and cartoonish sets allow readers to forget that *Pushing Daisies* is a show that is largely about death—even the title invokes death via a euphemism that plays on death and decay without actually describing the condition. In a way, this sweetness marks the series as distinct from traditional representations of undead creatures such as zombies and vampires: vampires and zombies kill and eat humans; the undead in *Pushing Daisies* stand in direct contrast to the fierceness exhibited by other, more malicious, forms of undead, and their chaste behavior (however forced upon them) recalls an earlier, less sexualized era of television.

Chuck's status as *some* kind of reanimated dead is a consistent topic in the series. The show's first episode deals with this question of terminology in one of its earliest scenes:

> NED: I asked you not to use the word zombie. It's disrespectful. Stumbling around, squawking for brains. It's not how they do. And un-dead? Who wants to be un-anything? Why do you got to stick with the negative? It's like saying "I don't disagree." Just say you agree.
> EMERSON: Are you comfortable with "living dead"?
> NED: You're either living or you're dead. When you're living you're alive. When you're dead, that's what you are. But when you're dead and then you're not, you're alive again. Can't we say "alive again"? Doesn't that sound nice?
> EMERSON: Sounds like you're a narcoleptic.
> NED: I suffer from sudden, uncontrollable attacks of deep sleep?
> EMERSON: What's the other one?
> NED: Necrophiliac.
> EMERSON: Words that sound alike get mixed up in my head.
> OLIVE: Me, too! I used to think that masturbation meant chewing your food! ["Pie-Lette"]

As this bit of dialogue makes clear, Fuller's characters are unsure how to classify the reanimated in the series. Ned rightly resists calling them zombies because the reanimated people he creates do not adhere to traditional zombie behaviors. Ned's rejection of "undead" is more curious, for it does not rely on traditional characteristics of the undead; instead, Ned simply asserts that the category is objectionable and unappealing. Ned's rejection, of course, does not negate the simple fact that these characters are reanimated corpses. Indeed, Emerson's invocation of necrophilia—however deflected it is by the joke about misunderstood words—draws attention to Ned's desire to avoid the idea that Chuck is dead. The dialogue ends with a fairly typical strategy of Fuller's to distract attention from troublesome issues with humor; Olive's humorous interjection keeps the discussion focused on sex while turning it away from the idea of sex with Chuck.

Later, Ned admits that his attraction to Chuck proves problematic for him. When Emerson asks whether Ned is in love with the alive-again Chuck, Ned attempts to describe the complexity of his feelings about their relationship:

> NED: I'll admit to being confused. It's a very confusing time. Childhood issues. Digging in the dirt. It's all coming up.

There is a great deal of wordplay here that implies necrophilia. Considering that he is talking about the complexities of his desire for his reanimated girlfriend, Ned's claim that he is "Digging in the dirt"—a common phrase used to mean that someone is engaging in the unpleasant task of determining the root causes of problems and eradicating them—also tangentially implies grave-digging. Additionally, his remark that "It's all coming up" again invokes death—but this time includes a suggestion of reanimation via the iconic image of a zombie hand reaching up from a grave.

In the end, however, Emerson is correct. Chuck is dead. But this raises questions about why Ned's attraction to her is acceptable. We might, perhaps, consider Ned's attraction to Chuck in terms of both its emotional and physical components. The emotional attraction Ned feels for Chuck is certainly a key element of the sweetness I discussed earlier; his emotional attraction, lacking a physical component, comes across as non-sexual and thus non-necrophiliac in nature, and thus as acceptable to the viewer.

While Chuck is certainly not a zombie, she is nevertheless dead and reanimated. Indeed, Chuck is the only reanimated character on the show who features no disfigurement due to the method of her death. We see this contrast a number of times over the course of the series, as other "alive-again" characters on the show retain their injuries and disfigurations upon being reanimated by Ned—ranging from a man missing half his face to a man with tire tracks across his face to a man with hoof marks on his face and torso to a woman who is so charred that she looks wooden to a man killed by a snow-plow and now encased in ice. As a reanimated murder victim, Chuck, in contrast, remains in "pristine" condition—unlike the other characters, who often die from puncture wounds, blunt force trauma, or exsanguination, Chuck's having drowned renders her reanimated body none the worse for wear. Thus, even in her re-animated state, she looks no different than she did when she was alive.

This is a crucial innovation in representing romance with the reanimated, for if the reanimated are to become potential objects of desire, they must be rendered aesthetically pleasing to the audience. While it may be possible that a *character* might be attracted to a slowly-decomposing zombie, presenting such a relationship to an *audience* runs the risk of disgusting them. In this sense, *Pushing Daisies* prefigures many of the transformations of the zombie figure that will follow in more recent depictions, such as *iZombie* and *Warm Bodies*. But even before these—generally popular and accepted—depictions of romantic zombies came CBS's failed pilot for *Babylon Fields* in 2007. According to the IMDB plot summary for the show, the pilot was about a world in which "The dead return to earth in an attempt to restore old wounds." James Hibberd's description of the pilot for *Advertising Age* describes how the series modified the traditional zombie representation: "the 'Babylon' brand of zombies are not all moany-stumbly like in most films about the living dead. But they remain, quite clearly, deceased—autopsy scars, open wounds, bad skin, worms, etc. The zombies walk back to their former homes. They talk to their former loved ones. *And have sex with them*" (Hibberd, *emphasis added*). While *Babylon Fields* is not alone in depicting the reanimated dead attempting to reintegrate into society. Other series, such as the French *Les Revenants* (2004) or the American adaptation, *The Returned* (2013), were based on a similar premise that the dead return. Likewise, the BBC's zombie apocalypse mini-series *In the Flesh* (2013) focused on a zombie character attempting to re-integrate into society with the help of cosmetics and medication to disguise his condition. Finally, Tim Seeley and Mike Norton's comic series *Revival* (2012) presents readers with people returning from the dead—in various conditions—and attempting to return to society.

This list of treatments of the returning dead suggests, I think obviously, that there is a market not only for zombies but for revenants who might hope to return to their former lives. While *The Returned* and *Revival* present us with reanimated characters who are aesthetically pleasing (insofar as they do not decay), it is important to note that earlier treatments of the theme such as *Pushing Daisies* and *Babylon Fields* were forced to confront the problem of reanimated romance; each show of course took a different approach to the problem, with *Babylon Fields* embracing the necrophiliac dimension of the plot (at one point even, as Hibberd explains, discussing the "erectile enhancing benefits of being dead") and *Pushing Daisies* avoiding it as often as possible. In this sense, we might consider these shows are attempts to push the boundaries of what is possible in a show featuring the reanimated dead. *Babylon Fields*'s failure to launch suggests that embracing zombie necrophilia repulsed viewers. A significant element of that repulsion, I contend, stems from how the show also maintained traditional zombie aesthetics.

Pushing Daisies, on the other hand, eschews any representation of Chuck that might remind viewers that she is reanimated dead. Because Chuck remains unmarred by her death, it is easy for the viewer to forget that Chuck is actually dead, despite the near-constant reminders about how she and Ned cannot touch one another. Thus, at the heart of *Pushing Daisies*, I want to suggest, is this fundamental tension. Here we have, as I have shown, a series that has, at its core, a strong attraction between the living and the dead which must, therefore, mount a serious prohibition against the sexual relationship of its lead couple. But the prohibition is dual. Yes, the show's overt message is that any contact with Ned (and not just sexual) carries with it the punishment of death. But the show's other condition is that physical contact (and especially the sexual) between Ned and Chuck would, in fact, be a kind of necrophilia. If the somewhat-acceptable sweetness of Ned's *emotional* attraction to Chuck is only so because of its non-sexual nature, the presence of a potential *physical* dimension of that attraction (and the show is unabashed in its consistent representations of their desire to engage in a physical relationship) results in a kind of sexual tension—between Ned and Chuck—that in turn places the viewer in the uncomfortable position of hoping for necrophilia.

The show seems relatively comfortable defining Chuck as dead. In "Girth," Olive, believing that Chuck has merely faked her death and wishing to indicate that she is aware of the scam, claims that, after Halloween, Chuck will be "One sorry little zombie. Seriously, you're going to be *dead*." Chuck's response to this, later, is to note that "Olive thinks I faked my death which is completely different to knowing that I'm dead." In "Girth," Chuck explains to Ned's Digby: "You know, if you think about it, we've already been murdered once. How many dogs or people can say that, huh? You know what we are? We're the walking dead on Halloween." "Bitches" begins with a dream sequence in which Chuck trips getting out of bed, falls onto Ned, and they realize that they can touch. After they strip off their clothes, Chuck strips off her skin to reveal that she is Olive, underneath, wearing a "Chuck suit." When Ned reveals this dream to Emerson, the response is "you feel guilty about kissing Olive when you want to be kissing some dead girl." In "Smell of Success," le Nez describes Chuck as "A girl smelling of honey … and death." Similarly, in "Smell of Success," Ned explains to Chuck and Emerson why he never talks about his former girlfriends before, as Emerson puts it, "Dead girl came long." It is clear, then, that the dead things Ned reanimates are, in fact, dead. To claim that Chuck—or any of the other alive-again characters—is a *zombie* is difficult to maintain. While the key zombie characteristic of being a reanimated corpse is certainly in place in *Pushing Daisies*, other features of the zombie genre are missing. The alive again in the series do not mindlessly hunger for and consume human flesh. They neither stagger nor run. They do not gather in groups. Nor does the setting of *Pushing Daisies* resemble the traditional post-apocalyptic landscape of the post–Romero zombie film. While the characters do retain whatever disfigurations that marked them before their deaths, they do not seem to decay if they remain alive-again—Chuck, it seems, neither ages nor decays. As I have already discussed, this aesthetic element of Chuck's representation in *Pushing Daisies* is crucial to viewers accepting the romantic relationship between Ned and Chuck.

Even more, the show masks its representation of necrophiliac desire by presenting the relationship as sweet and chaste. As Rebecca Feasey argues in "Beekeeper Suits, Plastic Casings, Rubber Gloves and Cling Film: Examining the Importance of 'No-sex' Sex in *Pushing Daisies*," the show occupies a curious space in a modern popular culture characterized by a "growing sexualization" (66). Feasey's argument pushes back against conservative claims that the series provides a kind of "'safe-sex' or 'no-sex' prime-time programming" (66). Feasey accomplishes this by pointing out the myriad ways that the series engaged in sexually-charged imagery or language, all in the service of exposing the ways that the show pushes back against an explicitly sexualized culture:

> *Pushing Daisies* makes it clear that sex can be fun, playful, and satisfying when you are forced to use your imagination, forced to find other ways to touch and be touched, to pleasure and be pleasured, to desire and be seen as desiring.... *Pushing Daisies* offers a playful wink in the direction of alternative sexual practices, far removed from the explicit sexual conquests that dominate the contemporary television landscape [74–75].

While it is certainly true that the series presents viewers with alternative approaches to sex and sexuality, Feasey's conclusion—that the show's cancellation "suggests that this charming sexual content cannot compete with the more aggressive sexualization of contemporary media culture" (75)—seems to ignore the larger problem of necrophiliac sex that lies at the heart of the show. Chuck is, after all, dead. Critics often acknowledge but quickly dismiss this issue. Allessandra Stanley, reviewing the show for *The New York Times* in 2007, remarks that "Though technically a member of the undead, Chuck is not in the least bit morbid or morose." Yet even Stanley's title—"Loner Finds He Has a Touch for Piemaking and Undeadmaking"—encodes the problem: Ned makes dead people "undead," and Chuck is one of those people. Her romantic relationship with Ned is acceptable largely—if not almost entirely—because she does not look dead.

Given the dramatic increase in the romantic undead—whether in *Twilight* (2008) or *Warm Bodies* (2013)—it is remarkable that this issue does not surface more often in discussions of such shows. Even Bishop, in his otherwise smart discussion of the emergence of the "Romantic Zombie," elides the issue. Focusing on the profoundly troublesome messages that texts such as *Warm Bodies* and *Twilight* send to women about "ideal" relationships, Bishop remarks that "The problem with paranormal romantic fantasy such as *Twilight* and *Warm Bodies*—to name just two of dozens of successful narratives featuring the monstrous boyfriend trope—lies in the messages such texts convey to young readers and viewers, both male and female" (179). This is certainly true, but I would argue that the primary "problem with paranormal romantic fantasy" is that one of the romantic partners is *dead* (and sometimes trying to eat the person).

It may seem odd that the status of the romantically-inclined revenant needs to be pointed out, but in romantic treatments of vampires, zombies, and Chuck, the physical condition of the revenant must be downplayed. In treatments such as *Twilight*, *True Blood* (2008–14), *Warm Bodies*, *Buffy the Vampire Slayer* (1997–2003), *Angel* (1999–2004), and *Pushing Daisies*, the undead are generally presented to viewers as aesthetically pleasing forms. Edward Cullen is—in Stephenie Meyer's own words—"fantastically beautiful" and "sparkly." Even in his vampire "mode," Bill Compton of *True Blood* is a relatively normal-looking and handsome man. R of *Warm Bodies* is pale and veiny, but otherwise handsome. Both Spike and Angel—our principal vampire romantic leads in both *Buffy* and *Angel*—are portrayed as handsome men. Because of the nature of her death, Chuck in *Pushing Daisies* sports no disfiguration from her murder. Their physical condition—indeed, their beauty—allows the viewer to forget that these romantic characters are actually dead people and thus allows viewers to interpret the lovers' physical union as a positive and romantic possibility instead of what it actually is: necrophilia.

This is less of an issue, it seems, when dealing with creatures such as vampires; like zombie films, innovations in vampire narratives have introduced infection as a cause of vampirism, which attenuates the emphasis on vampire-as-undead. Zombies—and whatever the reanimated dead are in *Pushing Daisies*—present a different set of problems. First, zombies are, traditionally, aesthetically unpleasing. They often feature advanced decomposition (which locates them uncomfortably in the uncanny valley), grey skin, missing body parts, open wounds, and deficits in motor function, speech, and mobility. In order to render the zombie sympathetic, these features must be downplayed. In order to render the zombie *romantic*, these features must be either eliminated or the zombie presented to the viewer in such a way that the viewer forgets that they are dead. *Pushing Daisies* excels at this act of forgetting, partly because of its magical realism and incredibly witty dialogue and partly because Chuck exhibits no apparent disfigurement from her murder. In the end, *Pushing Daisies* presents the romantic revenant to us as an essentially aesthetic problem—it does not matter that Chuck is dead so long as she does not *appear* dead. This is a particularly difficult problem for the zombie genre, which is closely associated with decay and disfigurement.

In his conclusion to *How Zombies Conquered Popular Culture*, musing on the future of the representation of the zombie, Bishop notes that "not all zombies have to be the hungry, reanimated dead. As a society, we need monsters to help us make sense of the world around us, and because our world is constantly changing, our monsters must change as well" (190). Indeed, if the zombie—or any revenant—is to make the transition from horror to romance, a significant aesthetic transformation such as the one that Chuck represents will be crucial. While *Pushing Daisies* is most certainly not claiming that Chuck is a zombie, the show nevertheless presents us with a reanimated corpse who is the love interest of our protagonist, in a way prefiguring the current issues associated with the romantic zombie, and pointing the way toward an aesthetic transformation of the zombie that no longer reminds viewers that when they hope for a union between Ned and Chuck, they are wishing for necrophilia.

Works Cited

"Babylon Fields." IMDB.com. n.d. www.imdb.com/title/tt0955219/.

Bishop, Kyle William. *American Zombie Gothic: The Rise and Fall (and Rise) of the Walking Dead in Popular Culture*. McFarland, 2010.

_____. *How Zombies Conquered Popular Culture: The Multifarious Walking Dead in the 21st Century.* McFarland, 2015.
Dead Like Me. Created by Bryan Fuller. MGM Television, 2003.
Dracula. Directed by Tod Browning and Karl Freund, Universal, 1931.
Feasey, Rebecca. "Beekeeper Suits, Plastic Casings, Rubber Gloves and Cling Film: Examining the Importance of 'No-Sex' Sex in *Pushing Daisies.*" *Television, Sex and Society: Analyzing Contemporary Representations,* edited by Basil Glynn, James Aston, and Beth Johnson, Continuum, 2012, pp. 65–78.
Hannibal. Created by Bryan Fuller. NBC, 2013.
Hibberd, James. "'Babylon Fields'—CBS's Buried Zombie Necrophilia Pilot Unearthed." *Advertising Age.com,* 15 Oct. 2007, adage.com/article/james-hibberd-rated/babylon-fields-cbs-s-buried-zombie-necrophilia-pilot-unearthed/121155/.
iZombie. Created by Rob Thomas and Diane Ruggiero-Wright. Warner Brothers, 2015.
Meyer, Stephenie. "The Story of Twilight Getting Published." StephenieMeyer.com. n.d. stepheniemeyer.com/the-story-of-twilight-getting-published/.
Night of the Living Dead. Directed by George A. Romero, Continental Distributing, 1968.
Nosferatu. Directed by F. W. Murnau. Film Arts Guild, 1922.
Pushing Daisies: The Complete First and Second Seasons. Created by Bryan Fuller. Warner Brothers, 2009.
_____. "Bitches." Written by Chad Gomez Creasey and Dara Resnik Creasey. 14 Nov. 2007.
_____. "Girth." Written by Katherine Lingenfelter. 31 Oct. 2007.
_____. "Pie-Lette." Written by Bryan Fuller. 3 Oct. 2007.
_____. "Smell of Success." Written by Scott Nimerfro. 21 Nov. 2007.
"Pushing Daisies First Look." *YouTube,* uploaded by ezazusernamefoglalt, 15 July 2007, www.youtube.com/watch?v=WEayMH7X3sc.
Stanley, Allessandra. "Loner Finds He Has a Touch for Piemaking and Undeadmaking." *New York Times,* 3 Oct. 2007. www.nytimes.com/2007/10/03/arts/television/03stan.html.
Warm Bodies. Directed by Jonathan Levine, Summit Entertainment, 2013.
Wonderfalls. Created by Bryan Fuller and Todd Holland. FOX, 2004.

The Idea of Love and the Reality of *Deadgirl*

WHITNEY COX *and* ASHLEY RUTH LIERMAN

Like zombies, "women," as a fictional category, are terrifying. They move in packs, swarming and making horrible screeching sounds. They have peculiar, inhuman appetites (i.e., shoes, romantic comedies, pumpkin spice lattes). They contaminate and emasculate, until all but the truly heroic men are subjugated and assimilated. They are almost human, yet not quite, inhabiting their own uncanny valley of difference. Individually, however, they are not too threatening. Under the right circumstances, they can be evaded, subdued, even controlled. Then the tamer does not have to live in fear. He can count his conquest as a win, assuring himself of his power not only in this situation, but in the rest of his life. One good headshot, and he can sleep peacefully.

The film *Deadgirl*, a critically acclaimed indie horror film released in 2008, presents itself as a coming-of-age narrative, billing itself with the tagline "[e]very generation has its story about the horror of growing up." In doing so, it places itself in the line of films such as *Carrie* (1976), *A Nightmare on Elm Street* (1984), and *It Follows* (2014) where the monstrous not only facilitates the plot, but represents the terror on the other side of childhood. Despite the tagline's attempt at universalizing language, however, *Deadgirl* is specifically a story about the horror of *boys'* growing up, turning them into men in the midst of a soup of toxic masculinity and (white) male entitlement. While the movie almost downplays the gendered aspects of its plot, they are in fact the movie's most critical element, because they bring to it the horror of heteronormative reality.

What makes this coming-of-age tale different from others is that the aforementioned horror is expressed largely through the brutal and repeated rape of the titular dead girl. Though we realize a movie with such graphic rape elements may seem a curious topic for inclusion in a collection focusing on romance, we contend that "romance" as a concept is so mired in patriarchal assumptions about gender and sexuality that its base form is more than appropriate to the horror genre. *Deadgirl* is not a movie wholly about sexual assault; throughout the film, the troubling, abusive relationship between JT (Noah Segan) and the dead girl (Jenny Spain) runs a direct parallel to the romanticized longing of Rickie (Shiloh Fernandez) for his childhood sweetheart Joann (Candice King). That they are the same relationship at different degrees of practical exploitation cannot be ignored, and that one is coded as evil while the other is coded as romantic indicates a persistent blind spot on the part of many other romance narratives as well. Thus, we do not contend that rape narratives should be considered romantic; instead, we wish to consider how significantly rape culture invisibly infects romantic tropes and structures.

There are, and have been through history, multiple categories of humanity where questions of consent were thought not to apply. Much of this categorization has of course been racialized; slaves in the Americas, for instance, were not considered human enough to require consent, while hypersexualized myths about their descendents suggested that their constant erotic appetites meant affirmative consent could be assumed (Bourke 76–77). Likewise, the "mentally subnormal" have often been easy targets for sexual predators who assume any complaints would be dismissed because of the victim's inherent untrustworthiness (79). What *Deadgirl* presents, however, is a situation where the consent-incapable woman is not merely a sexual target; rather, she is also a romantic ideal.

Deadgirl also presents itself as being subversive and edgy, which is not an unfair characterization, considering the level of gross-out gore *and* the use of rape as a repeated plot device. One of the ways it manifests its desire for subversion, however, is by combining heterosexual (non-consensual) sex and romantic elements with horror tropes to create a platonic-yet-fraught same-sex romance between two friends. While the film's two heterosexual pairings function as dark mirrors of one another, the real, tragic romance is the emotional indebtedness to one another of JT and Rickie. What might come of the queering of the traditional buddy dynamic, though, is soured by how these attempts at subversion come in ways that reinforce heteronormative and misogynistic power structures. In the end, *Deadgirl* says not something new, but something very old: that women are objects to be possessed, transferred, and, ultimately, replaced to better the men around them. This cruel economy perpetuates itself—in the film as in in real life—through heterosexual romantic tropes of male desire and female obligation, where men's journeys require a woman as a goal and eventual prize. What *she* wants, of course, is immaterial; it is his story, he deserves her, and, in the end, she is his to claim as the true, socially valid proof of his growth. It is an exchange so important that it calls itself love.

Living Dead Girl

"We never thought we were making a zombie movie. It isn't," says Gadi Harel, one of the film's co-directors, leaving the matter somewhat tersely at that (Gullién). This, however, is a difficult denial to make considering all the hallmarks of the genre the film preserves—primarily the contagious bite, which has been a pandemic-facilitating staple of zombie fiction for decades. The dead girl is at once dead and undying, animated and animalistic, surviving trauma and eventually decaying as other zombies do. She bears little resemblance to other traditional undead horror-movie fare, lacking a vampire's seductive bloodthirstiness, a mummy's embalming hallmarks, or a lich's magical intelligence. Likewise, neither is she a golem, a mindless animation of soulless clay; she is contagion, not creation, and not identifiably Jewish in any meaningful way. If she is not meant to be a zombie, she is not sufficiently distinguished from one either.

Harel's claim is perhaps easier to understand in light of how most of the genre-defining zombie stories consider loss of singularity a hallmark of the zombie. Since, as Kim Paffenroth points out, "individually zombies are not too threatening" (Paffenroth 5), zombie movies, such as George A. Romero's, focus on the tenacity and overwhelming force of a mass of bodies unable to be reasoned with; while specific infected individuals may be highlighted for pathos, the real horror comes from the sheer volume of the threat. Unimpressive alone but world-destroying cooperatively, the zombie horde becomes "a conceit for macho masculinism and conspicuous capitalist consumption" (Grant 202), "embodiments of the seven deadly sins" (Paffenroth 23), or manifestations of "anxieties about labor, especially the increasing precarity of employment the way immigrant workers displace (or appear to displace) economic opportunities" (McGlotten and Vangundy 109), depending on auteur and observer alike. Either way, the undifferentiated mass creates horror only in the context of said mass. In this sense, Harel is right to distinguish *Deadgirl* from zombie stories where the focus is on the living, uninfected protagonists and their often-futile efforts to stay that way.

But as evidenced by other pieces in this collection, the zombie genre is evolving to include zombie-as-individual works of fiction that get away from traditional shambling horde narratives. Zombies that retain some vestige of their identity—who can, perhaps, even be brought back to their full former selves—can no longer so easily stand in for the too-far-gone victims of communal errors. This switch in format facilitates a switch in metaphor. In *Deadgirl*, the traditional tables are somewhat turned: the dead is at the mercy of the living. Individually, the dead girl is indeed none too threatening; no matter her inherent danger, she is easily enough subdued. Despite the fact that she is singular, her identity is irrelevant. She has no name. We never discover how she got to be where she is. Her only features of interest to the boys are her sexual characteristics and her inability to prevent access to them. She has all the hallmarks of humanity, but she is not human.

And in these things, she is not manifestly different from Joann, the film's other significant female character. As the dead girl is to JT, so Joann is to Rickie—an object of fascination, but still an object. The two exchanged what was Rickie's first kiss (but not, it is implied, Joann's) when they were twelve, and Rickie has had a crush on her ever since, despite the fact that Joann has moved on. "That was a long time ago," she tells him. "I mean, another life" (*Deadgirl*). In the life they have now, Joann is dating a classmate named Johnny (Andrew DiPalma), while Rickie is left pining for a time the object of his affection barely remembers and certainly seems not want to recreate. We as the audience never really learn about Joann as a person; we see her mostly through Rickie's view, where she wavers between his masturbatory fantasy and an unattainable ideal. She is a classic romantic trope: the girl next door, the wholesome childhood crush grown up to ignore the "nice guy" in favor of an inexplicably cruel and domineering man.

Coming as it does from the perspective of the "nice guy," this love-triangle scenario can see nothing appealing about the love rival in question, nor can it understand why (beyond the arbitrary cruelty of feminine ways) the girl might be interested in him. Consequently, Johnny himself is not a character, but a joke; his primary plot-related function is to be a reason for Joann to reject Rickie on grounds that have nothing to do with Rickie himself. The horrifying toothed blowjob scene and his subsequent demise are over-the-top ridiculous underdog revenge fantasies, played as some of the movie's only true stabs at comedy. If anything, Johnny's exaggeratedly crass objectification of Joann is little more than Rickie's own attitude toward her, albeit disguised with off-color language; that the movie condemns Johnny for what it forgives as a defining, sympathy-generating trait of Rickie's character is telling. But Rickie is the hero, not Johnny, and romantic tropes teach us there is only one way these tales can go: He will achieve the girl as a prize by the end, regardless of her choice—or ability to choose.

What He Does Down There

GUILLÉN: [A] dead girl in the basement of an insane asylum is also a frustrated teenage boy's ideal, albeit a dark and misguided one. You see Rickie trying to deal with this in a way that he feels is right and—for himself—he perhaps makes the ethically-right decision.

HAREL: Yes. He's living with it.

GUILLÉN: My roommate and I watch a lot of genre flicks together and one of his favorite lines is, "Ah! The guy got rejected by that girl. That means he has to kill her."

HAREL: [Chuckles.] But in this instance, he saves her.
GUILLÉN: In some ways *substitutes* JoAnn [sic] for the dead girl.
HAREL: Some people would rather JoAnn [sic] just die; but, Rickie loves her. At least he thinks he does. People have asked us, What does Rickie *do* with her down there? And that's not for me to say. He's reading poetry? [Gullién]

Perhaps the most disturbing element of this section of Michael Guillén's interview with Gadi Harel is Harel's laugh at the genre convention that all but demands a man's response to romantic rejection be murder. And why should it not be? So many of these films, after all, are male fantasy-fulfillment, empowering those crushed under the politically correct demands of society to rise up and get what they deserve. Movies such as the genre films Guillén references are in part a realization of Margaret Atwood's oft-cited observation that men are most afraid that women will laugh at them, while women are most afraid that men will kill them (Atwood 413). In these genre films, both forms of terror are made manifest.

Zombie movies in particular provide the appropriate overturn of society to allow the meek to cowboy up and thus inherit the earth; from *Zombieland*'s (2009) Columbus to *The Walking Dead*'s (2010–present) Carl, the disruption of the normal social order becomes the fire in which boys become real men. While this disruption heightens peril by creating what Lars Schmeink describes as a "thanato-political reality in which no institutional security guarantees the players' status" (Schmeink 74), said reality also has the benefit of removing *others*' status, eliminating advantages of class, education, and wealth that oppresses the kind of people who always ultimately triumph in fictional survival situations. A prime example: The fifth season of *The Walking Dead* lands the party in a well-walled, self-sustaining city where some of the show's only fat, elderly, young, gay, and effete characters live; confronting one of the naïve compound-dwellers, multi-season survivor Glenn (Steven Yeun) tells him, "People like you are supposed to be dead" ("Try"). Part of the result of this is the removal of the constraining force that is our collective agreement to respect the humanity of other people. The visceral appeal of zombie destruction—whether experienced passively through film or actively in video games—cannot be separated from how these scenarios encourage the killing of other humans while removing the usual moral quandaries associated with that act. Zombification is a lost-cause condition, at least in more traditional narratives, meaning that the kindest thing one can often do for the infected is aim for the head.

The core conflict in *Deadgirl* happens at the intersection of these two genres, where the dehumanized is also the desired. JT does not—and perhaps does not have the ability to—take his revenge on others in a murderous rage, doing damage to those who damaged him. Instead, he channels his frustration into the dead girl. Though she did not, *could* not reject him, she becomes the stand-in for everyone who has. His violence against her is of instinct more than design; the first time he inflicts on her (what should be) mortal wounds, it is because she is struggling and trying to bite, and the only way JT knows to stop her is to punch her in the face. "So I hit her again and it felt good," JT explains to Rickie, telling his friend he killed the dead girl three times—and now look at her. (It is no coincidence that in the shot that accompanies that line, her bare nipple is prominently framed.) He strikes her first out of panic and fear, and once he learns that is a possible response, every blow after is deliberate.

At the film's climax, as Joann and the dead girl are bound, back to back, in the hospital basement, Joann sobs and insists that whatever is going on has nothing to do with her; JT counters and says that it has *everything* to do with her. Then he turns to Rickie and delivers lines that encompass both the zombie-genre ideal of social overthrow and the spurned-lover justification of violent retributive action: "Folks like us are just cannon fodder for the rest of the world. But down here, you see, we're in control. Now, we call the shots down here, man. Feels good, doesn't it? It's all right to say. You don't have to be the nice guy down here, Rickie" (*Deadgirl*). The existence of the dead girl creates a contained zombie apocalypse, a local phenomenon predicated on the idea that removing even one person's human agency absolves everyone else of moral responsibility. Rickie does not have to be the nice guy—neither to the dead girl, nor to Joann. After all, especially by the survivalist logic of post-apocalyptic narratives, one is not required to treat the undeserving with dignity. Paffenroth notes that, in Zac Snyder's rebooted *Dawn of the Dead* (2004), characters portrayed as incapable of positive human relationships before the crisis find themselves sinking deeper into these negative aspects in the new zombie-filled reality. Bart (Michael Barry), in particular, is an example of misplaced moral priorities: "The world has been reduced to a cannibalistic hell on earth, and all he cares about his having sex with a woman he admits he neither likes nor finds attractive" (Paffenroth 107). Disgusted though the film might be by Bart in general—his suggestion of raping a female character in a later scene is the most extreme, but not sole, demonstration of his sexist behavior—his aberrance is not his desire, but its degree. After all, there are several heroic heterosexual couples in the film, suggesting that finding love even under such dangerous conditions is a virtue instead of a vice. The problem here is that Bart has so little concept of women as human beings that when the customary niceties of society are no longer in place, he feels no need to disguise what he has wanted to do to them all along. As with JT and Rickie, crisis lays true intentions bare.

If *Deadgirl* is not a zombie movie, it is only because the dead girl's zombification is all but incidental, at least as far as JT and Rickie's estimation of her humanity goes. She is no less of a person than Joann is—because Joann is not much of a person either, at least in Rickie's eyes. The first thing that the audience knows about Rickie is that he likes Joann and she does not like him back, a classic setup that ensures the protagonist will have that girl (that he deserves) by the end; every moment of positive attention she pays him is a sign that she *really* wants to be with him, despite whatever else she might say or do.

A colossal sense of entitlement from both JT and Rickie propels the story forward, but it is most disturbingly manifested in Rickie, since the film is more willing to entertain the idea that Rickie should indeed get what he wants. "We always say that Rickie is our hero," Harel says, noting that his own views on romance are not dissimilar from Rickie's (Gullién). As laced with irony as the "hero" designation might be, it is not an incorrect representation of how the movie takes a much more sympathetic eye to Rickie's actions and inactions. His desires are presented as normative, perhaps even altruistic; Joann is, after all, a pretty girl in a relationship with a crass and violent partner, meaning Rickie's dating her would not only satisfy his own cravings but liberate her from a bad situation. Ultimately, he is the one who frees the dead girl, even if only as a distraction to save himself and Joann—a goal he only half accomplishes, as Joann is mortally wounded in the process. Rickie tries to comfort her as she dies, telling her again and again that he loves her, as might befit the end of a tragic romance. Joann, however, coughs blood into Rickie's face and tells him, "Fucking grow up." She wants no part of the love story he is writing; she consents to no part of it, least of all its ending this way. It literally has nothing to do with her.

The next time we see Joann, we do not see *her*; we see her reanimated corpse, bound to the same table in the same room as before, only now surrounded by homey touches and pretty dresses. Rickie has not only let her become the new dead girl, he has taken the initiative to make it so. By giving into JT's pleas to let him bite Joann "before it's too late," Rickie ultimately completes JT's original design for Joann—though now under extenuating circumstances that Harel characterizes as "sav[ing] her." While there is no doubt that neither the film nor Harel himself believe that Rickie ultimately made the right decision in choosing to infect and cage the dying Joann, what comes through time and again is the idea that Rickie's choices are ultimately not as bad as JT's. JT is the lost cause, the one who has the initial ideas to repeatedly physically and sexually abuse the dead girl, while Rickie's resistance to this stands in for the audience's own presumed discomfort; that he is powerless to stop it is seen only as a failure of courage mitigated by a cultural context where likely no one would have believed him anyway. Only when forced by circumstances would Rickie do such a thing to Joann—circumstances where Joann's bright future has already been ripped away from her, making him no longer responsible for the tragedy of her life cut short. Even in the section of the interview quoted above, Harel dodges the possibility that Rickie is raping Joann by first declining to speculate on what happens in the basement now, then suggesting the relatively innocuous activity of reading poetry. He loves her, so he cannot be hurting her.

This is wrong. Referencing an online review by feminist critic Sophie Mayer,[1] Harel acknowledges her correctness in noting that "what Rickie is doing to JoAnn [sic] is shades of the same sort of thing JT is doing to the dead girl." It is, in fact, the exact same thing. The only difference is access.

In a powerful piece entitled "Men See Themselves in Brock Turner—That's Why They Don't Condemn Him," author and activist Anne Theriault writes that one of the major problems with rape culture is that men understand rape both as a terrible crime and as an act that they themselves would *never* commit. Responding to a statement written both by the former Stanford student who received a six-month sentence for raping an unconscious woman and by his father, Theriault points out that this "nice guy" with a "bright future," having been found guilty of sexual assault, still cannot believe that what he did was actually rape. Turner insists in his description of the assault that the unnamed woman, intoxicated beyond consciousness, was enjoying herself, implying that his perception of her reaction should mitigate his culpability. Rape, after all, is something people like JT do: brutal, callous, violent, with no regard for the other person or their (ability to) consent. By identifying the crime so particularly with those aggressive, easily identifiable elements, however, rape culture glosses over the difficult truth that the majority of rapists are members of our communities:

> [R]apists are men we know and like: our neighbors and our colleagues and sometimes even our friends. Men who might admit that things got a little bit out of hand, or that they didn't mean to go that far but they got caught up in the heat of the moment. Men like my friend's boyfriend, who once referred to beer as liquid panty remover only to declare minutes later that rapists deserve to be castrated. Men who think that consent is a one-time binary, yes or no, and not an ongoing process of checking in with their partners [Theriault].

JT mocks Rickie when Rickie objects to the sight of Wheeler's raping the dead girl; Rickie, JT says, should go away and come back in a few hours to pick up where he and Wheeler left off: "You can have a nice private romantic time and do lots of nice sensitive things." This reinforces this clear binary of rape as the opposite of romance, two mutually exclusive conditions, with the one thought contemptible by the contemptible person obviously winning that particular moral dilemma. In fact, there is no such clear division between the two, and believing there is absolves many rapists of feeling they have done anything wrong. That a rapist's intentions are good does not mitigate the crime.

As she is dying, Joann does not care if Rickie loves her. His perception of their romantic potential does nothing to ease her passing. The nobility of his unrequited affection counts for nothing—in fact, the reason she is dying is that JT believed the narrative that says Rickie's love for Joann means Rickie deserves her. "You think she's going to choose you in the real world?" asks JT as he faces off against Rickie in the film's climax. "In the real world she'd rather die than be with you." While Rickie's morose reply to this is that he knows, whatever he knows obviously changes nothing about how much he feels his love should mean to her.

Furthermore, it is nearly impossible to believe by the end that Rickie is not somehow raping the infected Joann—only he would not think of it as rape. He loves her, after all, and would never treat her with the callousness JT showed the dead girl. However, Rickie comes from a culture where romance is at its core a commercial transaction, a case of a man's committing an unspecified amount of effort to impress a woman before she consents to being sexually available to him. Following her infection and imprisonment, Joann is no longer in a position to bargain that transaction on her own behalf. She is pliant now, submissive, just the way Rickie always wanted her. He may indeed be reading her poetry in that hospital basement, following the same conventional romantic script that likely prompted him to decorate the room for its unappreciative resident, but the fact that Harel skirts the issue suggests even he does not believe that would be the extent of their interaction.

If JT is a monster, he is one that only happens once in a proverbial blue moon. Without the perfect set of opportunistic circumstances, it is likely he would have never escalated to the destructive, damaging point he reaches by the film's climax. Rickie, however, is a more quotidian horror. He has been looking at Joann like this since long before meeting the dead girl, already imagining her pliant to his fantasies of what he deserves as a man in the world. He conflates objectification with romance, which then justifies whatever he does in the name of love.

Love and Power

In the immediate context they inhabit, Rickie and JT are positioned nearly at the bottom of the available social order.[2] Neither has much of a family support structure, and both are characterized as economically disadvantaged, with no sense from anyone that they will ever make anything of themselves in the real world. In the microcosm of high school, they also have little to no social capital, putting Joann far out of Rickie's reach while making both of them targets for bullies in their peer group. They have little agency, few support structures, and no role models. They are the kind of men who, because they have been beneath others their entire lives, cannot conceive of themselves as embodying privilege.

The introduction of the dead girl disrupts this previous understanding of power, however. If JT and Rickie already understand themselves as already at the bottom of their shared social ladder, their discovering her reveals an even lower rung. And because their only firsthand experiences of power have been through the exercise of it maliciously over them, their most logical way to deal with her is through subjugation and violence, letting her know "who's boss." She becomes the means through which JT, in particular, can elevate his social status: cementing his reputation, exploring his sexuality, even creating the possibility of a profitable franchise. This, the movie is quite clear, is abominable—at no point, it should be stressed, does *Deadgirl* ever condone the mistreatment the dead girl suffers, or imply in any way that she deserves it. Though the story understands the impulse to punch down, and even emphasizes the ugliness of it time and again, it does not provide it as an excuse for JT's behavior, only as an explanation. We as viewers are never supposed to see JT's actions as heroic; even his best intentions are so clouded by his poor judgment that they can come to no positive end.

Rickie, on the other hand, watches this new power dynamic unfold, but though he yearns on some level to participate, his reservations hold him back. For all the heterosexual rape taking place in the film, JT actually deals with the dead girl in a somewhat ungendered manner; one would not be hard-pressed to imagine a version of the film where the secret in the basement is a dead *boy* that JT treats in much the same fashion. Rape, after all, is not so much sex as it is violence, and male-male rape in particular is largely a display of dominance and submission.[3] Comments made by both JT and Wheeler about penetrating her anally show that her not having a vaginal entrance would not prevent her mistreatment. Given that JT assaults her physically before thinking to rape her, it stands to reason he might do the same to a similarly pliable male body. While considerations of gender cannot be separated from the way JT treats the dead girl, the more significant core of his response stems from his feelings of powerlessness and desire for empowerment over someone, *anyone*.

Rickie, on the other hand, sees her—at least in part—as a person, and a female person, at that; ironically, his ability to humanize her makes his subsequent action and inaction even more horrific. While he does not participate in the physical abuse of the dead girl, Rickie takes the lessons from the basement and brings them out into the daylight, until everything JT teaches him about the dead girl eventually winds up applying to Joann. Conflating Joann with the dead girl during a masturbatory sequence shows not only that the dead girl has infected Rickie's erotic imagination (likely the more deliberate effect), but juxtaposes the girl who will never say yes and the girl he does not even need to ask.

At the end of the film, when Joann uses a few of her dying breaths to reject Rickie, Rickie's fear and grief turn quickly to anger. Her death no longer makes him sad; it makes him *furious*, because not only has she rejected his heartfelt profession of love, her coming death will make her unavailable to him as a future conquest. In this moment, it becomes clear, that no matter what Rickie says he understands about how she would rather be dead than with him, he still feels he is owed.

Part of the audience's terror in Rickie's turning from declarations of love to rage should stem from the understanding women have that saying "no" to a romantic offer can lead to very real violence. As true as this was at the time the film was made, it remains true into the present; as with so many modern injustices, the digital age has not made these dangers more common, only better-documented. Normalizing this romantic script of desire and obligation that disregards women's agency creates a rape culture in which violence is never far beneath the surface of love. Sociologist Laura Finley connects this normalization in fiction to oft-violent entitlement in the real world: Finley writes, "In rape cultures, men feel entitled to grope women at bars or women who are wearing revealing clothing. These men believe they can get away with it because such behavior is considered normal for men; it's what they see on all their favorite shows, films, and music videos" (Finley 43). In fact, more dangerous than the certainty men can get away with harmful behavior is the assumption that romantic intent absolves the aggressor of their behavior in the first place. Stories of women assaulted and murdered for ignoring, spurning, and breaking up with men are not random, isolated incidents. They are the result of male entitlement that believes it is the woman who wrongs the man when she denies him what he wants, and treats the man's brutal and even murderous reaction as understandable. Whether in a relationship or just existing in a public space, women endanger themselves whenever they commit Joann's crime of refusing to fulfill a man's desires. That this resulting violence can happen between complete strangers shows that this entitlement is so powerful that these men understand these women as belonging to them absent any previous obligation; that it can happen with men desiring defined heterosexual relationships shows considering a woman as a potential romantic partner is not the same as regarding her as an independent, authentic human being. Once men such as Rickie and JT declare their ownership over a woman, she must submit to his authority or be punished for her rejections. "There is an answer to our no," writes Andrea Dworkin. "A semiautomatic gun is one answer. There are also knives. This is not a pleasant conversation that we're having" (Dworkin 106).

The normalization of men's inability to cope with rejection goes hand in hand with the idea that men should not be rejected at all. The term "friend zone" is a neologism to describe the state of disappointment where a man desires a romantic relationship with a woman, but the woman would rather remain nonromantic friends. However, this term is not a neutral description of varying levels of interest, but an active indictment of female behavior: A woman must actively *put* and *keep* a man in the friend zone, and this is due to a failure on her part to realize his availability and interest, not on his for arousing insufficient interest. Feminist author and blogger Amanda Marcotte characterizes a belief in the friend zone as resulting from a corresponding belief that establishing friendship with a woman is a sole and sufficient criterion for deserving a sexual relationship with her—and that said relationship is the sole goal of that friendship. Marcotte finds this message prevalent especially in certain online subcultures, where rhetoric and visual memes produce

> a relentless drumbeat of messages targeting young men that amount to framing sex not as an activity two people enjoy together for their own reasons, but as a commodity that women possess and dole out based on a metric that is viewed as "unfair." That when a woman you likes has sex with another man, he is taking something that "belongs" to you, something you "earned" by being meeting the minimum standard of human decency [Marcotte].

Perhaps it is a stretch to call where Rickie is in relation to Joann the "friend zone"—they are not, after all, precisely friends—but the corresponding entitlement on his part comes through so clearly, it infects JT as well. They have both bought into this narrative of effort and obligation, where men in their position *deserve* certain things, and when they find themselves without, they behave along these cultural presumptions "that it is natural for a man to use massive, grotesque violence against a woman, any woman, when he is upset" (Dworkin 64). Thus, as Rickie pleads during the climax for JT to let the tied-up and obviously terrified Joann go, JT responds, "Is that really what you want? You want what should have been yours a long time ago, and that's what I'm trying to do for you. I am doing this for your benefit, Rick. She's all yours" (*Deadgirl*).

The only way JT's claim can be true is if what Joann wants does not matter, and the only way either Rickie or JT can be justified in his behavior is if Rickie is indeed owed something. The movie imagines that Rickie is owed not only this woman's body, but recompense for whatever time he put into pursuing a relationship with her. Rickie does not—*cannot*—understand that Joann is in fact in a lower social position than he is by virtue of gender because she is still capable of humiliating him and hurting him emotionally. In the strict hierarchical understanding, Rickie and JT have of power: someone cannot be simultaneously above and below someone else. Rickie's self-pity over his helplessness does not allow him to realize the same helplessness in Joann herself, who is obviously trapped in a terrible, controlling relationship with Johnny she still does not feel capable of ending. She is locked inside the social roles of male dominance and female passivity that leave her even fewer options than Rickie has. Yet because Rickie does not see her as a person, but as an object whose ability to be desired is inextricable from its ability to harm, he cannot imagine for her any desires beyond the desires he has written for her in his head. If Joann has indicated (as she does through her rejection of him) that she is capable of doing emotional damage, then she has, to Rickie, abdicated any previous obligation he felt to protect her. Thus, Joann is for Rickie the same thing the dead girl is for JT: the subjugated other through which a man may establish dominance.

Living Dead Girls

The idea that entering into committed heterosexual relationships is what "civilizes" men is a supposition at the core of much Western culture, particularly in places influenced by Christian narratives of heteronormativity. Love is presented time and again as the taming force for men, causing them to "settle down" and take responsibility for the lives of others. Marriage and family life are seen as incredible male-stabilizing forces; married men earn more money and more promotions than their single counterparts, often through the perception that they are more reliable on account of having families to provide for. Some studies also suggest that this "marriage premium" is not only given, but is earned, because a man who is comfortable and contented in a marriage will work harder and perform better (see Correll et al., Toutkoushian, Antonovics). *Deadgirl* surely seems to believe in this interpretation of the marriage premium, presenting it at the film's close as a direct contrast to JT's earlier violent stabs at elevating his own position. Ultimately, JT could not become a man because his responsibility was to Rickie, not to the dead girl; this juvenile "bros before hos" mentality is not the "proper" way to mature, and one cannot reap the proper benefits from clinging to it. Correct responsibility correctly shouldered, however, can do wonders for a struggling young man—namely Rickie.

These ideas of agency and obligation are important in light of the film's conceit that it is a coming-of-age tale. Indeed, we do see a transformation in Rickie, one of the movie's few survivors—who not only lives through the ordeal but thrives as a result of it. The last shots of the movie, played over the near-hypnotic indie strains of the Liars' "The Other Side of Mt. Heart Attack," show a much happier, more socially acceptable Rickie moving through the world. Wearing a polo shirt and smiling, he walks down the street in the sunshine, seeming miles away from the sullen, grungy teenager seen for most of the movie. He now no longer struggles against society, but embraces his place in it, groomed and content to live among the people around him. Through love and marriage, he has bettered himself and become respectable.

However, this is not a love story; this is set of self-aggrandizing lies told about the corpse of someone Rickie used to know. In considering that such an end could turn out so well for one of the participants and so catastrophically for the other, we have to consider that romance, when pursued from this perspective of male entitlement, has no need of mutuality. In fact, Rickie benefits even more from how mutuality is no longer even a concept for consideration here. He can gain all the benefits of a relationship without having to live in fear that his true love will leave him; he can also set the parameters of his own obligation to her without fear of complaint from her end.

Thus, we arrive at the final question hinted at yet never addressed by the film, which is this: How much self-awareness *does* this particular strain of zombification remove? Are the infected reduced, as they are in so many other films, to mindless drives and basic hindbrain response? Or is there a bit more *there* there?

This is difficult to assess, considering how little evidence the movie presents either way about the dead girl's behavior or condition. There is no attempt to explain the biological or supernatural origins of the infection; as with the epidemic fueling *The Walking Dead*, the cause is incidental and the symptoms are self-evident. There are, however, a few moments that hint at a more significant retention of intelligence than anyone in the movie assumes. On repeated occasions, the dead girl bides her time, choosing to lie still until her target is close enough to attack. She remains docile while JT applies her lipstick, then moments later uses her newly painted mouth to savage the dog that climbs on top of her. When she is finally let loose at the film's climax, she mauls JT, but then bypasses Rickie in favor of running for the door and her freedom. While she seems to display no coherent master plan of action, there is certainly more to her behavior than sheer stimulus and response.

This is the thing of nightmares: that she is at some level aware of what is happening to her, yet all but powerless to do anything about it. Yet when male power is premium and violent retribution is always at hand, passivity is often the only choice women have for survival. "In our society men are expected to take the leading role and women to acquiesce with faint protest. Male aggressive dominance and female passive submission are cultural ideals" (Hanmer 41). By playing into these expectations—by literally not biting the hand that feeds her—the dead girl endures unthinkable abuse, yet also secures her escape when the moment is right. If her consciousness is gone, her instincts are still good, muscle memory from a culture that values female deference to men in all things. We have only to look to Joann throughout the film to see how one does not have to be a zombie to lose agency in a relationship. Joann and the dead girl are subject to the violence of a culture that teaches men that both what they want and what they deserve operate independent of women's humanity. It has nothing to do with either of them.

Finally, as the last shot closes on her bloodshot gaze, we are left to wonder: What will Joann do? What *can* she do? Will she accept her imprisonment as affection? Will she rebel against her abuser? Is there enough of her left in there for her one day to rise up and go? And would Harel then blame her for breaking his hero's heart?

Notes

1. This review, quite tragically, seems to have disappeared from the internet before the authors got a chance to read it. From references to it, however, it seems that Mayer's read of the film was an overall positive one that challenged many of the larger gender constructions found in the horror genre.

2. It is at this point we must note that there are factors of privilege not addressed here, most notably race–no matter what else they are, Rickie and JT are both white. (Though Rickie has "Hecho in Mexico" visibly tattooed on his forearm in one scene, it exists without comment or explanation, and there are no other indicators in text or casting that the character is intended to be a person of color.) However, the all-but-all-white setting of the film means that this gives them no particular immediate advantage.

3. For a larger discussion of this point, see Susan Brownmiller's seminal text, *Against Our Will* (1975), particularly the section titled "Prison Rape: The Homosexual Experience."

Works Cited

Antonovics, Kate, and Robert Town. "Are All the Good Men Married? Uncovering the Sources of the Marital Wage Premium." *The American Economic Review*, vol. 94, no. 2, Papers and Proceedings of the One Hundred Sixteenth Annual Meeting of the American Economic Association, San Diego, CA, Jan. 3–5, 2004, pp. 317–21.

Atwood, Margaret. "Writing the Male Character." *Second Words: Selected Critical Prose, 1960–1982*. House of Anansi, 1982, pp. 412–32.

Brownmiller, Susan. *Against Our Will: Men, Women and Rape*. Fawcett, 2010.

Correll, Shelley J., Stephen Benard, and In Paik. "Getting a Job: Is There a Motherhood Penalty?" *American Journal of Sociology*, vol. 112, no. 5, March 2007, pp. 1297–1339 www.jstor.org/stable/10.1086/511799.

Deadgirl. Directed by Marcel Sarmiento and Gadi Harel, Hollywoodmade, 2008.

Dworkin, Andrea. *Life and Death*. The Free Press, 1997.

Finley, Laura L. *Domestic Abuse and Sexual Assault in Popular Culture*. Praeger, 2016.

Grant, Barry Keith. "Taking Back the Night of the Living Dead: George Romero, Feminism, and the Horror Film." *The Dread of Difference: Gender and the Horror Film*, edited by Barry Keith Grant. University of Texas Press, 1996, pp. 200–212.

Gullién, Michael. *DEADGIRL—Interview with Gadi Harel*. 8 March 2009.

Hanmer, Jalna and Sheila Saunters. *Well-Founded Fear: A Community Study of Violence to Women*. Hutchinson Publishing Group, 1984.

Marcotte, Amanda. "The Dangerous Discourse of 'the Friend Zone.'" *RawStory*. 27 May 2014. www.rawstory.com/2014/05/the-dangerous-discourse-of-the-friend-zone/.

McGlotten, Shaka, and Sarah Vangundy. "Zombie Porn 1.0: or, Some Queer Things Zombie Sex Can Teach Us." *Qui Parle: Critical Humanities and Social Sciences*, vol. 21, no. 2, Spring/Summer 2013, pp. 101–125.

Paffenroth, Kim. *Gospel of the Living Dead: George Romero's Visions of Hell on Earth*. Baylor University Press, 2006.

Schmeink, Lars. "'Scavenge, Slay, Survive': The Zombie Apocalypse, Exploration, and Lived Experience in DayZ." *Science Fiction Studies*. vol. 43, no. 1, March 2016, pp. 67–84.
Theriault, Anne. "Men See Themselves in Brock Turner—That's Why They Don't Condemn Him." *The Establishment*. 7 June 2016. www.theestablishment.co/men-see-themselves-in-brock-turner-thats-why-they-don-t-condemn-him-902a2a619db3#.u736neoxa.
Toutkoushian, Robert K. "Racial and Marital Status Differences in Faculty Pay." *The Journal of Higher Education*, vol. 69, no. 5, Sep.-Oct. 1998, pp. 513–541.

La Petite Mort
Death and Desire in Pride and Prejudice and Zombies

AMY CAROL REEVES

There is a long and well-documented frustration among readers regarding the lack of sexual passion in Jane Austen's novels.[1] Always in Austen's world, a young heroine's sexual desire remains subordinate to considerations of intellectual compatibility and economic stability of a marriage partner.[2] The women who break these rules end up worse off as evidenced by *Pride and Prejudice*'s Lydia Bennet and *Mansfield Parks*'s Maria Bertram. I argue that Seth Grahame-Smith's *Pride and Prejudice and Zombies,* as a parody of Austen's work, plays with the concept of *la petite mort*—the "little death" most often referring to orgasm—to invoke a landscape teeming with death and to thus showcase sexual tensions for popular audiences, particularly for young adult readers. Burr Steers's 2016 film, *Pride and Prejudice and Zombies,* takes this idea even further.

Although the French phrase *la petite mort* has often historically been used to refer to nonsexual "little deaths," as evidenced by its use in *Tess of d'Urbervilles,*[3] the term was first used to signify orgasm in 1882 (*"petite mort"*) and is most often understood today as referencing orgasm. This connection is likely due to the advent of Freudian theory in the late nineteenth-century. Specifically, the Oedipal Complex rests upon the assumption that sexual urges intertwine with murderous desires. Furthermore, Freud's speculations in *Beyond the Pleasure Principle* (1920), that living organisms have the dual drives to create (embodied in sexual instincts) and to self-destruct (embodied in the death wish) further solidify these connections. He asserts that there are two types of instincts in every human being: "those which seek to lead what is living to death, and others, the sexual instincts which are perpetually attempting and achieving a renewal of life" (Freud 52). In this post–Freud world, authors such as Jean Rhys, who wrote *Wide Sargasso Sea* (1966), effectively take full-advantage of these connotations, and death imagery abounds in her sexual scenes. Rhys's Mr. Rochester referring to Antoinette's orgasms as deaths and drownings reinforces this emphasis on death and sexuality.[4]

Even well before Freud, the connection between chills and erotic thrills is also evident in the popularity of the Gothic novel in the late eighteenth-century. Coleridge famously made the connections between sensual pleasure and Gothic novel reading.[5] Austen inadvertently demonstrates these links in *Northanger Abbey* (1817) as inexperienced Catherine Morland moves to coded sexual experience through her Gothic novel reading. Her fear of rogue "noblemen and baronets" (26) paves the way for her to learn about the real-life liar, John Thorpe, and the controlling and selfish General Tilney. Indeed, when Henry Tilney mocks Eleanor and Catherine's reading habits for creating a riot in their brains (Austen 113), he is equally mocking the riot in their *bodies* brought on by reading. The Gothic tales fire the young women's passions and imaginations in ways threatening to the general patriarchy. Margaret Drabble points out the sexual nature of Catherine's move towards experience: "*Northanger Abbey* is clearly a story of initiation rites, of a young woman's post-pubertal and at times painful induction into society and adult life" (viii).

Grahame-Smith establishes these foundational links between sexual desire and concepts of fear and death through his setup of core plot tensions in the opening page of *Pride and Prejudice and Zombies*. The original novel's opening lines, "It is a truth universally acknowledged, that a single man in possession of a good fortune, must be in want of a wife" (Austen 5), foreshadows the plot problem of securing an economically stable husband. Grahame-Smith explicitly links Austen's matrimonial plot tension with the zombie apocalypse survival tension through blending these original lines with references to zombie attacks: "It is a truth universally acknowledged that a zombie in possession of brains must be in want of more brains" (Grahame-Smith 9). Furthermore, whereas Mrs. Bennet presents all of the original character's concerns over marrying her daughters to wealthy men, Mr. Bennet rebuffs her with his main concern that his daughters survive the zombie apocalypse:

> "If I can but see one of my daughters happily settled at Netherfield," said Mrs. Bennet to her husband, "and the others equally well married, I shall have nothing to wish for."
>
> "And if I can see all five of them survive England's present difficulties, then neither shall I," he replied [11].

Their sparring in these opening pages sets up the sex and death dichotomy and immediately thickens the goals of the original novel's protagonists. Marry well, but one must also physically survive long enough to marry at all.

Mr. Bennet's essential concern that his daughters survive, also acknowledges "new rules" for men and women in Grahame-Smith's revision. In Austen's world, marriage represents the only acceptable realm for sexual experience. However, the post-zombie apocalyptic landscape, where the Bennet sisters must fight for their own survival, metaphorically bleeds out matrimonial sexual ecstasy into their everyday lives. *La petite mort* plays heavily here as the threat of death increases elements of sexual desire in otherwise traditional Austen scenes.

The Netherfield Ball most pointedly demonstrates *la petite mort*. In *Pride and Prejudice and Zombies*, Bingley and Darcy carry out the original Austen exchange where Darcy finds himself challenged by his friend to dance with Elizabeth Bennet. Mr. Darcy's famous insult plays out: "She is tolerable, but not handsome enough to tempt, *me;* I am in no humour at present to give consequence to young ladies who are slighted by other men" (Grahame-Smith 13). However, whereas Austen's Elizabeth felt, "no very cordial feelings towards him" (Austen 13), laughing off the slight with friends, Grahame-Smith's Elizabeth burns with fury. Her response is much more physically-rooted than in the original text:

> As Mr. Darcy walked off, Elizabeth felt her blood turn cold. She had never in her life been so insulted. The warrior code demanded she avenge her honour. Elizabeth reached down to her ankle, taking care not to draw attention. There, her hand met the dagger concealed beneath her dress. She meant to follow this proud Mr. Darcy outside and open his throat [Grahame-Smith 13–14].

The fact that Darcy's insult can incite such a physical reaction within Elizabeth, where she becomes set on killing him for a slight, reveals the orgasmic nature of her murderous intentions. Whereas Austen heroines seek to *control* bodily feelings—a slighted Elizabeth feels "no very cordial feelings"—this revised Elizabeth is *ignited* by her feelings. She makes no attempt to reign in desire but instead chases it (reaching immediately for her concealed dagger, a blatant phallic object) towards its logical conclusion: death. The moment here is nothing less than coded sexual fantasy where she desires not only opening Darcy's throat, but also bringing about another "death" for him and for herself—orgasm.

This coded sexual fantasy continues to build as the novel progresses towards Mr. Darcy's first proposal to Elizabeth. Namely, Elizabeth psychologically links matrimony/sexual desire with death. When Mr. Bennet advises her to pursue Wickham as a romantic interest, Elizabeth responds with: "I am perfectly content being the bride of death" (105). She also sees her role as a fierce warrior as an alternative to becoming a bride, "My talents and my times demand my service, and I believe the Crown more pleased to have me on the front lines than at the altar" (115). Both "passions," murderous and matrimonial desires, are equally fueling to *Zombies*'s Elizabeth Bennet. She explicitly seems to admit this when, after finding out about Wickham's rumored engagement, she says to Mrs. Gardiner, "I have never been much in love; for had I really experienced that pure and elevating passion, I should at present detest [Wickham's] very name, and wish him all manner of evil" (115). Interestingly, although she seems here to connect love with rage, she fails to recognize these connections in her own building desire for Mr. Darcy. Yet, she exhibits what Freud describes as the intermingling of the life (sexual drive) and death drive as "the presence of the sadistic component of the sexual instinct" (Freud 59).

From the point where Elizabeth Bennet fantasizes at the Netherfield Ball about bringing Darcy closer to *la petite mort*, Darcy's love for Elizabeth grows as he recognizes her murderous skills. Death and sexual desire are joined in the same moment as he seems himself in "some danger of falling in love" (42). He realizes in this moment, that her skills as a warrior are advanced enough that she might be a dangerous opponent for him: "for never had he seen a lady more gifted in the ways of vanquishing the undead" (42). The idea titillates Grahame-Smith's Mr. Darcy as an ideal woman is also the woman who brings about death. He lists off traditional Regency era accomplishments for a wife, "knowledge of music, singing, drawing, dancing, and the modern languages," but he adds that she should also understand the deadly arts of battle: "she must be well trained in the fighting styles of the Kyoto masters and the modern tactics and weaponry of Europe" (34). His sexual fantasy of Elizabeth as a skillful murderer becomes increasingly overt. After Lady Catherine suggests that Elizabeth would be highly skilled at using the Leopard's Claw with more practice as, "she has a very good notion of fingering," Darcy replies, "'That she does,' ... in a manner such as to make Elizabeth's face quite red" (138). Such an innuendo obviously would make no appearance in Austen's original text, but the pressing drive of *la petite mort* banishes conventional boundaries of propriety. Indeed Tiffany Potter affirms the significance that the zombies are referred to as "unmentionables" (17). What would be "unmentionable"—sexual tension, murderous fury—in Austen's text, surfaces boldly in this violent reimagined Regency era world.

Author of *Everybody's Jane* (2011), Juliette Wells notes that *Zombies* is a pleasurable read as "the physical dimensions added by Grahame-Smith ... intensify the tension established by Austen" (188). Certainly the first proposal scene where Darcy and Elizabeth battle each other, not only through sparring words but through a physical fight, exposes the building sexual fantasy. Because she knows now that Darcy was behind the plot to keep Bingley away from Jane, Elizabeth's desire for his "death" is even greater at this point. Immediately before the scene, she imagines bringing Darcy's head and heart to Jane after slaying him with her sword (148). This desire for his death symbolizes her desire for his body, and the first proposal scene unfolds with their attraction playing out in the orgasmic fury of Darcy and Elizabeth's fight.

After Darcy's insulting proposal, "In vain I have struggled…" (148), Elizabeth feels the stirring of "her deeply rooted bloodlust" (149). Bloodlust, the perfectly coined word in this instance, unites her literal lust for Darcy's blood with her lust for his body. *La petite mort* surfaces here as the moment's foreplay builds towards physical and sexual "death." Even Elizabeth's feelings seem perfectly conflicted with both desires: "she could not be insensible to the compliment of such a man's affection, and though her intention of killing him did not vary for an instant, she was somewhat sorry for the pain he was to receive; till, roused to resentment by his subsequent language, she lost all compassion in anger" (149). She is set on killing him while yet still moved by the "compliment" of his affection; she feels "sorry" about the death she plans to inflict even while she is simultaneously enraged by his insults. These unsettling dual drives spark the physical battle fueled by sexual tension.

After announcing that she will cause his death, "Before you walked through that door, I had resolved to strike you down" (149), *Zombies*'s Elizabeth Bennet lifts her skirt to fight Darcy. She becomes the sexual aggressor in this scene, assuming the first fighting pose, the "basic crane pose" (149), and putting an unsettled Darcy into a defensive position. When she does strike him, sending him into the mantelpiece, his reaction is not only physical pain, but increased desire—an essential *approval* of her violence: "Wiping the blood from his mouth, he looked at her with a smile of affected incredulity" (151). She responds by taking the fireplace poker, a phallic object of sexual penetration, and threatening him with it. The orgasmic fury building since the Netherfield Ball fully surfaces here as she swings "the poker at him with renewed vigour" (152). Elizabeth's "vigour" represents the flourishing of her dual desires for Darcy's "death." The fighting is interspersed between word-for-word Austen text, and Darcy returns the sexual play through grabbing the poker from her (152). But when he bows out, "throwing the poker in the fire" (152), Elizabeth's climactic rage remains unsatisfied and she still burns with desire, "The tumult of her mind was now painfully great" (153). The physical fighting here allows for pre-marital erotic play, the manifestation of the "unmentionable" sexual tension between Darcy and Elizabeth in the original text's first proposal scene. Furthermore, the sexual encounter is as failed as the marriage proposal, evidenced by Elizabeth's frustration when Darcy leaves as she fails to bring about "death" in both senses of the word.

The infiltration of *la petite mort* in *Zombies* shows not only through the interactions between Elizabeth and Darcy, but through Lady Catherine's role as well. In Austen's *Pride and Prejudice,* she tries to control and manipulate all of the romantic relationships—desiring her own daughter to marry Darcy and overseeing Mr. Collins's choice in a marriage partner, "A clergyman like you must marry.—Chuse properly, chuse a gentlewoman for *my* sake; and for your *own*, let her be an active, useful sort of person, not brought up high, but able to make a small income go a good way" (Austen 89). Most blatantly, she exercises her control through attempting to intimidate Elizabeth into rejecting Darcy should he propose to her. The fact that the zombie infection is the main vehicle for *la petite mort* becomes evident in Lady Catherine de Bourgh's drive to control the plague.

Specifically, Lady Catherine is known as much for her warrior skills as she is for her fortune and rank. Collins describes Lady Catherine's warrior skills, "[her] skill with blade and musket are unmatched, and [she] has slain more unmentionables than any woman known" (51). He also claims that she "has a singular dedication to the art of killing zombies" (53). Although Collins tends to inflate Lady Catherine's qualities, Elizabeth knows of her reputation, "she had been regaled with stories of Lady Catherine's accomplishments from the time she had been old enough to hold her first dagger ... the presence of a woman who had slain ninety dreadfuls with nothing more than a rain-soaked envelope was an intimidating prospect indeed" (124). Additionally, Lady Catherine knows that her reputation as a zombie-slayer and her team of deadly ninjas give her power and control in a landscape awry with traditional rules, particularly regarding love and marriage. She also seems to know that the ability to wield death is where women's power lies in this world. In *Pride and Prejudice*, she judges Elizabeth's status through interrogating her about her sisters, her ability to play an instrument, and not having a governess during her childhood (137). In *Zombies*, Lady Catherine challenges Elizabeth to fight her ninjas "for the amusement of the party" (129). Elizabeth passes her test, violently murdering all three ninjas and establishing herself as a threatening opponent to Lady Catherine's power.

The final confrontation between Lady Catherine and Elizabeth further highlights this idea that power is located in the ability to kill. Elizabeth hits at the heart of this in her retort to Lady Catherine's argument that her daughter should have Mr. Darcy: "Has she even strength to lift a Katana?" (288) Grahame-Smith's Lady Catherine has all of the power-hungry nature of Austen's Lady Catherine, and thus realizes the importance of warrior skills in the new landscape. Hence warrior-Elizabeth truly is the greatest threat to Lady Catherine's influence over the *petite mort* landscape. Elizabeth realizes this and presents her fighting power as her strongest weapon, "My master ... taught me that the shortest path to ruin was underestimating one's opponent" (292).

Lady Catherine fails to control warrior-Elizabeth, and she also cannot control the zombie infection. *Pride and Prejudice*'s Lady Catherine's drive to manipulate romantic relationships remains and is demonstrated through her attempt to manipulate and control the plague. Not only does she try to wield power as a zombie-slayer, but she seeks to control the infection itself through creating a cure. In the final confrontation scene, she boasts to Elizabeth about dropping serum into an infected Charlotte's tea to cure her and to give her "new priest ... some measure of happiness" (287). In the same way that she likes to have power by controlling who those around her marry, holding a viable "cure" for the zombie plague would allow her to control who lives and who succumbs to the infection. But her efforts to regulate the infection fail as much as her efforts to regulate matrimony. *La petite mort* resists control. The last paragraph of *Zombies* places emphasis on this: "her ladyship's serum proved folly, for while it slowed some effects of the strange plague, it was helpless to stop them" (316–17).

Finally, I must note, that after Darcy's successful marriage proposal, Elizabeth identifies precisely what made him fall in love with her. It was her murderous drive, representative of her thriving sexual desire—the characteristic absent from more proper young women. Elizabeth speaks plainly of the *petite mort* building between them:

> The fact is, that you were sick of civility, of deference, of officious attention. You were disgusted with the women who were always speaking, and looking, and thinking for *your* approbation alone. I roused, and interested you, because I was so unlike *them*. I knew the joy of standing over a vanquished foe; of painting my face and arms with their blood, yet warm, and screaming to the heavens—begging, nay daring, God to send me more enemies to kill. The gentle ladies who so assiduously courted you knew nothing of this joy, and therefore, could never offer you true happiness [311].

It was her swelling bloodlust, pushing both of them towards orgasm or the little death that fueled his love for her. She boldly asserts here that she "roused" and "interested" Darcy with her warrior skills. The orgasm imagery in Elizabeth's description of a kill is blatant—her "joy" at standing over a defeated enemy, her intense physical pleasure of the kill where she paints her "face and arms with their blood," her screams "to the heavens, begging" for more "enemies to kill." It is significant that when she accepts Darcy's proposal, they immediately come upon a large herd of zombies and "sharing a glance, and a smile, [they] realised they had stumbled onto their first opportunity to fight side by side" (302). In this instance, bringing death to these zombies, functions as the physical consummation of Darcy and Elizabeth's love. Given the failure of the first proposal to bring about "death," the second proposal is successful, and their zombie kill here is nothing less than a representation of intercourse. The fact that Grahame-Smith has a "fade to black" moment, non-descriptive of Darcy and Elizabeth's first moment of fighting side by side supports this reading. When they realize this is "their first opportunity to fight side by side" Grahame-Smith follows this up simply with, "And so they did" (302).

Burr Steers's 2016 film, *Pride and Prejudice and Zombies,* pushes these ideas of sexual desire and death/violence even further, which is particularly evident in the visual images of the Bennet sisters' fighting scenes. The attractiveness of the warrior Bennet sisters' bodies *is* present in the novel, Elizabeth Bennet is described as equally "ferocious" and "fetching" (74). Furthermore, Andrea Ruthven points out that in the novel:

> Despite the fact that her militarized body and violence are constructed as being first and foremost for the defense of herself and her loved ones, her finely tuned body *is* heteronormatively attractive, though this is presented as an added bonus, the result of so much training for the defense of others and not the primary motive of her training [342].

However, in the novel, Elizabeth Bennet still pays a fair amount of attention to modesty, using a "modesty string" (136–137) to keep her legs concealed when she stands on her head. But the film takes full advantage of visual media to sexualize the Bennet sisters' bodies. Specifically, the film fetishizes the Bennet sisters as warriors—giving significant time in the opening scenes to shots of the young women dressing and carefully sheathing daggers into their satiny undergarments.

The scene at the Netherfield Ball, where the sisters assume the "Pentagram Shape," to ward off a zombie attack in the ballroom, plays out like a dance with the sisters fanning out into specific positions. The film emphasizes the sexualized nature of the battle, paralleling the violence with a ballroom dance. Instead of waltzing with romantic partners, the Bennet sisters bring death to approaching zombies as they wield daggers and a quarterstaff. Although Darcy (Sam Riley) had moments earlier elicited his famous slight against Elizabeth (Lily James), the film here clearly roots his sexual desire for her in his observance of her fighting abilities. While Darcy and Bingley (Douglas Boothe) watch voyeuristically from the side of the ballroom as the Bennet sisters fight the undead, Darcy praises Elizabeth's figure, deciding that "Her arms are surprisingly muscular and yet not so much as to be unfeminine."

The film emphasizes the intermingling of erotic play and violence in Darcy's first proposal to Elizabeth. In Steers's film, *la petite mort* flourishes as Riley depicts perhaps the darkest and broodiest Darcy of any previous film. He maintains a near sneer on his face as he delivers his insulting proposal. Furthermore, he assumes a kneeling posture, a parallel pose mingling a traditional marriage proposal posture with a battle posture signaling defeat; particularly given Elizabeth's warrior skills, the posture *invites* her to slay him. In Austen's *Pride and Prejudice,* the first marriage proposal represents Darcy's "defeat" as he confesses to Elizabeth, "In vain have I struggled" (Austen 157). Riley's Darcy physically demonstrates this defeat and seemingly postures himself to Elizabeth to bring on his "death," a brilliantly symbolic moment where he invites not only her physical attack, but the little death promised through sexual play.

It is immediately after he stands from his kneeling position, when she delivers her first blow, kicking him in the chest and then throwing books at him. As in Grahame-Smith's novel, here Elizabeth works as the sexual aggressor, advancing on him with the symbolically phallic fireplace poker. But the film shows him restraining her and glancing down at her bosom—a detail *not* in the novel. The scene also emphasizes a certain amount of "undressing" where her skirts fly up and she crushes his head between her legs revealing both her flesh and stockings as they argue about Wickham's "misfortunes." When they rise, she slices through the buttons on his shirt with a letter opener before he grabs the poker and slices through the top of her dress exposing her bosom. They proceed to wrestle on the floor until she plunges the letter opener towards his heart, but here, as in the novel, though the scene is ripe with erotic play, everything remains unconsummated; Elizabeth stops short of driving the letter opener into his heart to deliver "death." There is no penetration, and when he leaves the room she remains agitated and unsatisfied, the ending shot shows her breathless and teary and making no move to cover her nearly exposed breasts as Mr. Collins (Matt Smith) and Charlotte (Aisling Loftus) return to the cottage.

A zombie-slaying Lady Catherine de Bourgh, played by Lena Headey, depicts the most sexualized, youthful de Bourgh of any film. She is an obvious break from the Lady Catherine de Bourgh in the *Zombies* novel, described as fifty years older than Elizabeth in the final confrontation (289). Rather, the film's de Bourgh is much younger. Her long dark hair, form-fitting dresses, and black leather pantaloons position her against the Bennet sisters almost as a viable romantic rival in the *petite mort* landscape. Even the eye-patch, absent from the illustrations and descriptions of Lady Catherine in Grahame-Smith's novel, works here as an accessory. The eyepatch accentuates the same pattern of heteronormative attractiveness Ruthven attributes to *Zombies* Elizabeth Bennet's "finely tuned body"—the eyepatch accentuates the battle wound as a sexual symbol, an aesthetic "added bonus" resulting from war triumph. Even Mrs. Bennet (Sally Phillips) notices the appeal of the eye patch, timidly asking Lady Catherine if it is for "function or fashion." Additionally, in the same way that the poker is used as a phallic symbol of erotic play in the first proposal's fight scene, Headey's Lady Catherine wields her katana as a symbol of sexual power throughout the film. Her grand house showcases a portrait of her wielding a katana sword over an undead Lucifer. Furthermore, when Headey's Lady Catherine confronts Elizabeth to make her promise to refuse a proposal of marriage from Mr. Darcy, she holds the katana to her throat in a threatening play to demonstrate her sexual power on the *petite mort* playing field. At this point, when the film's Lady Catherine says, "I do not know which I admire more Elizabeth Bennet, your skill as a warrior or your resolve as a woman," she is emphasizing the dual nature of their battle; they fight not only as warriors to slay zombies, but they fight each other as women for agency in the realm of sexual politics.

One interesting departure from Grahame-Smith's novel is the film's characterization of the zombies. Whereas in the novel the zombies are inarticulate and unintelligent, driven only to consume the living, in Steers's film version, zombies in various stages of decay have agency and can speak to the living. This intensifies the *petite mort* where the zombies can actually become objects of desire. In the novel, George Wickham (Jack Huston) becomes wheelchair bound and unable to control his bowels after Darcy beats him for bringing shame to the Bennet family. The film transforms dashing and insouciant George Wickham into a dashing and insouciant infected zombie, thus making the popular object of desire also an undead. Although Elizabeth does not know for most of the film that he is infected, she desires him nonetheless.

As both an undead and an alluring sexual object, Huston's Wickham holds power over *both* death and desire and is thus much more dangerous than the Wickham character in both novels. Whereas Lady Catherine futilely attempts to control the sexual relationships in the film and novels, Huston's Wickham holds complete control, including the ability to open the door to the apocalypse. He is the only character who seems to know that the normal boundaries of sexual relations and death are banished in the presence of *la petite mort*. This is demonstrated most effectively on a night when during her stay at Rosings Park, a restless Elizabeth Bennet gets out of bed with very little covering over her nightgown and leaves the cottage for a walk in the middle of the night. In the scene's neo-Gothic atmosphere, Elizabeth senses danger before drawing her dagger and assuming a fighting stance; Wickham then steps out from a spreading fog, accentuating the scene's thick tensions of fear and sexual desire.

If Elizabeth Bennet breaks Regency rules of sexual propriety by walking alone outside at night, Wickham breaks these rules as well by approaching her and standing improperly close to her body. After predicting the downfall of Rosings Park and telling Elizabeth that Darcy has persuaded Bingley to stay away from Jane (Bella Heathcote), Wickham takes her hand and proposes that she run away with him. The move is not only intimate, but it is a bold seduction attempt. As an undead and a desirable man, he asserts the free reign of sexual desire and death in a chaotic apocalyptic world. In a pivotal moment, Elizabeth pulls away. Although she does not know at this point that he is an undead, she helped him access Lady Catherine earlier to argue that the undead might be civilized rather than slain if they are raised on pigs' brains. But here Elizabeth is deeply unsettled by the very fact that Wickham makes no attempt to recognize boundaries upon desire and death. She might engage in coded erotic fight play with Darcy; she and her sisters might expose flesh and satin stockings while slaying zombies; Lady Catherine might seek to regulate the surging passions between the characters around her; but the introduction of a character who radically *embraces* the chaos without any attempt at control disturbs her, and she points out his lack of boundaries, "You have crossed a line, sir." Wickham, before leaving her, remains unscathed by her critique; he knows that sexual desire and death are at this point far beyond containment: "We are far beyond lines now, Miss Bennet."

The final scenes of the film initially seem to depict a world where both death and sexual desire seem to be in their proper places—in a dramatic battle scene London is saved from being overrun by zombies and Jane and Elizabeth marry Bingley and Darcy. But the film's end also shows Wickham overturning these victories. As Darcy, Elizabeth, Jane, and Bingley leave their wedding ceremony, he leads a zombie army towards them. Here Wickham functions as the *embodiment* of *la petite mort* and the other characters, though they might resist him, remain powerless to stop his force on the apocalyptic landscape.

Both Grahame-Smith's novel and Steers's *Pride and Prejudice and Zombies* use the *petite mort* to portray sexual tension otherwise absent in Austen's texts. Specifically, the *petite mort* updates *Pride and Prejudice* for popular audiences, namely young adult audiences. In a blog post after the 2016 release of Steers's film, Jason Rekulak, the Quirk Books editor who brainstormed the mashup, admitted that finding an audience was a challenge, "I hoped we'd sell the book to Jane Austen fans and zombie fans, but my friends were quick to point out that 'Jane Austen fans won't tolerate all of the gory zombie bloodshed' and 'Zombie fans won't tolerate all of the Regency courtship and melodrama'" (Rekulak). Given the booming marketplace for young adult literature,[6] aside from popular audiences, Quirk Books most certainly had young adult readers in mind. Furthermore, the very fact that Steers's film has a PG-13 rating as opposed to an R rating shows that the viewers of the *Twilight* (2008) and *Hunger Games* (2012–15) films were a target audience. Indeed, both Rekulak and Grahame-Smith acknowledged the challenge of getting young adults to care about Austen texts. Rekulak stated in 2010:

> When I was sixteen years old and my English teacher assigned *Sense and Sensibility*, I just thought it was about the most boring book in the world. Later I read some remarks by Richard Price, the really famous New York writer, who was growing up in the Bronx, and his teachers were pushing Jane Austen on him. And he had the same reaction: "I don't understand … who these people are, I can't relate to this" [Qtd. in Wells 186–87].

When Rekulak contacted him about writing the book, Grahame-Smith admitted he had not read *Pride and Prejudice* since age fourteen and, as a teenager, he had not "particularly cared for Elizabeth Bennet's love life and Regency mannerisms, nor for Austen's 19th-century prose, on his first readthrough" (Dunn). These comments indicate that he likely had a dual audience in mind for the book—both adult Austen-philes as well as young adult readers who might have difficulty connecting to Austen's works.

Additionally, Austen's novels have wide popular appeal[7] and young adult readers might like the plot and characters, but the notorious lack of sexual desire in an essentially romantic story line would remain a problem. For a generation of teenagers consuming the *Twilight* series (2005–08) where a significant storyline revolves around Edward Cullen's virginity and the consummation of his relationship with Bella in *Breaking Dawn* (2008), the lack of sexual passion in *Pride and Prejudice* presents a void to young adult readers. However, unless the *Pride and Prejudice* storyline is removed completely from the Regency era setting as in the case of Helen Fielding's *Bridget Jones's Diary* (1996), including too much sexual material in a non-erotica mashup would be unbelievable. The inclusion of the zombie apocalypse allows for popular appeal to teenagers, but the elements of *la petite mort*, infused in the violent atmosphere, breakdown Regency era rules of sexual propriety and provide a believable place, both in the film and novel, for sexual tension otherwise absent.

Pride and Prejudice and Zombies represents a bold and brilliant creative move updating Austen's novel for an evolving marketplace. Rekulak, Grahame-Smith, and Steers strategically pitch the story to the widest possible audience including teenage consumers of young adult books and films. *La petite mort* becomes the means of catapulting both sex and violence into a widely read work to engage not only Austen fans, but otherwise reluctant readers of her novels.

Ironically, the *Pride and Prejudice* mashup aimed at meeting the expectations of young adult consumers parallels the Gothic novels pitched to Catherine Morland and her friends. Zombies, violence, and sexual desire satiate readers' needs for "powerful stimulants," and yet again popular literature is written for a reading public's particular appetites. *Northanger Abbey* represents nothing less than Austen's shrewd observation of the transformative power of novel-reading on young adult minds. It seems entirely fitting therefore, that her most famous and beloved novel be updated to fit the expectations of twenty-first century Catherine Morlands in an evolving literary scene where zombies, apocalypse, and sexual desire replace the drafty castles and scoundrel baronets of the popular Regency era Gothic novel.

Notes

1. Juliette Wells in *Everybody's Jane* (2012) covers this topic extensively: "The absence of physical passion in Austen's novels, which accords with her contemporaries' ideas of what

lady novelists should represent, has long irritated those readers who yearn for a more inclusive, and arguably more realistic, depiction of human life" (181). She even points to Charlotte Brontë's well-known complaint to her publisher: "the Passions are perfectly unknown to [Austen]" (qtd. in Wells 181).

2. Anne Mellor elaborates upon Austen's caution surrounding female sexual passion and desire: "Given the economic dependence of women upon men, it follows that women cannot obey the impulses and dictates of their feelings. Sexual desire and passionate love too easily lead women into unhappy marriages, as we see when Lydia Bennet is punished for her 'high animal spirits' and promiscuous desire by the indifferent contempt of Wickham. Or they can threaten a woman's life, as when Marianne Dashwood almost dies after Willoughby cruelly rejects her ardent love. Or worse, they can condemn women to the perpetual disgrace and ostracism endured by Maria Bertram and the two Elizas in *Sense and Sensibility*" (59).

3. When Tess learns the morbid background of the pillar that Alec d'Urberville misidentifies as a Holy Cross: "She felt the *petite mort* at this unexpectedly gruesome information" (259).

4. "'Die then! Die!' I watched her die many times. In my way, not in hers. In sunlight, in shadow, by moonlight, by candlelight. In the long afternoons when the house was empty. Only the sun was there to keep us company. We shut him out. And why not? Very soon she was as eager for what's called loving as I was—more lost and drowned afterwards" (Rhys 55).

5. Coleridge refers, in his review of *The Monk*, to Gothic novels as "Most powerful stimulants" (608).

6. "With sales up 24 percent, the fastest growing market for publishers is young adult books" ("Young adult books").

7. About Austen's popular appeal, Rekulak states, "People love Jane Austen.... They love that book in a way they don't love other books. Austen fans are a special bunch. If there's a more loved novel in the English language, I don't know it. It's the template for so many stories, like a Rosetta Stone of Hollywood rom-coms" (Dunn).

Works Cited

Austen, Jane. *Northanger Abbey*. Introduction by Margaret Drabble, Signey, 1989.

_____. *Pride and Prejudice*. Introduction by Vivien Jones, Penguin, 1996.

_____, and Seth Grahame-Smith. *Pride and Prejudice and Zombies*. Quirk Books, 2009.

Coleridge, Samuel Taylor. "Review of *The Monk* by Matthew Lewis." *The Norton Anthology of English Literature*, edited by Stephen Greenblatt et al., 9th ed., vol. D, Norton, 2012, pp. 608–11.

Dunn, Thom. "*Pride and Prejudice and Zombies*: Part 1 of 3." *Quirk Books*, 11 Mar. 2014, www.quirkbooks.com/post/pride-prejudice-zombies-part-1-3.

Freud, Sigmund. *Beyond the Pleasure Principle. On Freud's Beyond the Pleasure Principle*, edited by Salman Akhtar and Mary Kay O'Neil, Karnac, 2011, pp. 13–64.

Hardy, Thomas. *Tess of the d'Urbervilles*, edited by Scott Elledge, Norton, 1979.

Mellor, Anne K. *Romanticism and Gender*. Routledge, 1992.

Meyer, Stephenie. The *Twilight* Series. Little Brown, 2005–2008.

"*petite mort.*" *Oxford English Dictionary Online*, 3rd ed., Dec. 2005, www.oed.com/view/Entry/260928?rskey=eiOod2&result=1#eid10651807.

Potter, Tiffany. "Historicizing the Popular and the Feminine: *The Rape of the Lock* and *Pride and Prejudice and Zombies*." *Women, Popular Culture, and the Eighteenth Century*, edited by Tiffany Potter, University of Toronto Press, 2012, pp. 5–21.

Pride and Prejudice and Zombies. Directed by Burr Steers, Lionsgate, 2016.

Rekulak, Jason. "Undeniable and Inevitable: The Untold Origins of *Pride and Prejudice and Zombies*." *Quirk Books*, 5 Feb. 2016, www.quirkbooks.com/post/undeniable-and-inevitable-untold-origins-pride-and-prejudice-and-zombies.

Rhys, Jean. *Wide Sargasso Sea*, edited by Judith L. Raiskin, Norton, 1999.

Ruthven, Andrea. "Zombie Postfeminism." *This Year's Work at the Zombie Research Center*,

edited by Edward P. Comentale and Aaron Jaffe, Indiana University Press, 2014, pp. 341–60.
Wells, Juliette. *Everybody's Jane: Austen in the Popular Imagination.* Bloomsbury, 2012.
"Young Adult Books Are Fastest-Growing Market for Publishers." *CBS News,* 8 Dec. 2013, www.cbsnews.com/videos/young-adult-books-are-fastest-growing-market-for-publishers.

Love and Marriage in the Time of *The Walking Dead*

Amanda Taylor

Total societal breakdown is a typical trope in zombie apocalypse texts. Frank Darabont's televised adaptation of Robert Kirkman's series, *The Walking Dead* (*TWD*) (2010–present), is no exception to this.[1] As seen in the episode "Sick," explaining this breakdown to someone who has not seen it firsthand can be particularly difficult. In this episode, Rick Grimes (Andrew Lincoln), Daryl Dixon (Norman Reedus), and T-Dog (Irone Singleton) must explain the end of the world to a group of inmates they find in an abandoned prison that is mostly overrun by walkers (the show's term for zombies). The inmates have been trapped in the prison cafeteria for ten months. When they ask Rick's group about using a cell phone to call their families, or when the Army or National Guard is coming, Rick, Daryl, and T-Dog realize how much the inmates do not know. "There is no Army," Rick explains. "No government, no hospitals, no police. It's all gone." All social institutions as the inmates knew them are gone. While it is easy to see the crumbled infrastructure and lack of government in *TWD*, we can, upon further examination, also see the breakdown and reconstruction of social structures, particularly that of marriage.

What does marriage look like in a zombie apocalypse? Specifically, what do marriage and romance look like in *TWD*, and how might they affect group dynamics? How are gender roles affected, especially if viewed as a binary between the archetypal masculine Warrior and feminine Caregiver? This essay investigates the place and shape of marriage and romance in *TWD*. As *TWD* reflects its cultural moment, we can expect to see a variety of romantic relationships, including those that are nonconsensual and those that are sex-only. I wish, however, to go beyond the more casual relationships and focus on two core romantic relationships in *TWD*: the marriage of Rick and Lori

Grimes (Sarah Wayne Callies) and the marriage-like relationship between Glenn Rhee (Steven Yeun) and Maggie Greene (Lauren Cohan). Both relationships have definite effects on group dynamics and showcase different attitudes toward marriage itself. I draw on triangulation theory, attachment theory, personality archetypes, and a close analysis of episodes in my examination. I argue that while *TWD* does privilege heteronormative, monogamous romantic relationships, it ultimately shows that romantic relationships between archetypally balanced individuals are the key to preserving both hope and (a sense of) humanity in the time of zombies.

First, we must explore and/or clarify a few terms and concepts, starting with romance. While the term is ably explained and discussed in this volume's introduction and in other essays, we must remember that a romantic relationship does not equal or require a sexual relationship, though sex may be part of the relationship. Sexual relationships can be romance-free just as romantic relationships can be sex-free. Rather, I want us to equate romance with intimacy. There are eight possible "spheres" of intimacy: aesthetic, affectional, emotional, intellectual, physical, social, spiritual, and sexual (Skyler). Individuals can share different types of intimacy with multiple partners. For example, spouses may be sexually, emotionally, and affectionally intimate, but have different aesthetic tastes. These different tastes lead them to friends who share those tastes, with whom they then form aesthetically intimate relationships. This multiplicity, especially when it involves sexual and/or emotional intimacy, can complicate a marriage relationship.

Marriage can be thought of as institutionalized, regulated, or partitioned romance. Marriage is, or has traditionally been, considered the ultimate intimate relationship, fulfilling all spheres of intimacy. Marriage has a place in every culture, although what marriage looks like and entails varies. Though marriage differs from culture to culture—and not everyone within a culture will marry—"marriage across societies is a publicly acknowledged and supported sexual union that creates kinship obligation and resource pooling" between those within the marriage bonds, including children (Wilcox, et al. 15). Three things are particularly important in this definition.

First is the idea of public acknowledgment or sanction of the marriage relationship. This is, according to Wilcox, et al., one of the primary things separating marriage from cohabitation. It is not enough for two people to live together or just to call each other husband or wife—the relationship must be publicly recognized as a marriage, even if, as in *TWD*, there is no means to officially solemnize the relationship. This recognition includes acknowledgment that the marriage partners are (now) exclusive in their intimate relationship, that no other partners will be entertained, and that the marriage relationship is the prime relationship among any others each partner may have.

Second, sexual intimacy is both an expected part of marriage and to be kept within the bonds of that marriage only. No other sexual partners will be or should be considered. This helps to both maintain the boundaries acknowledged by others and establish clear paternal lines and kinship claims. Where a child (almost) always clearly belongs to its mother, ambiguous paternity can strain a relationship to say the very least, as seen in the "Who is the father of Lori's baby?" storyline of Seasons Two and Three of *TWD*.

Third, marriage sets up an obligation to pool resources and work together. Thus, marriage becomes a microcosm of the society. As the marriage partners fulfill their mini-social contract with each other, they, in turn, help to promote social stability and uphold the larger social contract of living harmoniously with others. Wilcox, et al. argue that "a strong normative commitment to marriage makes married adults less likely to look for alternative partners" (16). Ideally, this commitment drives both partners to sacrifice for the other's good and to care for any offspring produced within the union, strengthening and maintaining the kinship bonds created with the marriage. These kinship bonds reinforce the primacy of the marriage relationship and, when healthy, perpetuate strong families. For Wilcox, et al., strong families are the backbone of strong and close-knit communities. Thus, preserving marriage as an institution protects and preserves the family as the fundamental unit of society. The question remains if this preservation is possible in the face of the zombie apocalypse.

Marriage is often expected to fulfill all spheres of intimacy all the time, which is an unrealistic expectation. This expectation can cause stress in a relationship, potentially resulting in triangulation. Triangulation, or triangle theory, suggests that "a two-person relationship under stress will 'triangle in' a third person" (Leupnitz, qtd. in Young 92) to help bring stability to the relationship. This triangulation can happen in any type of two-party relationship: parents may triangulate with a child, one parent and the child could triangulate with the other parent, or a couple may triangulate with a close friend. The triangulated party may act as a buffer, a sounding board, a referee, or fill other roles that will help the stressed relationship find balance and, ideally, recover.

Triangulation is not without possible complication. The main danger is that the triangulated party may lose his/her objectivity and choose sides. This can happen from argument to argument or as a general rule and could end up sowing more discord in the already strained relationship. This is because "the possibility of a couple emerging that excludes the third is always there" (Young 93). The triangulated party may have an individual relationship with both of the other people involved and may not wish to lose either of them. Yet, sides are almost always drawn, and all parties will work not to be excluded. So, while triangulation may be helpful, it is fraught with difficulties for all involved, especially if allegiances change. Triangulation is even more complex when there are other parties, such as children, whose security relies on the strained relationship that the triangulation is supposed to stabilize. Adding to the complexity of triangulation are the various ways people form attachments, which can affect the durability of romantic, kinship, and other bonds.

Attachment theory seeks to explain how we bond with other people and suggests that the types of attachments we made as infants affects the type of bonds we make as adults, including romantic bonds. Attachment theory "explains how both healthy and unhealthy forms of love originate as adaptations to specific social circumstances" (Hazan and Shaver 511). There are three styles of attachment: secure, anxious/ambivalent, and avoidant. Each style has different and specific approaches to and expectations of romantic attachments in adulthood.

Secure adults, such as Rick Grimes and Glenn Rhee, will characterize their "most important love experience" by "trust, friendship, and positive emotions" (Hazan and Shaver 513). Additionally, secure adults "believe in enduring love, generally find others trustworthy, and have confidence" that they themselves are likable (513). Secure adults tend to be more fulfilled in their relationships.

Anxious/ambivalent adults, such as Shane Walsh (Jon Bernthal), "experience love as a preoccupying, almost painfully exciting struggle to merge with another person." They also "fall in love frequently and easily but have difficulty finding true love" (513). Anxious/ambivalents like the idea of true love and want it, but are unlikely to believe that they will find it or, once they do, that true love will last. Anxious/ambivalents "experienc[e] love as involving obsession, desire for reciprocation and union, emotional highs and lows, and extreme sexual attraction and jealousy" (513). Maggie Greene has anxious/ambivalent tendencies.

Avoidant adults fear closeness and do not trust (in) romantic relationships. They also are "more doubtful of the existence or durability of romantic love and believe that they do not need a love partner in order to be happy" (513). Additionally, avoidant adults are "characterized by fear of intimacy, emotional highs and lows, and jealousy" and believe that "the kind of head-over-heels romantic love depicted in novels and movies [do] not exist in real life, romantic love seldom lasts, and it is rare to find a person one can really fall in love with" (515). Avoidant adults may have difficulty forming any type of intimate attachment, romantic or otherwise. Daryl Dixon is an avoidant adult.

The use of and reliance on archetypes in fiction complements both triangulation theory and attachment theory. A form of shorthand, archetypes allow audiences to quickly distinguish characters and anticipate some of their reactions. Of the twelve archetypes discussed in Carols S. Pearson's *Awakening the Heroes Within* (1991), the Warrior and Caregiver are the most germane. Pearson argues that all the archetypes must be developed and balanced within a single individual for lasting self-awareness and self-fulfillment. While it is possible to find a balance within an intimate relationship, this is not Pearson's ideal. All of the archetypes are present in *TWD*, but in its world, the balance between Warrior and Caregiver is the hardest, yet most important, to achieve: The Warrior will do anything to survive; the Caregiver will do anything to protect and preserve the bonds between the family, biological or chosen.

According to Pearson, the Warrior is "associated in our cultural mind with masculinity." Furthermore, we are "likely to think of the [Warrior] as male—and often (in Western culture) as a white male at that. Women and men who are not white are seen as supporting characters on the journey: sidekicks, villains, victims to be rescued, servants, and so on" (Pearson). The Warrior is often a leader, and is "called upon to slay many dragons" while showing "courage and subscrib[ing] to high ideals" (Pearson). Warriors "are willing to risk their very lives to defend" what is theirs "or to protect the weak from harm" (Pearson). The Warrior also has a high level of integrity and will fight for "their own principles or values even when doing so is economically or socially costly" (Pearson). Warriors are planners and, generally, good strategists. They can hold multiple scenarios in their minds and improvise as needed. Once Warriors set a goal, they will do all in their power to achieve it.

Pearson cautions us that Warriors—and all archetypes—have a Shadow side, or a "dark" side. The Shadow Warrior has all of the general characteristics of the Warrior, but is self-serving instead of altruistic. The Shadow Warrior is ruthless, has an "unprincipled and obsessive need to win," uses "power for conquest" and views "all difference as a threat" (Pearson). Rick and Shane are predominantly Warriors, as are Andrea (Laurie Holden) and Michonne (Danai Gurira).

Caregivers are traditionally seen as the "natural" balance or counterpart to Warriors. For Pearson, the ideal Caregiver "is the perfect, caring parent—generative, loving, attentive to noticing and developing the child's talents and interests, so devoted to this new life that he or she would die, if necessary, that it might thrive." In addition to parenting, the Caregiver "creates community by helping people feel that they belong and are valued and cared for.... Caregivers create atmospheres and environments in which people feel safe and at home" (Pearson). While Beth Greene (Emily Kinney) is also a Caregiver, Lori Grimes is the clearest example of the Caregiver in *TWD*.

Lori spends her energy on making a home wherever she is. She takes photo albums and keepsakes as part of her survival gear; she vainly fights to preserve Carl's innocence and childhood in a world gone mad. Notably, in

"Chupacabra," Lori fights with Andrea about traditional gender roles and the place of domesticity in this mad world. Lori implies that the women should be taking care of the domestic work, and that Andrea is not doing her share:

> ANDREA: Are you serious? Everything falls apart, and you're in my face about skipping *laundry*?
>
> LORI: [It] puts a burden on the rest of us.... You, you don't care about anyone but yourself. You sit up on that RV working on your tan with a shotgun in your lap.
>
> ANDREA: No, I am on watch against walkers. *That* is what matters, not fresh mint leaves in the lemonade.
>
> LORI: And *we* are providing stability. *We* are trying to create a life worth living.

Unsurprisingly, Andrea does not buy into Lori's Caregiving exhortations. Like many Warriors with un(der)developed Caregiver sensibilities, Andrea is unable or unwilling to see the work of the Caregiver as important or something she should engage in, even as she benefits from their work. That this tension arises between two women is not a mistake and clearly reflects the current push-pull many women face in modern society. In this push-pull, women are often told to choose between being a Warrior or Caregiver rather than encouraged to develop both archetypes.

From an archetypal point of view, the Warrior/Caregiver balance can be achieved through marriage or a relationship. Pearson reminds us that "In the past, archetypal functions were assigned to different roles in family systems. Mothers were Caregivers. Fathers were Warriors." These roles reinforce a traditional heteronormative setup where both labor and general social interactions are divided: women stay in and tend the home and children. Men earn a living outside of the home to supply the family's needs. Caregiving is largely un(der)paid, un(der)valued, and persistently coded feminine.

Taken together, triangulation theory, attachment theory, and the Warrior/Caregiver dichotomy help explain the complex relationship between Rick, Lori, and Shane. This triangle and its aftermath illustrates how *TWD* first heralds the death of traditional, legally encumbered marriage and then presents a new, more flexible conception of marriage. This triangle is particularly interesting because there are three separate but tightly intertwined relationships within it, each of which affect the others.

Rick and Lori were married pre-zombie apocalypse. This means they went through a formal ceremony and have paperwork attesting to their mutual legal obligations. Rick and Lori embody the heteronormative, traditional marriage. Rick makes his living by leaving his home to protect, defend, and serve others. Lori is a stay at home mother and, from what we hear and see in flashbacks, is concerned about making her family comfortable. We find out from Rick that she had definite ideas about what the Grimes family should be like. "Every Sunday," he tells Carol, "she'd make pancakes. [They were] god-awful, with clumps of flour not mixed in right. But she kept at it" ("Indifference"). After Carol questions why Lori would go through such trouble, Rick responds with a slight smile, "She wanted us to be the kind of family who ate pancakes on Sunday." Lori's focus was her home and family. She wanted to care for them. Her perseverance with the pancakes demonstrates her desire to build a home and serve her family, prime characteristics of a Caregiver.

Yet, we also find out that Lori is not satisfied within her marriage. We learn from Rick that she wants him to speak more ("Days Gone Bye"), that he does not always say what is on his mind. This stoicism is characteristic of Warriors (Pearson). Rick is also loath to cause conflict in his home. He is always calm and collected, even when he and Lori fight, something that also bothers Lori ("Bloodletting").

What she and Rick may have lacked in matrimonial harmony, Lori tried to make up for in domestic harmony. In fact, as they stand on the prison catwalk considering their relationship in "Sick," the one consolation Rick offers her is that he "doesn't think [she is] a bad mother." Left unspoken, and what Lori immediately picks up on, is that "Wife is another story." They stand in silence for a moment before Lori's attempt to see where she and Rick stand: "For better or for worse, right? I mean, what are we gonna do? Hire a lawyer and divide up our assets?" What she really wants to know is: with everything crumbled and collapsed around them, is there still a marriage to be had? Despite her many mistakes, did he still want her as his wife? She chose him in the end, returning to honor the promises she had made before the world went to hell.

We see the hope in her eyes as Rick moves closer and lays a hand on her shoulder. To her disappointment, he does not give her the answer she seeks, and she takes that as rejection. Now seemingly without a partner, Lori turns her attentions to her unborn child and prepares for its birth. Sadly, but perhaps fittingly for a professed Caregiver, Lori's death during Judith's (Anniston and Tinsley Price) birth is her final attempt at redemption. For actress Sarah Wayne Callies, who portrayed Lori, Season Three was all about Lori's failed attempts at redemption:

> There were some very specific things that mattered to me to find with Lori in the third season. And redemption was a big part of that—a sense of redemption in her marriage and a sense of redemption with Carl. And while I don't think either of those were ever achieved completely—because that would tie things up in a package that's far too neat for our show, and I don't think honest in life—I think we took steps down that path [Ocasio].

It is, perhaps, this incomplete attempt that contributes to the ongoing division between fans about Lori.

Complicating the Grimes' already troubled marriage was the fact that both Rick and Lori triangulated Shane Walsh into the relationship. One reason that Lori seems to bear the brunt of fans' ire in this triangulation has to do with relationship history; Rick and Shane had a longer history together than Lori and Rick did. The series implies that Rick and Shane grew up together; we know at the very least that they went to high school together ("What Lies Ahead"). Thus, their relationship pre-dates Rick's marriage to Lori. We also know that Rick and Shane have a brother-like relationship, as seen in the first scenes of "Days Gone Bye." As the two men talk about the differences between men and women, we come to realize that Rick is really asking about his and Lori's relationship—confiding in his brother (in-arms) that all is not well in the Grimes household. This is a clear, and probably not the first, instance of Rick triangulating Shane into his and Lori's relationship. Likely already aware of the situation, Shane listens and offers vague advice before a dispatch call interrupts the conversation. The men's fraternal bond is most evident in Shane's reaction to Rick being shot. Each time, Shane reacts immediately to neutralize the threat and is the first to attend Rick after the second, more life-threatening shot. Shane is also the main person to attend Rick in the hospital, either by Lori's request or his own insistence, and clearly struggles with the fact that he cannot seem to save Rick when the moment calls for it ("TS-19").

Their brotherhood faces the ultimate test in "Tell It to the Frogs" where Rick joins a group of survivors and finds Lori, Carl, and Shane. We discover Lori and Shane's sexual intimacy in this episode, while Rick remains seemingly unaware until Season Two ("Secrets"). The narrative timeline between Rick's injury and his appearance in this episode is not set—some estimates have it as high as 45 days—but many fans were quick to judge Lori and Shane for the speed of their relationship. Lori tends to bear the brunt of this judgment, as seen in different fan forums that respond to questions such as "Is Lori a skank?" (Kontrol) or "Lori/Shane affair before the ZA?" (divinitysbreath). Lori also faces a seemingly inordinate amount of dislike in the fandom, as seen in the question "Why all the hate for Lori?" (RickFan22). Suffice to say that fans have multiple and varied reasons for their dislike, though Lori does have her fair share of supporters.

No matter how one feels about Lori and Shane's relationship, it is logical that Lori would turn to Shane after Rick's assumed death. Whether or not Lori and Shane were sexually intimate before then—Shane insists in "18 Miles Out" that nothing ever happened before Rick "died"—Lori and Shane shared an emotional bond. Due to his friendship and working relationship with Rick, Shane was likely a regular fixture at the Grimes home. This emotional bond is particularly apparent in the beginning of "Bloodletting." Lori, in conversation with a friend, sees Shane approach in the cruiser and knows instantly that something is wrong. The two exchange a long, searching look in which Lori's fears are confirmed. It only takes a short conversation to establish the specifics, and then Lori must explain to Carl what happened, depending on Shane for emotional support.

The longer Rick is incapacitated, the more heavily dependent Lori becomes on Shane. As a Caregiver, she is ultimately driven by what is best for her family. In Rick's absence, Shane offers the protection and stability that she and Carl need; Lori's acceptance is both understandable and logical. Shane is a Warrior—he will do what he must for those under his care. When his sphere of responsibility widens with the camp's establishment, Lori's calming influence helps keep the peace. Her penchant for overseeing domestic affairs, such as cooking, cleaning, laundry, and arranging schoolwork/chores for the children in the group, allows Shane to oversee and manage larger aspects of day-to-day survival, such as providing food, shelter, and protection from walkers. In Shane and Lori's relationship, as also in Rick and Lori's relationship, the balance between Warrior and Caregiver is achieved. Additionally, Lori offers a secure attachment, soothing Shane's anxious/ambivalent tendencies.

Rick's appearance at the camp is akin to Lazarus rising and immediately, though not necessarily obviously, upsets its balance ("Tell it to the Frogs"). Lori returns to Rick's side without hesitation and is clearly haunted by her actions with Shane. She also clearly believes Shane lied about Rick's death and took advantage of her while Shane insists that "what [they] had was real" and Lori knew it ("Better Angels"). On the surface, it may seem that Lori returns to Rick to save face. Because all the adults know she had been sleeping with Shane, there is no way she can reject her husband. Marriage holds an expectation of fidelity and monogamy; without a legally dissolved union, Lori *should* (if not *must*) return to Rick if he is alive. Death has not parted them after all, and she has vows to honor.

However, Lori is motivated by more than just saving face. First, Rick is Carl's father. Shane may be an acceptable substitute, but the biological bond matters to Caregivers. Second, Rick represents life before the zombie apocalypse. Lori's history with Rick is far more intimate than her history with Shane, and having that back is priceless to her. Rick's death showed Lori how much she did love him, and now she could try to prove that. Finally, Lori's reunion with Rick suggests that marriage as an institution still matters in *TWD*. They made vows; the legal obligations associated with those vows still pertain. This further suggests that social contracts may persist even in the absence of government or other enforcing bodies. Lori will honor the contract, and that means relegating Shane back to friend, a move Shane does not take kindly to.

In "TS-19," Shane confronts Lori in the CDC's recreation room, telling her that he is better for her than Rick. His insistence turns into attempted rape, resulting in Lori clawing his face. This should be a clear signal to stay away, but he really only bides his time. As an anxious/ambivalent, he misses the security he had in his romantic attachment to Lori. With that attachment gone, he becomes obsessive and clearly cannot let go. Eventually, Lori recognizes Shane's obsession with her and Carl, one that she arguably helped to fuel, and tries to get Rick to recognize the threat in "Triggerfinger." She tells Rick that he is "going to have to make" Shane see reason because Shane will not listen to her. Indeed, by this point in the series, Shane is unlikely to respond to anything but violence. Finally, after hearing Rick describe how he killed two men for her sake and Carl's, Lori realizes what Rick needs to hear:

> LORI: You killed the living to protect what's yours?
> RICK: Yes.
> LORI: Shane thinks I'm his. He thinks the baby is his. And he says you can't protect us.

Though Rick does not reply, he has received the message: Shane is a threat, and, as the Warrior, Rick must protect and defend what is his from that threat.

After a failed confrontation in "18 Miles Out," Rick and Shane finally face off in "Better Angels." Shane concocts and executes a detailed plan to get Rick alone in a clearing away from Hershel's farm. The two men, once brothers, are committed to a fight to the death. Someone will die. To the victor: Lori, Carl, the baby, and, presumably, uncontested leadership over the remaining group. As they circle each other, Rick tries to talk Shane down, but Shane will have none of it. Instead, he tries to goad Rick into striking:

> SHANE: What happened, Rick? I thought you weren't the good guy anymore. Ain't that what you said? Even right here, right now, you ain't gonna fight for 'em? I'm a better father than you are, Rick. I'm better for Lori than you, man. It's 'cause I'm a better *man* than you, Rick. 'Cause I can be here, and I'll fight for it. But you come back here, and you just destroy everything! You got a broken woman. You got a weak boy. You ain't got the first clue how to fix it. (Cocks and raises weapon again.) Raise your gun.

Here, Shane attacks Rick on all fronts, insulting his manhood, his wife, and his son, implying that Rick should have died, or at least never found the group. The two Warriors are now mirrors of each other. Shane, having lost all attachments he held dear, has descended into Shadow Warrior territory. Everything is a fight that he must win. Anyone who disagrees with him is an enemy. Rick, still mostly secure in his attachments, refuses the descent. Rick is everything and has everything that Shane cannot be and cannot have. At the same time, Shane is everything that Rick may still become. Ultimately, though, Rick can no longer abide Shane's presence. For the good of his family, the group and his own sanity, Rick kills Shane.

Shane's death drives the final wedge between Lori and Rick. When Rick admits that he both wanted to and did kill Shane, Lori's expression is one of grief, betrayal, anger, and surprise. Rick approaches her to offer comfort, but she continually backs away, her expression dark and accusatory. Rick holds her gaze, searching for something left unarticulated—perhaps forgiveness or understanding or confirmation that she really had not chosen Shane over him like he now thinks. Communication never was a strong point in the Grimes marriage, and this is one of the few times that they are so open in their discussions. Lori's reaction suggests that she cannot handle his honesty. Indeed, the division between them remains until Lori's death in childbirth. Rick is the only survivor of this triangle, and it colors his other relationships, both romantic and platonic as best seen in his relationship with Michonne.

It takes most of Season Three for Rick to recover from Lori's death. After a short-lived relationship with Jessie Anderson (Alexandra Breckenridge) that ends in her death ("No Way Out"), Rick takes some time to heal from that and help rebuild Alexandria. We see in "The Next World" that some time has passed and that Rick, Carl, Judith, and Michonne are now sharing a house together. There is no apparent indication of romance between Rick and Michonne, but they do have an ease about them, a familiarity seen between a long-married couple with a good relationship. They banter, tell each other about their upcoming plans; Michonne asks Rick to find her some toothpaste on his supply run because she has used all of his. At the end of a long, trying day for each of them, they come back together and commiserate on the couch. Rick hands Michonne a package of mint Lifesavers in lieu of toothpaste. She takes it and holds his hand for a long moment. They share a look that turns into passion, solidifying a relationship that has been building since they first met.

Actors Andrew Lincoln (Rick) and Danai Gurira (Michonne) were excited about the relationship. Lincoln said, "I sat there and screamed when I read [the script]. I ran to [Danai's] trailer, banged on her door, and screamed, 'Why didn't you tell me?!' It's insane and I loved it" (Goldberg). In Michonne, Rick finds the ideal partner for the zombie apocalypse. As a Warrior, she can take care of herself and is not above putting Rick in his place, even if it means violence. Yet, Michonne yearns for domestic safety, a place she can call home. She has the capacity and wants the chance to be a Caregiver. She will fight to make a home, and she will fight to keep it. She has that home in Alexandria and with Rick. Even Carl accepts her as family, which is of utmost importance to Rick.

Though the Rick/Michonne dynamic, also known as "Richonne," is very new, it appears to be the most stable relationship Rick has had through the series. Where there were secrets and distrust with Lori and Shane, Michonne has consistently proven herself to be reliable and, most importantly, able to fend for herself. She does not need Rick's protection, though she will take it if offered, and can protect Rick as needed. He does not have to be the Warrior all the time, allowing his underdeveloped Caregiver to resurface. With the Warrior-Caregiver balance achieved, Alexandria is peaceful. Once they discover Negan (Jeffrey Dean Morgan) and the Saviors, however, the Caregiver must submit to the Warrior as both Michonne and Rick prepare again to fight.

The balance between Warrior and Caregiver is also the strength of Glenn and Maggie's relationship. In contrast to Rick and Lori (and Lori and Shane), Glenn and Maggie balance the archetypes within themselves rather than between them. For Pearson, this is the ideal and, arguably, allows Glenn and Maggie's relationship to flourish in a time where attachments can be fleeting and are often self-serving. It is highly likely that without a zombie apocalypse, these two would have never met. Glenn delivered pizzas in the city before somehow becoming part of Shane's camp. Maggie remained on the family farm outside of the city, generally sheltered from the brunt of the dead and mayhem.

By the time these two meet, Glenn has established himself as a valuable resource for his group. He has an uncanny knack for survival—a Warrior trait—and is good at gathering supplies (scavenging really), which is a Caregiver trait. We see all of this early in Season One, especially in the episode "Guts." Glenn does what he must do to help the group, and can call upon his Warrior to help him through the more perilous tasks. He is also "without guile" and "suck[s] at lying" ("Secrets") which enables him to be the general "go-to guy" for Rick's group. People trust Glenn, even if they cannot fully articulate why.

In "Bloodletting," he is part of the group searching for Carol's daughter, Sophia (Madison Lintz), when Maggie rides in on a horse and clubs a walker in the head that is trying to kill Andrea. She barks orders out to Lori to come with her, brooking no argument, and once Lori is secure on the horse, hurriedly gives directions to the farm, and immediately returns to the farmhouse. Glenn is visibly gobsmacked as he watches this unfold. He is clearly attracted to this Warrior woman and, once he processes her instructions, realizes he may get the chance to get to know her better.

For her part, Maggie has lost family members and friends in what she and her father see at first as a plague. She has had to continually make a home on the farm—cooking, cleaning, caring for the animals and land—and has thus developed her inner Caregiver. In the face of the plague, she has also had opportunity to corral, if not kill, walkers, suggesting that she developed a Warrior side as well. She can and will fight for what she considers hers, especially when she is secure in her attachments.

Glenn and Maggie first meaningfully interact in "Cherokee Rose" during

Glenn's attempt to secure a rope around a grotesque walker at the bottom of a well. After this encounter, Maggie starts calling him "Walker Bait," almost as a term of endearment. This could be seen as flirting, though Glenn takes issue with the nickname, and is Maggie's way of marking Glenn as her territory, a definite Warrior-like move.

Later in this episode, Glenn and Maggie make a run to the nearest pharmacy for some medications and general supplies. Lori has asked Glenn to retrieve a pregnancy test if possible, but Glenn does not want to tell Maggie what he is looking for. There is still a distinct "us" and "them" sentiment between the groups; Glenn went with Maggie because he is "good at getting stuff" and because Rick wanted one of his group to look out for their interests. When Maggie finds Glenn in the remnants of the feminine hygiene aisle, he quickly stuffs the pregnancy test in his bag and grabs the nearest box as she asks him what he has. He stammers a reply, "Uh, nothing. Like I said, just some general stuff" and holds up a box of condoms. The ensuing exchange is worth examining in detail, as it shows, again, how Maggie and Glenn balance both archetypes within themselves.

> MAGGIE: Condoms?
> GLENN: (hangs head and gasps, unable to articulate a reply)
> MAGGIE: You got a girlfriend I don't know about?
> GLENN: Me? No. No.
> MAGGIE: Then you're a pretty confident guy.
> GLENN: (smile fades) No. No no no. I–I–I wasn't.... I would never.
> MAGGIE: Something wrong with me?
> GLENN: No ... (incredulous) I would never have sex.... Uh. I'm lost. (shakes his head, still clearly confused and wanting her to explain)
> MAGGIE: I'll have sex with you.
> GLENN: Really? Why?
> MAGGIE: You're asking questions?
> GLENN: Okay, I can't help wondering.
> MAGGIE: It's not like our options are vast these days.

Maggie's challenging tone signals her Warrior—she is ready to fight, or at least spar, with Glenn. Indeed, many of Maggie's confrontations early in Season Two are verbal. She is not averse to Glenn's inadvertent proposition, but she needs to get him to think it is his idea. Intriguingly, Glenn's accidental possession of condoms further illustrates his Caregiver side. Ever mindful of his (potential) partner, Glenn would, of course, do what is best and use protection. Additionally, we can already see that Glenn and Maggie's relationship is more open and communicative than Rick and Lori's.

Hershel (Scott Wilson), Maggie's father, does not approve of Maggie's budding relationship with Glenn, but Maggie, ever the Warrior, fights Hershel on his prohibitions. "I'm a little old for us to be having this conversation," she argues in "Chupacabra" before walking away. Later in that episode, Glenn channels his inner Warrior by clumsily propositioning Maggie by telling her they have eleven condoms left. Her response implies a rebuff, and Glenn immediately backs off. He is willing to give Maggie some space, but he is also clearly signaling his interest. He is securely attaching himself to Maggie, though Maggie, interestingly, remains anxious/ambivalent about him.

It is not until after the barn-cleansing in "Pretty Much Dead Already" that we see the strength of their attachment. We see in "Triggerfinger" that Maggie now prioritizes Glenn over Hershel. When Rick, Glenn, and Hershel return from town—where Hershel had gone to drink after the barn-cleansing—Maggie runs out to greet them. Instead of running to Hershel, she runs to Glenn. She has already declared her love for Glenn, which unnerved him enough to ask Rick for help, a minor but successful triangulation that soon sets things right ("Nebraska"). For his part, Rick is encouraged by Glenn and Maggie's relationship. After listening to Glenn explain the problem—he did not return Maggie's declaration of love—Rick tells Glenn, "Hey. Hey, this is a good thing, something we don't get enough of these days. Enjoy it. And when we get back, return the favor." Even in the face of his own crumbling marriage, Rick finds hope in Glenn and Maggie's budding romance. Clearly, love is still possible in the time of zombies, even if others resist it or, like Hershel, disapprove of it.

Eventually, Hershel comes to realize and admit that Glenn is right for Maggie. In "Judge, Jury, and Executioner," he tells Glenn about his Irish heritage and the good woman his wife Josephine, Maggie's mother, was. When Hershel pawned a family heirloom pocket watch to buy alcohol, Josephine bought it back and saved it until he sobered up. "Maggie's a lot like her," Hershel explains as he holds the pocket watch. "You become a father someday, you'll understand. No man is good enough for your little girl until one is." He hands the pocket watch to Glenn, signaling his acceptance of the relationship and a tacit welcome to the family as the pocket watch had traditionally been passed from father to son. Hershel's blessing helps both Maggie and Glenn securely attach, alleviating any anxiety Maggie had over the relationship.

The pocket watch resurfaces during another poignant conversation between Glenn and Hershel in "This Sorrowful Life." By this point, the group has made a home in the prison and is trying to figure out what to do about the Governor. Glenn approaches Hershel, the watch in his hand:

GLENN: When you gave me this, I didn't fully understand what it meant. Such a simple thing. I know what it means now. I know what it takes. I want to marry Maggie. And we don't have to have a wedding. I don't even know if we'll last the week. But I want her to know before ... who knows?

HERSHEL: You have my blessing.

On the surface, this seems like a throwback to the patriarchal exchange of women as property. However, in *TWD*, it is very clear that Maggie is no one's property. While Glenn seeks Hershel's blessing, he is not really asking permission or setting up a contract. Instead, he declares himself to a man he sees as a father figure—explaining to Hershel how he sees Maggie, how he views their relationship. He acknowledges Hershel's gift and sentiment in the pocket watch. Glenn knows how much Maggie means to Hershel and vice versa. Starting a new life together requires Maggie leaning on Glenn more than Hershel. She has already willingly shifted her alliances, so to speak. Hershel smiles as Glenn leaves. This nod to tradition satisfies Hershel immensely and appeals to his belief in the Bible: "Therefore shall a [wo]man leave [her] father and [her] mother, and shall cleave unto [her husband]" (Genesis 2:24, KJV). Maggie and Glenn are securely attached now. Only death will separate them, even if there is no formal wedding.

The fact that Glenn tells Hershel that there need not be a wedding—who has the "authority" to perform weddings, anyway?—both reflects a 21st century attitude and illustrates the idea of marriage-as-consent, or continued consent rather than a legal and social institution. In this vein, marriage is between the two individuals involved—they define the relationship and use terms to signify their level of commitment. Maggie calls Glenn her husband; Glenn calls Maggie his wife. To them, their consent to these terms enacts all the privileges, rights, and exclusions of marriage. They are monogamous because they choose to be, not because marriage vows and societal customs mandate this behavior. Additionally, those in the group acknowledge their relationship as they define it, fulfilling all the requirements, save legal paperwork, for marriage.

Interestingly, Glenn and Maggie's most controversial decision is not their marriage, but having a baby together. Both saw what pregnancy did to Lori; Maggie performed Lori's C-section and watched her die. Not everyone sees Maggie's pregnancy as desirable, as seen in "Knots Untie." Abraham (Michael Cudlitz) is particularly curious about whether or not the pregnancy was intended. On the way to The Hilltop, he tells Glenn that he "can't stop thinking about Maggie having a pup" and tries to satisfy his curiosity:

> ABRAHAM: When you were pouring the Bisquick ... were you trying to make pancakes?"
>
> GLENN: Uh.... Yes? Oh, okay, um ... it's something that we talked about.
>
> ABRAHAM: Yeah.
>
> GLENN: Why?
>
> ABRAHAM: No, I just.... Well, given the precarious state of affairs on any given Sunday, I am damn near floored that you or anyone else would have the cojones to make a call like that.
>
> GLENN: I mean, well, we're trying to build something, me and her. All of us.
>
> ABRAHAM: For the record, I see rain coming, I'm wearing galoshes. I double up.

Clearly, Abraham is not as sanguine about Maggie's pregnancy as Glenn and Maggie are. Yet, their confidence suggests that *TWD* not only values romance, marriage, and family creation, but sees them as acts of hope. While Abraham may have well-protected sex with Rosita, he is in no rush to rebuild or replace the family he lost earlier in the apocalypse ("Self Help"). However, Glenn and Maggie's confidence in their relationship eventually affects Abraham enough to end his relationship with Rosita—no longer "the last woman on earth"—(Christian Serratos) and pursue one with Sasha (Sonequa Martin-Green) ("Not Tomorrow Yet"). What may come of that relationship remains to be seen.

With the collapse of almost all other social structures, love, romance, and marriage in the time of zombies are all vital in preserving a sense humanity and providing hope for the future. Additionally, as the face of marriage continues to change in the 21st century, *TWD* models ways to adapt to and come to terms with these changes. In Rick and Lori, we see the death of traditional, contractual marriage with well-defined and gender-divided roles of Warrior and Caregiver. In Glenn and Maggie, we see the rise of the "new" marriage—marriage by consent and a balance of Warrior and Caregiver in each of both parties. We also see this potential in "Richonne." Though Glenn and Maggie and "Richonne" are monogamous, heteronormative relationships: one man, one woman, and clear relationship roles, the roles are interchangeable and fluid dependent on the situation. Both parties can inhabit the same role—Warrior or Caregiver—at the same time, or they can share roles as needed. More importantly, the roles do not have to be divided along gender: Rick or Glenn can be the Caregiver while Michonne and Maggie are the Warrior. This fluidity allows *TWD* to champion some marriage traditions while clearly reflecting its cultural context.

Kirkman and David Erickson's new series, *Fear the Walking Dead* (*Fear*) (2015–present) continues an examination of romance and marriage. By focusing on a single blended family in the making, *Fear* highlights the difficulties and stigma associated with this type of love and family formation, compounding the microcosm blended family with the more typical "group of fellow survivors become family, too" trope in zombie texts. *Fear* is too new to offer definitive conclusions. However, it seems to have a similar triangular set up in the Madison (Kim Dickens)/Travis (Cliff Curtis)/Liza (Elizabeth Rodriguez) relationship and a look at a more traditional relationship in Daniel (Rubén Blades) and Griselda Salazar (Patricia Reyes Spíndola). It would be interesting to revisit these ideas as *Fear* matures. It would also be interesting to do a more in-depth analysis of what constitutes "family" in both *TWD* and *Fear*.

Ultimately, while Kirkman's vision of the world in both series is undoubtedly bleak, it is not entirely without hope. There is still room for intimacy, for romance, for marriage in Kirkman's world. Social institutions may have collapsed, but at least some individuals in *TWD* fight to preserve society and humanity. If, as Dale Horvath (Jeffrey DeMunn) reminds us, "The world is gone, but keeping our humanity" is a choice ("Judge, Jury, and Executioner"), then the choices to love, to marry, and to build families in the time of zombies may be (among) the most important choices we make.

Note

1. At the time of writing, Season 7 of the television series had not yet premiered. Unfortunately, due to time constraints, this essay cannot incorporate the developments in that season. I hope to take those up in future work.

Works Cited

Darabont, Frank, creator. *The Walking Dead.* AMC, 2010–present.

Divinitysbreath. "Lori/Shane Affair Before the ZA?" *Walking Dead Forums.* 2 May 2014. www.walkingdeadforums.com/forum/f49/lori-shane-affair-za-68822.html.

Goldberg, Lesley. "*Walking Dead* Stars on Rick and Michonne's Surprising New Dynamic." *The Hollywood Reporter.* 21 Feb. 2016. www.hollywoodreporter.com/live-feed/walking-dead-rick-michonne-romance-868046.

Hazan, Cindy, and Phillip Shaver. "Romantic Love Conceptualized as an Attachment Process." *Journal of Personality and Social Psychology,* vol. 52, no. 3, 1987, pp. 511–24.

Kirkman, Robert, and Dave Erickson, creators. *Fear the Walking Dead.* AMC, 2016.

Kontrol. "Is Lori a Skank?" *Roamers and Lurkers: The Walking Dead Community.* 14 Nov. 2011. www.roamersandlurkers.com/topic/1317-is-lori-a-skank/.

Ocasio, Anthony. "*Walking Dead* Star Admits Lori Never Redeemed Herself." *Screen Rant.* 5 Nov. 2012. screenrant.com/walking-dead-season-3-lori-death/.

Pearson, Carol S. *Awakening the Heroes Within: Twelve Archetypes to Help Us Find Ourselves and Transform the World.* HarperCollins, 1991.

RickFan22. "Why All the Hate for Lori?" *Walking Dead Forums.* 8 Mar. 2012. www.walkingdeadforums.com/forum/f37/hate-lori-1894.html.

Skyler, Jenni, and Carey Roth Bayer. "Eight Spheres of Intimacy." *American Journal of Sexuality Education*, vol. 5, 2010, pp. 290–99.

Wilcox, W. Bradford, et al. "Why Marriage Matters, Second Edition: Twenty-Six Conclusions from the Social Sciences." *Institute for American Values*, 2005, pp. 1–44.

Young, Sally. "Two's Company, Three's a Crowd: Revisiting Triangles in Family Therapy." *The Australian and New Zealand Journal of Family Therapy*, vol. 31, no. 1, 2010, pp. 92–9.

Memories of You
The Undying Love of the Zombie in Harold's Going Stiff

Simon Bacon

Harold's Going Stiff (2011) is an unusual zombie film. Unusual in that it does not feature the cinematically ubiquitous, "undirected, predatory, cannibalistic ... and larger horde of the collaborative undead" (Mantz 183), but a retiree who lives in a bungalow in Yorkshire. Harold Gimble (Stan Rowe) lives alone as he has no surviving family. His is a solitary life typical of many old people in 21st-century England who no longer socialize but refuse, or cannot afford, a care home. What marks him out as unusual is that he is patient zero of the mysterious ORD (Onset Rigors Disease) that affects older men. The disease begins with stiffness in the joints, memory loss, and, eventually, uncontrollable aggression. Set oppositionally to Harold are a group of self-styled zombie killers, three Millennials, men who do not seem to work but sit in their car drinking tea, waiting for a zombie/old man to stagger past so they can kill it/him, creating a real life zombie killing game with Harold set as their ultimate prize. The inevitable conclusion to the narrative—Harold's demise at the hands of the zombie-hunters—is given meaning by the introduction of Penny (Sarah Spencer), a young nurse who calls on Harold to give him a series of massage therapy treatments for his increasingly stiff joints and who eventually forms a romantic relationship with the old man. The relationship between her and Harold restores the old man's connection to the past and the world around him, while also making the hunters realize their own loss of humanity, largely through acts of remembrance and memory-making. This study looks at the film to show the importance of memory, not just for the zombies that lose them but for a society that is increasingly separated from them.

Harold's Going Stiff equates memory loss, such as that seen in Alzheimer's or senile dementia, with zombiism, just as it also intimates how contemporary Millennial society is equally, and as catastrophically, separated from their own past. The film simultaneously connects and resolves the equivalence and homicidal disparity between the two categories through love and romantic connection to others which restores both memory and common humanity to each. Ultimately, the narrative shows that the connection to the past and the quality of humanity is directly related to memory and the importance of making new ones together, before we all become zombies in an increasingly violent and isolating world. Consequently, the notion of memory constituting what is human, or humanness, is central to this study where memory not only creates identity but links one to the wider culture and society. As Liliane Weissberg comments, citing the work of sociologist Maurice Halbwachs, "people acquire or construct memory not as isolated individuals but as members of a society, and they recall their memories in society" (Weissberg 13). As such, humanity is made by one's connection to the world, as well the narrative progression of this memory through time. Zombies traditionally have issues with this definition, and as I have mentioned elsewhere, while "they are monstrous because they refuse to remain dead, what they actually configure is the more horrifying death of memory and identity" (Bacon 216). Roger Luckhurst continues from this to show the way that this monstrosity removes them both from their own lives and also their own culture: "the zombie is the loved one who has somehow catastrophically *turned*, in the same body yet a stranger to themselves and their kin" (Luckhurst 10). In this way, zombiism, and particularly that as seen in *Harold*, is a lack of memory that disconnects the subject both from their past as well as that of the society around them.

Interestingly, in the film the vigilantes appear as disconnected as Harold. The three of them spend all their time in the remote Yorkshire countryside and talk only of killing zombies. In line with the common conception of Millennials, they spend much time on their phones and seem to be living in some form of first-person shooter video game (Luttrell and McGraph 74), which both disconnects them from the real world around them and in memory formation with family, friends, or wider society. This situates them as being of the same order as Harold in not being actively human/alive—in being disconnected from the narrative flow of the society around them—but equally not dead, which resultantly sees the zombie and zombie-killer as undead entities.

Curiously, Penny, who, as mentioned, provides some form of resolution to this memoryless aporia created between Harold and his pursuers, is equally disconnected from the world around her. The only indication that she sees anyone other than Harold is her use of online dating sites. For the early parts of the film, these sites are shown as the only means she has to interact with other people, revealing a typically Millennial dependence upon technology and a resultant diminishing of physical contact, so much so that "actually seeing the other person is not as important, or necessary" (Stubbe 8), which configures a similarity to the hunters, though deep down she longs to be connected to someone and be part of the world around her. Before exploring how Penny resolves these issues, it is worth examining more closely the creeping forms of zombiism that are consuming the environment she lives in.

The Death of Memory

Like many pensioners living on their own, Harold Gimble is surrounded by memories. His bungalow is full of lacy lampshades, ornaments, and pictures that are testaments of his former life with his now dead wife. In this aspect, Harold represents a connection to the past, and while his age is never mentioned, it is assumed he is in his late 70s and so born slightly before or during the Second World War. This sees him on the cusp of the Boomer generation or the one viewed "in clouds of idealism and nostalgia" (Henger and Henger 93). As such, he keeps these personal artifacts so that, like others of his age group, he remains in the continuing line of history, "as a means of anchoring themselves in a rapidly changing and unstable present" (Noakes 48), but also "because the act involved in throwing them away would constitute some sort of ritual symbolizing the disposal of ... [his] past" (Prizer 191). Harold's dependence on the objects around him is increased as he appears to have no children, family, or friends to speak of, and so it is only through these items of remembrance that he finds meaning and maintains his identity. The film never reveals just how long ago Harold's wife passed away, but his condition began at some point after that with the steady stiffening of his joints preventing him from continuing the rituals which linked him to his former life, such as gardening, hanging out the washing, etc. In many ways, the onset of ORD is directly linked to his wife's death as the disease's cause links to a particular kind of fast food called "meat-a-rina" that he only began to eat when he was no longer having his meals prepared for him by his partner. Harold ate these sausage-like snacks "morning, noon, and night" (*Harold's Going Stiff*), and later scientific tests on mice proved that it was the savory sauce in them that caused the disease, though only in men. Consequently, the film shows Harold slowly being removed from his own life, no longer being able to interact meaningfully with his memory filled surroundings, so much so that he begins to forget what they mean and how they fit into the rituals that reinforced their significance. As he forgets how to negotiate the space of his kitchen, he forgets the ritual of how to make a cup of tea properly, and he continually adds the wrong ingredients instead of either sugar or milk. The process continues until Penny comes to visit.

At this point Penny, who is part of the Home Nursing Team, begins to massage Harold's joints to help loosen them up, but, more importantly, she begins to help him to reconnect to the space around him and, consequently, his memories. Very quickly, Harold begins to be able to do his own laundry and washing-up again, re-inhabiting his living space and, subsequently, his memories. This gives substance to Karlfried Graf Von Dürckheim's observation as quoted in Bronfen.

> The living subject realises and preserves his innermost self in the plethora of content and meaningful multiplicity of his space, and lived space has a momentary or more permanent psychological reality in the living subject. He is to the same extent "in it" as it is "in him" [Bronfen 39].

As such, Harold inhabits the memories of the space in which he lives, and the ability to re-enactment the rituals of his "living" in that space, which make its memories live in him. Dürckheim speaks in terms of the "living subject" which sees those that can inhabit their space as "living," with the inference that to not be able to do so makes one not "living," though obviously not dead either—the inability to inhabit one's memories constructs the subject as undead. Harold's inability to remember how to negotiate the spaces he lives in links him to more traditional zombies (traditional in the sense of the post–Romero era) who similarly seem to lose all memory and, consequently, their ability to recognize familiar environments. However, this situation has changed within certain narratives and even Romero himself began to use the idea of ritual/habit memory in relation to particular spaces as capable of restoring a modicum of remembrance to the zombie. In *Dawn of the Dead* (1978), the survivors take refuge in a shopping mall, which similarly seems to attract the zombies. One of the survivors explains this phenomena by relating it to an innate instinct, "a memory of what they used to do," in a previously "important place in their lives." The idea of instinct or habit memory returning to the undead corpse is used in *Land of the Dead* (2005) where one zombie in particular is seen to return to his job as a gas attendant and regains enough memory to think beyond just consuming human flesh—and which is similarly used in *Resident Evil: Extinction* (2007). As such, movement within a known space, one which the subject has "lived" in, in the sense intimated by Dürckheim, can link them back to the past and to their memories. This linkage, while not making them human again—they are after all largely dead when becoming a zombie—sees them regaining some measure of humanity.[1] Within the structure of the zombie narrative, then, memory is posited as a key factor in re-humanizing the undead with the environment and the subject's relation to it being central.[2] Harold, not being dead, is caught in this liminal space held between memory and amnesia, human and zombie.

The Protectors

The would-be zombie killers, and others like them, are actually encouraged by local police forces to help in the rounding up and, if necessary, killing of those infected with ORD. The three featured in the film, Jon (Andy Pandini), Mike (Lee Thompson), and Colin (Richard Harrison), call themselves the Protectors, and they see it as their job to "protect the innocent" (*Harold's Going Stiff*). As mentioned earlier, they mirror Harold in their ongoing failing connection to memory, though it is configured in a very different way to the old man's. The three men are roughly the same age of about 30-ish, though Colin looks a little older, while behaving somewhat younger. They appear to spend all their time together, and only Jon is mentioned as having a wife and a son, but he is never seen speaking to them, constructing the Protectors as largely separate or removed from the world around them—a self-contained unit. A point reinforced by their lack of interaction with the landscape around them and which becomes just a zone to move through rather than a place to interact on an emotional level. Subsequently the car, which they spend the majority of their time in becomes something of a metaphor for the disconnected mobility that characterizes the Millennial experience. This kind of emotional detachment is graphically illustrated in one scene, where Jon speaks to the camera—much of the film is shot as a mock-documentary—describing Colin as someone who "only wants to make the world a better place" (*Harold's Going Stiff*), while behind him Mike and Colin brutally club an old man/zombie to death. Much of this sees them configured as typical Millennials who "lack connections to nature" (Barton and Collens 257), and exhibit a "lack of empathy" (Knowlton 21), but more easily experience life through technology. Curiously, the three exhibit all the characteristics of the Millennial generation while having a very limited amount of access to technological equipment but still live their zombie-hunting lives as if in a game—in line with this "living in a game" idea is the sudden appearance of night vision glasses while hunting a prospective zombie. This configures to the Millennial need to be "immersed" and "connected ... like in a video game" (Childs et al. 308)—indeed when they hear that Harold has gone "zombie," they celebrate as he is like "the World Cup" and "worth 1,000 points," and much of their experience in the Yorkshire Dales correlates to this gaming style where the fields and farmyards become anonymous hunting and killing grounds. Two other scenes in particular make the gaming analogy explicit. In the first, they chase a younger zombie into an underground cavern where Colin dons night vision glasses to track and attach a wire to their prey. The scene is shot just like a single-shooter game winding through tunnels, with sudden green flashes across the screen of the zombie's face in the light of night vision glasses. The second is when they set out to catch Harold and speed along a road. The camera focuses on the back of Mike's head and the road speeds past either side of his head as seen in the car's windshield—the little country lane is transformed into totally anonymous highway. As such, the landscape and their spatial experience of it is memoryless and is only delineated by their "mission" to kill zombies. The detachment of the Protectors from their environment is shown in one scene which sees Penny and Harold walking through the same landscape but admiring the view, while the old man remembers trips there with his wife seeing them fully engaged with their surroundings.

This last scene illustrates the difference, or oppositional nature, of the two views of zombiism in the film. Harold, who in many ways is too full of memory from all the experiences of his long life, becomes disconnected from them primarily due to his inability to inhabit the space within which they were made and, consequently, reside. In contrast, the hunters do not make, or store, memories like Harold. They have little connection to the real places around them, which function as blank spaces for them to pass through rather than meaningfully interact with, which, on one level, makes them seem as undead as Romero's zombies. However, like them, the hunters do retain habitual memory, or memories created and stored in the repetition of tasks or rituals. As such, their memory storage is formed in the virtual, or imaginative space, linked between each other and the fulfillment of their quest. As Birdsall, quoting Casey, notes, "habit memory involves moments where the past is re-encountered in the present ... and play an important role in contributing to a sense of self and belonging" (Birdsall 116). The hunters participate in this sort of habit memory, finding their identity in a world outside of the physical reality of the one in which they live. Interestingly, Penny exemplifies both these forms of zombiism, or at least bridges the gap between them, but unlike either Harold or the hunters, she manages to reconnect memory to the space around her and take it into the future.

Nursing the Past

In many ways, Penny is shown as being as cut off from her surroundings as much as both Harold and the Protectors. She used to work in a hospital, but was a little squeamish about what she saw there, so now she does home visits, spending the majority of her time alone in her car not unlike the hunters. Like Harold, she appears to have no family, friends, or even a pet, and she is shown to live in something of a small studio apartment with little furniture in it. Therein, she seems to spend most of her time on online dating sites, arranging a string of disastrous dates with men who are abusive, disrespectful, or just want sex. In part, this behavior is blamed on her strong desire for an immediate and meaningful relationship but also on her size, as she is somewhat overweight. But it is even more possibly due to her being out of step with the world around her. The film depicts her as slightly younger than the hunters, so still part of the Millennial generation, but she yearns for actual physical contact and direct human interaction, though in a very structured way. She desires old fashioned ideas of courtship and romance. While this can be seen as a fairly stereotypical character construction—a lazy narrative shorthand—within the film, it has a more purposeful intent and it influences in the way that Penny relates to the environment around her and what kinds of memories she wishes to make/retain. Consequently, when she first visits Harold, Penny is struck by how much memory there is contained in his surroundings, and largely from time with his wife. Harold's surroundings embody long term companionship and an idealized view of partnerships that last forever, which is something that Penny deeply desires—seen in her repeated attempts to find a boyfriend, no matter how rude or insulting the last blind date was.

Not unsurprisingly, Penny's relationship to Harold changes after a disastrous non-date where she is "stood up," and the prospective boyfriend leaves a particularly insulting phone message. After receiving this call, an extremely upset Penny goes to see Harold for a shoulder to cry on. Unlike any of the other men she seems to know, Harold sits and listens to her and tells her that such things never happened in his day and that women were always treated with respect—one suspects Harold might be just talking about himself. Although this is something of an idealized view of the past, as indeed are Harold's reminiscences of his wife, it describes a meaningful connection to the past and the spaces within which one lives. These are the qualities that are indicative of the Baby Boomer generation, and ones that Penny very much wants to take as her own. The disparity between the past and the present, Boomers and the Millennials, is shown later the following day when Penny's next date comes to Harold's house to collect her before going out. Sitting on Harold's sofa by himself, the young man is on the phone, speaking loudly and telling his friend that he thinks he is "on a promise" (certain to have sex). Not only does this show how disrespectful the young man is but that he needs to relay his experience immediately to a friend to give it meaning, seeing him more connected to technology and/or virtual space than he is to Harold's living room. Penny and Harold share a knowing look at the end of this scene signaling both her decision to forgo the views of her own generation for the earlier one but also a shared view on the importance of being in the world.

Harold and Penny's increased time together brings great improvement to the old man's condition, but two events signal that it is not going to last: the first is Penny's volunteering to help at a center caring for ORD sufferers, and the second is Dr. Shuttleworth (Phil Gascoyne) contacting his former patient about coming to his center for some further tests. The former sees Penny traveling to what looks like a large wooden hut out in the dales, where seven men in various stages of ORD are housed as their families are no longer able to cope with them. The illness in the "inmates"—and they do appear to be in some form of incarceration—varies in degree from those who are vaguely confused to one, simply known as "No. 7," (Richard Atkinson) who is almost uncontrollable. Penny, possibly ill advisedly, takes Harold with her one day so he can see her at work, but it shows Harold, "patient zero," just how bad he will become and that it might happen suddenly and without warning.[3] The latter scene sees Harold and Penny traveling to the Doctor's Institute for further tests to see why the old man is suddenly improving. When they first arrive, in what appears like a large house, they are given a double room and all seems well. The positivity increases when Dr. Shuttleworth gives Harold some new pills he has developed and, suddenly, the remaining stiffness in his limbs disappears. Harold is so excited by this that he starts running around and jumping, chasing Penny around the Institute's garden and up to their room. Interestingly, there is nothing sexual in his increased vigor, and, although the pair jump up and down on their beds, their relationship is one of like-mindedness and intellectual connection, which again reinforces Penny's separation from her own generation. Unfortunately, the following morning, Harold is not feeling so well and the symptoms have returned but even worse than before. Penny overhears Dr. Shuttleworth talking to his assistant explaining that he does not think Harold will survive the week and that he will need to contact the authorities to warn them that the old man is dangerous. Penny goes to Harold and tells him they are leaving. She asks him to show her where he proposed to his wife, as a last grasp at his memory before it vanishes forever. And it is these final scenes that join the past to the present to describe a future that will continue the ongoing flow of memory.

Remembering the End

As the film draws to a close, the disparities between Harold and the Protectors are shown more clearly. As mentioned earlier, the self-styled Protectors speed to Harold and Penny's position as if they were in a game, becoming increasingly removed from any real connection to the landscape they are passing through, or even the ambiguities in the quest they are undertaking. Meanwhile the unlikely couple increase their relationship to each other and the environs around them. Before beginning on their walk to the place Harold proposed to his wife, he promises to look after Penny no matter what. As they leave Penny's car and embark on this pilgrimage of remembrance—and that is very much what it is for Harold, being his own final quest to connect with his wife, the land, and his memory—he is increasingly wracked with fits. While curled in a ball from his latest spasm, Penny is suddenly attacked by No. 7, who has escaped from the care facility. Harold suddenly leaps to the rescue and saves her, but not before receiving severe injuries from the encounter. In the meantime, the hunters, who have been running through the woods shouting "Gimble, Gimble" as if involved in a children's game, arrive and kill No. 7. They then surround Harold and Penny, intent on killing him, even though the nurse tries to protect him. Caught in something of a standoff, Penny faces them all repeatedly crying "No, no!" and pleading the case for Harold, as her "best friend," a person who has loved and is loved and who represents the past and the kind of memory and connection to place that the hunters do not have. Momentarily, Jon pauses—he was shown earlier briefly contemplating the family photos in the wallet of a "zombie" they had just clubbed to death—and they allow Penny to hug Harold goodbye as she turns and walks away. Harold, knowing he is on the verge of losing himself totally, attacks his attackers, knocking two of them to the ground. However, Colin avoids Harold's blows and surprises the old man and kills him. As Penny walks away, there is the feeling that the hunters have somehow killed the past and lost all connection to it, cutting themselves adrift. In destroying their ultimate goal, they have completed their quest, which was not killing zombies but to replace them in their memoryless state.

Indeed, something of this is borne out as the film ends and a cure for ORD is found due to the tests carried out on Harold. Even the most extreme cases are shown to be in remission, or even taking part in charity runs. While killing Harold when they did had no real effect on the cure being found, the construction of the film suggests differently—that killing the original zombie somehow ended the game so that all the others affected are cured, cutting off the hunters not only from the past but their own quest. With no memory and no purpose, even their connection through the "game" is gone, they have become the equivalent of the undead. While we learn of the subsequent lives of all the other protagonists in the film, nothing is shown of Jon, Mike, and Colin—they have quite literally vanished from memory. Conversely, Penny is now full of memory. Harold's passing has left her the only receptacle of his past, a veritable living archive that will carry his memory and memories into the future. Penny shows this by lovingly tidying and packing all his belongings back in the bungalow. Her subsequent return to the spot where Harold proposed to his wife marks it not only as a place of remembrance of that event, but also where Penny lost the person she loved but found herself.

Conclusion

Harold's Going Stiff is a continuation in the evolution of the zombie in what Kyle William Bishop calls the "post-millennial climate," but like earlier films, in particular those of Romero, it also creates a world where "the humans are not necessarily humane" (Bishop 159). In fact, Wright's film blurs many of these boundaries, further intimating that zombiism is not so much a disease/contagion that brings people back from the dead, but rather a condition that separates people from their lives and memories. Further, it posits that zombiism does not just point to those that act the way that popular culture intimates that they should—mindless, lumbering, flesh-eating monsters—but as a theoretical category that can include much of contemporary society. Consequently, *Harold* begins to embody cultural anxieties about technological advances, generational differences, and the perceived speeding up of the future, leaving the past behind. As Alexander Etkind observes, "Some cultures proliferate their ghosts, vampires and zombies in response to the catastrophes of the past; other cultures generate this imagery in anticipation of the catastrophes of the future" (Etkind 260). This catastrophe in the future is one of memory, built on the anxiety that the current generation, the Millennials, are no longer meaningfully connected to the environments they live in or have a physical connection, not only to their peers, but also their parents and grandparents, representing the past. The future in this construction becomes a world of individuals who are primarily driven by their own desires and are totally focused on their quest to fulfill that desire, living in the moment with little recourse to the past—effectively making them zombies. *Harold* specifically configures this in relation to the perceived difference between the Baby Boomer and the Millennial generations, with the former seen as an integral part of historical memory which holds everyone in the flow of the past into the future, while the latter holds itself separate from that temporal stream, creating a fracture in the timeline that will destroy it forever. However, the film sees the coming together of Harold and Penny as something of a suture that heals this wound in the stream of memory. Coming from either side of the generational gap, Penny crosses over to take on board Harold's memories and carry them with her into the future. More so, this involves not just being a personal archive, but equally posits the importance of space to memory and the ways in which meaning creates and continues in terms of the inhabiting of places and the memories and memorials one makes there. As such, their love not only makes the "zombies" more humane but also humanizes the world as a space where we can once more be at home.

Notes

1. The films *Fido* (2006) and *Colin* (2008) both posit something of the same, where a connection between the zombie and its surroundings, usually familiar in their previous life, begins to cause something of a return of their memory.

2. *Warm Bodies* (2013) takes this even further, making its hero virtually human again.

3. While Harold was the first person to be identified with the disease, he is also the longest suffering without the more extreme symptoms presenting themselves, and this is why the head of the Shuttleworth Institute is so interested in him.

Works Cited

Bacon, Simon. "'Six Impossible Things Before Breakfast': Living Memory and Undead History." *Unraveling Resident Evil: Essays on the Complex Universe of the Games and Films,* edited by Nadine Farghaly. McFarland, 2014, 216–34.

Barton, Karen S., and Charles O. Collens. "Millennials' and Baby Boomers' Perceptions and Use of Nature." *21st Century Geography: A Reference Handbook*, edited by Joseph P. Stoltmam. Sage, 2012, pp. 255–65.

Birdsall, Carolyn. "Sound Memory: A Critical Concept for Researching Memories of Conflict and War." *Memory, Place and Identity: Commemoration and Remembrance of War and Conflict*, edited by Danielle Drozdzewski, Sarah De Nardi and Emma Waterton. Routledge, 2016, pp. 111–29.

Bishop, Kyle William. *American Zombie Gothic: The Rise and Fall (and Rise) of the Walking Dead in Popular Culture.* McFarland, 2010.

Bronfen, Elizabeth. *Dorothy Richardson's Art of Memory: Space, Identity, Text.* Translated by Victoria Applebe. Manchester University Press, 1999.

Childs, Robert D., Paulette Robinson, Terry M. McGovern, and Gerry Gringich. "The Millennial Generation," *Transforming American Governance: Rebooting the Public Square*, edited by Alun P. Balutis, Terry F. Buss, and Dwight Ink. Routledge, 2011, pp. 307–21.

Dawn of the Dead. Directed by George A. Romero, United Film Distribution Company, 1978.

Etkind, Alexander. "Post-Stalinist Russia: Memory and Mourning." *The Ashgate Research Companion to Memory Studies*, edited by Siobhan Kattago. Routledge, 2015, pp. 251–64.

Harold's Going Stiff. Directed by Kevin Wright, Frisson Films, 2011.

Henger, Bob, and Jan Henger. *The Silent Generation 1925–1945.* Authorhouse, 2012.

Knowlton, Dave S. "Navigating the Paradox of Student Ego." *New Directions for Teaching and Learning*, no. 135, Autumn 2013, pp. 19–30.

Land of the Dead. Directed by George A. Romero, Universal Pictures, 2005.

Luckhurst, Roger. *Zombies: A Cultural History.* Reaktion Books, 2015.

Luttrell, Regina, and Karen McGraph. *The Millennial Mindset: Unraveling Fact from Fiction.* Rowman & Littlefield, 2015.

Mantz, Jeffrey W. "On the Frontlines of the Zombie War in the Congo: Digital Technology, the Trade in Conflict Materials, and Zombification." *Monster Culture in the 21st Century: A Reader*, edited by Marina Levina and Diem-My T. Bui. Bloomsbury, 2013, pp. 177–92.

Noakes, Lucy. "'War on the Web,': The BBC's 'People's War' Website and Memories of Fear in 21st-Century Britain." *British Cultural Memory and the Second World War*, edited by Lucy Noakes and Juliette Pattinson. Bloomsbury, 2014, pp. 47–66.

Prizer, Timothy C. *Pining for Turpentine: Critical Nostalgia, Memory, and Commemorative Expression in the Wake of Industrial Decline.* Proquest, 2009.

Stubbe, Emily. "Loving Online." *Reddex: Spring 2015 Cross Media Graphics Management Program Review.* University of Wisconsin, 2015, p. 8.

Weissberg, Liliane. "Introduction." *Cultural Memory and the Construction of Identity*, edited by Dan Ben-Amos and Liliane Weissberg. Wayne State University Press, 1999, pp. 7–26.

The Sexy Millennial Reinvention of the Undead in *Warm Bodies* and *iZombie*

Ashley Szanter *and* Jessica K. Richards

Contemporary zombie storytelling has turned away from the tangible to emphasize more personal concerns, but, while previous generations needed their zombies to act as scapegoats for seemingly unconquerable events (e.g., disease, death, nuclear war), new zombies turn away from that kind of abject horror to embody interiority and questions of identity and belonging. While these thematic shifts reflect changes at the sociocultural level, they also coincide with the maturation of the Millennial generation. Reaching adulthood in the late 1990s and 2000s, Millennials began shaping popular culture right as zombies garnered mainstream attention. Shifts in zombie genre tropes and storylines come as no surprise when juxtaposed with Millennial concerns and contributions to popular culture.

Raised on a diet of individualism, Millennials do not connect with the "united front" imagery of the traditional zombie horde. Because of this, narratives like *Warm Bodies* (2013) and *iZombie* (2015–present) present a new and attractive alternative by speaking to Millennial concerns about identity and the self. Defining questions for this generation are "Who am I?" and "Where do I fit?" rather than an individual's contribution to the continued success of a group. If zombies are to represent the concerns and preoccupations of the Millennial generation, the horde is useless. But, within new zombie universes where even the humans are half dead, there is another, unprecedented development. The tendency to romanticize and sexualize zombies now stands front and center in both *Warm Bodies*, crafted as a Romeo and Juliet-esque rom-com, and the television series *iZombie*, whose characters can contract zombiism as a sexually transmitted disease. Based on a novel and a graphic novel respectively, promos for both *Warm Bodies* and *iZombie* take liberties with their source material and increasingly emphasize the sexuality of both zombie protagonists. Millennials remain unfazed by the implied necrophilia of sexy zombies, but this generation's cultural consumption of other "dead" heartthrobs, more specifically vampires, desensitizes young audiences and sheds some light on our recent tendency to sexualize the dead.

In light of these recent developments, we discuss the Millennial appropriation of the zombie genre as a way of communicating and grappling with generational anxieties through this monster of the moment. The continued popularity of zombies allows Millennials to consistently express concerns about the problematic world we inherited from our predecessors while also addressing issues of how we can exist within contexts that limit self-expression and self-identification. Through this essay, we argue how recent incarnations of the zombie in both the source material and the adaptations of *Warm Bodies* and *iZombie* are the direct result of Millennial representation and engagement in popular culture and why these new, individualized characterizations of zombies captivate Millennial audiences.

Pre-Millennial concerns of the zombie genre often address questions of identity in contexts of social collapse: when society breaks down, do social roles (e.g., race, class, gender, occupation) retain any significance? Often, the answer is an unequivocal "No." The breakdown of socially defined identity takes center stage in Danny Boyle's *28 Days Later* (2002), Zac Snyder's *Dawn of the Dead* (2004), and Robert Kirkman's *The Walking Dead* (2003–present) as well as AMC's televised adaptation (2010–present). These zombie narratives present characters trapped between pre-existing social constructions of trustworthiness and responsibility and new, undefined borders of how those constructions crumble under epidemic collapse, or a zombie apocalypse. But current changes in the zombie genre tend to deal with individual, rather than social, identity politics. Rather than questioning how an individual fits in with others, new incarnations of the zombie deal with how individuals define and express themselves. We believe these zombies and their various presentations reveal the shifting landscape of American cultural anxiety, and these ideas appear in several other pieces of zombie scholarship and popular culture; the most relevant of these comes from Peter Dendle.

Often cited for his creation of *The Zombie Movie Encyclopedia* (2010) and *The Zombie Movie Encyclopedia, Volume 2: 2000–2010* (2012), Dendle's "Zombie Movies and the 'Millennial Generation'" is the first attempt at a new approach to zombie studies and opens up conversations about how Millennials, the generation just now entering adulthood, transformed the zombie genre. Taking a clear generational stance, Dendle defines Millennials as a "technologically savvy, fast-paced generation of young people in the 1990s and 2000s" but questions how the zombie, a "shambling, slow revenant," became the Millennial's monster of choice (175). Ultimately, Dendle asserts Millennials crave the simplicity of a zombie's existence; "For the zombie, choices are easy and the world is uncomplicated" (186). But he also pushes a step further to claim young people no longer have a strong foundation for appearances and truth. The idea of zombies "as outwardly human and familiar—but completely alien within" speaks to post–9/11 concerns of terrorism and cyberwarfare—both defining the sociopolitical climate of Millennial upbringings (186). However, Dendle's analysis falls just short of making serious claims about the shifting taxonomies of Millennial identity politics.

While critiques of this generation are not in short supply, there are those pushing back against critics to examine why Millennials are the way we are.[1] Sophia A. McClennen's article "America's Millennials are in crisis—and it's not all in their heads," leans on the research of Russell Dalton, a political scientist and member of the Baby Boomer generation, who argues that "millennial Americans may be the most disparaged generation of young people in their nation's history." McClennen also claims, "Dalton's research shows that Millennials may be the most publicly denounced generation of all time." It seems Millennials are crafting a response to this criticism through pop culture, and it has had an impact on characterizations of the undead. Presenting characters who experience and express decay allows Millennials the opportunity to commiserate over less than ideal circumstances.

As such, "Millennial zombie narratives" like *Warm Bodies* and *iZombie* feature characters who happen to be both zombies and attractive 20-somethings. R (Nicholas Hoult) and Olivia "Liv" Moore (Rose McIver) are the central characters of these two recent adaptations who share many traits of the newly individualized zombie. They have logical thoughts, emotions, desires, and consciences—none of which are typical of the traditional zombie. While both R and Liv represent laziness, apathy, and aimlessness, they embody these in slightly different ways. One particular anxiety expressed through these two zombies is their inability to articulate their shared condition. Both are subjected to involuntary zombification but cannot place blame on either themselves or those around them for their condition.

"I'm dead, but it's not so bad."

These anxieties surrounding successful communication are also present in Isaac Marion's novel *Warm Bodies*—the source material for the cinematic adaptation. Marion's first major publication garnered widespread attention from American and international readership. The story chronicles R, a 20-something male zombie struggling to come to terms with his zombie existence. R lives in an airport where he shambles from place to place with little direction but has a striking ability to experience complex thought. Often a stream of consciousness, R's introspection reimagines the traditional archetype of zombiism. Avoiding a traditionally one-dimensional creature, zombies in Marion's novel form relationships (R's best friend's name is M, played by Rob Corddry) and rationalize the world around them. The novel's interiority puts readers in R's conscious as he relays the context of the apocalypse, the nature of zombie existence, and grapples with his identity crisis as he struggles to remember his pre-zombie life. However, zombies in the novel are still constrained by their physical condition as R continually expresses frustration about his limited ability to speak and his inability to read. While Marion's zombies are moderately fast, perhaps entering a light jog at full speed, they have lost most fine motor skills, have limited speech, and exhibit some signs of physical decay—though not to extent of other, similar zombie creatures.

A member of the Millennial generation himself, Marion's novel articulates a crisis of identity and belonging above all else: R exists outside of "community" and instead lives alone with very few options, or desires, for companionship. He surrounds himself with trinkets and artifacts from the past. Most notably, R's collection of vinyl records speaks to a nostalgic desire for a different time and place. When confronted by Julie for his collection, R claims the vinyl is "More real. More ... alive" (Marion 52). R is a zombie hipster longing for the past. Unable to resign himself fully to this new, undead existence, R tries to recapture humanness through music and the memories he experiences through consuming brains. The book takes a specifically Millennial view of the post-apocalyptic space.

The film only emphasizes these Millennial concerns and strives to make more explicit connections to them within the visual text. First, R's character design taps into conceptions of Millennials as lazy (LaFrance) with his costume consisting of sneakers, jeans, a white t-shirt, and a red hoodie: none of which indicate success or ambition. This representation of R taps into an extreme view of Millennial stereotypes: he does not move or work unless he absolutely has to. But this is precisely where the film takes liberties with the source material as director Jonathan Levine deviates from the source material in terms of R's appearance. In Marion's novel, R narrates, "Before I became a zombie I must have been a businessman, a banker or broker or some young temp learning the ropes, because I'm wearing fairly nice clothes. Black slacks, grey shirt, red tie" (Marion 4). R later states, "these final fashion choices are the only indication of who we were before we became no one" (Marion 4). Rather than characterizing R as a "lazy Millennial" stereotype, Marion's treatment of R's appearance conveys a sense of accomplishment, or at least ambition.

Levine's adaptation changed a few key elements of the text but kept the plot largely intact. R falls in love with human girl Julie (Teresa Palmer) and embarks on a Romeo and Juliet story of "star-crossed lovers" against all odds. So, the cinematic choice to restyle R as a stereotype of Millennial informality garners attention from fans of both the novel and film. Perhaps capitalizing on public opinion of this generation, Levine's decision to restyle R seems to make a more pointed critique than Marion's novel. However, it can also function to develop clear connections between the zombie protagonist and the Millennial audience. Crafting R as an extreme representation of Millennial stereotypes, young audiences form a bond with R in not only his thought processes but also the ways in which others must view him. Levine's visual choices reinforce this reading as M, an older, Generation X zombie character, wears a business casual suit jacket and khakis as opposed to R's jeans and t-shirt ensemble.

Compounding these crises of character, *Warm Bodies* increases the emphasis on generational conflict. The constant disapproval of Julie's father, General Grigio (John Malkovich), makes generational conflict a secondary theme in *Warm Bodies*. Spurred on by her father's inability to listen to her, Julie must convince her father that R can be healed, renewed, and redeemed. Grigio's objection to R, and to corpses in general, is their difference. They are the "Other" he cannot abide. R and Julie as Millennial characters cannot convince Baby Boomer Grigio of R's humanity. Mimicking the rhetoric of older generations, Grigio's othering of Millennials skews his objectivity, and he views his daughter's defense of R as naïve and infantile because he cannot see past R's exterior or Julie's youth. These artistic choices reflect an underlying message present in both text and film: characters reflect and embody generationally defined identities that speak to both motivation and culturally defined roles. But *Warm Bodies* is not the only narrative dealing directly with zombie identity politics.

iZombies These Days

Released in 2015, Rob Thomas[2] and Diane Ruggiero-Wright's *iZombie* retains few elements from its source material. Originally, the graphic novel series, developed by Chris Roberson and Michael Allred in 2011, details the exploits of Gwen Dylan, a gravedigger and revenant in Eugene, Oregon. The comic contains a unique mythos with a host of supernatural characters including mummies, ghosts, vampires, and were-beasts. Once a month, Gwen digs up a newly buried body from the graveyard where she lives and works. Consuming brains allows her to retain human-like characteristics and prevents her from becoming "all mindless and shambling. Total *Night of the Living Dead*" (Roberson and Allred), while also adding the complication of experiencing the memories and impulses of the recently deceased. Gwen's zombie-related identity crisis is made more poignant by her limited memories of her human life.

While Thomas and Ruggiero-Wright's adaptation retains Gwen Dylan's powers of memory and identity absorption for each of their zombies, they transform the narrative into a murder-of-the-week procedural with hints that a full-fledged zombie apocalypse is waiting in the wings. Rather than Gwen Dylan, we have Liv Moore, who falls short of her pre-zombie human potential. In the pilot episode of *iZombie*, Liv's family hosts an intervention expressing concern over her recent behavior. After attending an apocalyptic boat party that leaves her zombified, Liv breaks off an engagement, leaves a promising medical career, appears depressed and lethargic, and works a dead-end job as a medical examiner—her answer to the ethical dilemma of how to procure brains. Her family and friends express their concern about her lost potential and seemingly erratic choices, including her new side job as a consulting detective. Unlike Gwen, who retains little to no memory of her past, Liv Moore is painfully aware of how her life was and what it should have become.

In *iZombie*, Liv can cook, go to work, get dressed, and live "normally." But she also faces concern from family and friends about her abandoned potential. For Millennials, this is a common occurrence. Even while completing medical school and becoming a successful medical examiner, Liv cannot achieve the potential expected of her. Her best friend, Peyton (Aly Michalka), is a law school graduate and district attorney in her mid-twenties who embodies an unrealistic level of "success." Though this accomplishment is a virtual impossibility for someone so young, its inclusion in the show condemns Liv to fall short of Generation X and Baby Boomer expectations. Liv, while able to speak easily, internalizes her lack of apparent success as a personal failure, and, early on in the series, her condition hangs on her as a secret she cannot reveal for fear of being misunderstood.

Generational conflict is also present in *iZombie* where Liv's mother, Eva Moore (Molly Hagan), continues to express her concern over Liv's wasted potential. This tension culminates in an estrangement at the conclusion of the first season. Blaine (David Anders), the central antagonist in Liv's world and another Millennial, also fights a generational war. Early in the second season, the show introduces Blaine's father, Angus McDonough (Robert Knepper). Blaine transforms his father into a zombie to supplement his income, and, in an ambitious moment, Blaine attempts to extort a further half million from his father. Angus, while ultimately forced to comply, complains about Blaine's lack of success:

> ANGUS: You should learn to live within your means. If you don't mind what shortcut are you taking this time, huh? It's always the same for you isn't it? Always looking for the easy way out? Least amount of talent required. Least amount of effort.... The strings I pulled to get my party boy son into Wharton.

> You couldn't make it one semester. "Dad, Dad, Dad, Dad, Dad, Dad this widget is going to revolutionize the way we listen to music, rent apartments, hookup. I just need some startup capital." I always knew the request was coming, because you'd manage to hide your hate for me a few weeks leading up to the pitch. And I would just give in, I guess that's how this story ends ["Zombie Bro"].

The insults Baby Boomer Angus lobs at Blaine resonate with Millennial audiences. By labeling his son as a "party boy" and suggesting that Blaine takes the "easy way out," Angus taps into Millennial anxieties about laziness. He also attacks Blaine's lack of formal education. While Millennials obtain more years of education than any other generation (Patten), they are also disparaged for their lack of common knowledge (Bauerlein). Despite Blaine occupying the role of "The Big Bad" throughout the first season, this scene cultivates sympathy for Blaine. The apparent animosity already present in this father/son relationship suggests that Blaine's villainous tendencies stem from rejection and misunderstanding, rather than strictly from his own agency. *iZombie* seems to place some of the blame for Millennial anxieties about their own decay at the feet of the Baby Boomers.[3] The tenuous intergenerational relations[4] in *iZombie* reflect a growing sentiment among Millennials that their failures manifest most noticeably in the condemnation of their elders. Referring back to McClellan's article, the Millennial internalization of their elder's disapproval is "not all in their heads."

Really, Really Bad Tabula Rasa

While the Millennial tendency to extend adolescence is seen as an unwillingness to contribute meaningfully to society, it is also rooted in a terrible anxiety surrounding the formation of character. Identity used to come with commitment and expectation, but as Wesley Morris recently pointed out in his article "The Year We Obsessed Over Identity," while we have collectively celebrated the "smashing of binaries," we also question who we are, as the assumptions accompanying specific gender, racial, and social behaviors become fuzzy and more malleable—an unprecedented freedom. However, the obliteration of these institutions also leaves Millennials with fewer ways to organize and develop identity. The shift in these cultural boundaries leaves Millennials without the ability to take on concrete roles, resulting in a craving to experience a fully fleshed out character.

As Morris's article indicates, there is another side effect to constantly reevaluating our identity: we become obsessed with ourselves. In addition to being considered lazy and entitled, Millennials are also defined by their tendency towards narcissism and self-obsession. As Joel Stein details, "The National Institutes of Health reported that '58% more college students scored higher on a narcissism scale in 2009 than in 1982.'" Technology is partially to blame for this over inflated sense of self. Millennials constantly connect and relate to the world through a narrow lens. A Pew Research Study from 2010 entitled "Millennials: Confident. Connected. Open to Change," reported that approximately 75 percent of the Millennial generation have accounts on social media compared to 50 percent of Gen-Xers and only 30 percent of Baby Boomers.

Millennial self-consciousness about narcissism helps identify the process of "knowing" a person as fundamentally destructive. In a pivotal moment of the *iZombie* series, Liv's zombie boyfriend declares "Liv, we.... We eat people. We eat people" ("Patriot Brains"). The poignancy of these words does not stem from their simplicity, but rather the character's recognition that his continued existence requires consuming identity to retain a false humanity. This is a defining conflict of "Millennial zombie narratives": brain-eating allows zombies to retain humanness. In *Warm Bodies*, the consumption of brains serves as a substitute for the inability to dream and communicate. Brain eating in *Warm Bodies* allows the zombie to experience flashbacks and memories of the person being consumed. Zombies can experience emotion and human connection through the life experiences of another. R eats the brains of a young man, providing him with a deeper emotional connection to a human girl, and eventually paving the way for him to defeat zombiism through love. Millennial zombie narratives use brains as an adjusted perspective, a mask, allowing characters to try on various identities and engage Millennial anxiety about the formation of their own character.

It is particularly through Liv that we access Thomas and Ruggiero-Wright's treatment of Millennial empathy—which clearly connects to *Warm Bodies*. While the types of memories experienced are still unpredictable, Liv's "visions" come when triggered by external stimuli. When someone or something activates this trigger, Liv sees snippets of the deceased's memories, though in a less reliable way than that in *Warm Bodies* as the memories do not immediately follow consumption. Liv's own victimization, or her involuntary zombification, causes her to feel satisfied when seeking justice for the others suffering from a similar death, an utter loss of potential. Liv's pursuit of justice makes her feel restored. In one of the most unfortunate creative choices of the *iZombie* series, Liv expresses the traits of the deceased through hackneyed stereotypes. (For example, Liv's consumption of an Asian gang member's brain leaves her with a knowledge of Kung Fu.) In many ways, this problematic representation of identity underscores a central Millennial conflict. Because the "smashing of binaries" dismantles conventional ways of understanding identity and because Millennials are self-conscious about their narcissistic tendencies, the exploration of identity takes on horrific significance in "Millennial Zombie Narratives." In these narratives, zombies destroy the object of their desire, their human counterparts, so they can retain a false sense of their human-like qualities.

Warm Bodies *Romanticized It: "I've learned to live with it."*

Kyle William Bishop's book, *How Zombies Conquered Popular Culture: The Multifarious Walking Dead in the 21st Century* (2015), approaches ideas of individual expression in the penultimate chapter, "The Romantic Zombie: *Warm Bodies* and the Monstrous Boyfriend," but does not fully address the Millennial commitment to self-identification. In fact, the chapter provides Bishop's scathing review of Jonathan Levine's *Warm Bodies* adaptation as a narrative romanticizing abusive relationships.[5] Bishop eviscerates the story and its characters, equating them to little more than a zombified *Twilight* (166). Again, Bishop, like Peter Dendle, tends to neglect the real question of Millennial identity politics in conjunction with newer zombies. R's questions about his identity as a zombie, as well as Julie's ability to connect with R in spite of his zombification, mimic concerns over interpersonal connections and collapsing identity.

Though the movie was popular with audiences, earning over $66 million dollars at the box office, many were upset with the seemingly abusive portrayal of R's and Julie's relationship ("Warm Bodies (2013)"). In this most recent criticism of *Warm Bodies*, Bishop attacks the film as depicting a newly defanged monstrous boyfriend in zombie protagonist R. Bishop categorizes R as "decidedly antisocial, dangerous, and disturbing" and continues the critique to Julie who "allows herself to be manipulated and endangered" (169–70). While in certain terms Bishop's analysis reveals problematic elements of R's and Julie's unorthodox courtship, he fails to take into consideration *why* depictions of "monstrous relationships" attract Millennial audiences. Bishop's chapter builds on Glennis Byron's assertion that audiences defanged modern monsters in an attempt to completely romanticize them as is the case with many vampire narratives. Bishop, citing Byron, claims,

> "the quintessential Gothic monster and the iconic 'star-crossed lovers' have been simplified and commodified, emptied of threat and tragedy, welcomed into the collective iconography of popular culture, and now, merged together." This lessening of threat and tragedy for modern readers is problematic; yet, not surprisingly, this kind of merger has made its way into the world of the zombie apocalypse narrative as well [166].

The assertion that defanged monsters represent a Millennial unwillingness to acknowledge the danger inherent in monstrous relationships neglects to take into consideration Millennial perceptions of the omnipresence of violence.

Rather than defanging the monstrous boyfriend, narratives like *Warm Bodies* instead present Millennials as accepting of the danger of everyday life. Julie's attraction to R stems from an understanding that danger constantly surrounds her. Existing in a post-apocalyptic space, Julie cannot hope to live without fear of death or danger. Rather than "defanging" as suggested by Bishop and Byron, we argue Julie's Millennial perceptions of the world as an increasingly dangerous place replaces her fear of harm. Julie even tells Perry, her even more abusive ex-boyfriend, "There is no ideal world for you to wait around for. The world is always just what it is now, and it's up to you how you respond to it" (Marion 113). Lines like this indicate Millennial zombie narratives have not removed "threat and tragedy." Instead, these monstrous Millennial characters retain all the horror they are meant to convey—and Bishop explores this horror in great detail. Even Peter Dendle acknowledges "Millennials have grown up in a world in which violence is often spontaneous and inexplicable" (Dendle 185). "Because of the unique face of violence in the modern age" Millennials also have a perception of contemporary violence as omnipresent (Dendle 179). Accounting for this awareness, the fundamental change is that Millennials like Julie recognize, but do not concede to, violence because it corresponds to our developing worldview.

Though the Millennial perception of violence seems to indicate an inherent pessimism about the world, the reality is quite different. The difference lies in the positive, optimistic view of the world Millennials cling to (Tanenhaus). Julie's affection for R stems from her desire to redefine the pessimistic tone of her apocalyptic life. R, attempting to navigate Julie through an airport full of zombies, observes, "to my amazement, Julie's fear seems to be *diminishing* as we walk, despite the obvious peril of her situation" (39). Rather than dismissing the "obvious peril" of her situation, Julie decides to simply adapt to the presence or feelings of fear and not let them dictate her behavior. For Julie and other Millennials, fear is a given and does not define this generation's attitudes or conduct. Instead, she quite literally embraces the fear and uses it to mobilize her desire to change the world around her for the better.

Julie's decision to pursue an emotional connection with R comes under scrutiny for characterizing her as a woman who desires emotional distance in this heteronormative context. As a young woman, her options for male companionship in both the novel and film present her with few good choices. The emotional distance of her father and boyfriend Perry as well as the aggressive rhetoric of men in bars who desire "loose" women actually place R in a safer emotional category. Because his most aggressive action towards Julie is a constant "male gaze," Julie actually saves herself from the emotional abuse received at the hands of her father and Perry. In fact, R's commitment to speech throughout the course of the narrative implies a dedication to breaking down the barriers implicit in male identity. The detached, contested nature of masculine identity (especially in American culture) reinforce R's mute characterization (Rosin). As the only male character who overcomes that emotional distance, R actually transcends his masculine identity in his endeavor to be a better mate to Julie. Every strained attempt at communication speaks to R's dedication to participating in their, albeit unconventional, romance.

Millennial interpretations of *Warm Bodies* as distinctly romantic reveal anxieties present in modern dating and relationships.[6] However, R's and Julie's transcendence of their less than ideal situation falls in line with Millennial desires for a better future. Again, the Pew Research Center, in "Millennials: Confident. Connected. Open to Change," claims Millennials "are more upbeat than their elders about their own economic futures as well as about the overall state of the nation." Pew's assertion that Millennials have a distinct optimism about the future reinforces R's and Julie's belief that they have a chance, however slim, to change their own fates. The narrative confirms this notion as R transforms from "corpse" to human and, in this process, changes the entire world as they know it—including the opinions of older generations. Going from post-apocalyptic dystopia to the cusp of a bright new world, R's and Julie's trust in a better future ultimately marks the story as one of unrelenting Millennial optimism.

iZombie *Sexualized It*

While we have established that *iZombie* takes very little from its graphic novel source material, the show explores some interesting new angles by keeping the protagonist a Millennial female zombie. Liv Moore maintains her identity as a 20-something woman in modern day Seattle, Washington. However, her appearance, much like R's, represents her characterization. Once an ambitious medical student, Liv's opening shots of the series show her "perfect" life: she is beautiful, thin, engaged to an attractive man, and deeply intelligent ("Pilot"). However, her zombification turns her life upside down and audiences are now left with a single young female who binge watches infomercials, eats an exorbitant amount of junk food, and only gets up to go to work as a medical examiner—a far cry from the prestigious job viewers know she was on track to achieve. Liv is now a recluse whose family worries about her wasted potential. However, her new characterization, while reinforced by her new wardrobe of muted, ill-fitted clothing, comes with some odd physical changes. Whereas human Liv is nicely tanned with medium brown hair, zombie Liv is now extremely pale with almost white-blonde hair ("Pilot").

Strangely, her zombification more closely aligns her appearance with Western standards of physical beauty. But Liv's physical transformation is not the only example of attractive zombie physicality.

"Flight of the Living Dead" introduces Lowell Tracey (Bradley James) as a British heartthrob and Liv's new zombie love interest. Though he goes to great lengths to hide his zombiism (e.g., dying hair, spray tans), his first appearance on screen showcases the "The CW Smolder"—a trademark of *iZombie*'s network where attractive actors, particularly males, stare intently at another individual with a seductive look, a "smolder." After enduring police questioning because of his suspected involvement with another girl's murder, Lowell realizes that Liv suffers from the same zombification he does. As a result, he gives a romantic speech at the end of the episode which preludes their fiery courtship: "no one can really know, you now. Kissing, touching, sex, love, yelling at someone for stealing the blankets ... out of the question, forever" ("Flight of the Living Dead"). Lowell's attempt to connect with Liv underscores the nature of their burgeoning relationship. While he does list "love," the focus is on physical intimacy—the piece parts of a sexual relationship. Though Liv worries about sharing her disease, she finds liberation in a sexual zombie relationship with Lowell. Both of these zombie characters possess undeniably human desires for sexual companionship.

iZombie is far more liberal with its characters' sexual expressions than either Marion's or Levine's *Warm Bodies*. The impetus behind the sexualization of these zombies stems from their shared disease. Thomas and Ruggiero's story arc involves zombiism as a communicable disease—particularly through fluid exchange. Because of this, the disease in *iZombie* can function like a sexually transmitted disease.[7] Viewers learn that this realization prompts Liv to break off her engagement with Major Lilywhite (Robert Buckley). While Liv and Major decide to rekindle their romance despite her zombification, the absence of a sexual relationship paired with her erratic personality changes proves too complicated, and Liv ends their brief courtship in the mid-season finale episode, "Cape Town."

Whereas Liv's narrative arc includes several ruminations about the moral grey area of zombie/human sexual relationships, the series also presents sex as threatening and power dynamics play out as humans enter relationships with the undead. While their initial bond centers on their shared zombiism, Liv learns Blaine operates a side business where he kills homeless teenagers and harvests their brains to serve his "clients," but Blaine is not just a middle man. In episode two, "Brother, Can You Spare a Brain?," Blaine seduces an older woman named Jackie (Sarah-Jane Redmond) effectively turning her into one of the living dead. When she realizes her transformation, Blaine offers her his services at the cost of $25,000 per month for an ongoing supply of brains in a variety of restaurant quality preparations.

Blaine's seduction of Jackie represents more than simple villainy. Whereas Liv's and Lowell's relationship explores the positive side of zombie sexuality, Blaine's reveals the inherent dangers of casual sexuality. With zombiism as a sexually transmitted disease, Blaine targeting Jackie now becomes a premeditated sexual assault, but Jackie chooses to continue her relationship with Blaine making him a "zombie booty call." Trying to extract more from their relationship, Jackie inquires as to whether they can work out an arrangement so she can avoid the monthly payment for brain delivery. Nonchalantly, Blaine states, "Oh, Jackie, I made you a zombie, but I'd never make you a whore" ("Live and Let Clive"). Considering Blaine's connection to Millennials, his targeting of Jackie, a Boomer character, underscores the tenuous generational conflicts throughout the series. Though Blaine acts on his aggression towards Boomers, his violent sexuality becomes a tool to retaliate against a generation that fundamentally misunderstands him. By taking away Jackie's sexual agency, Blaine literally and figuratively screws the Boomer generation; while Blaine's actions against his father tend to be calculated towards his business empire, the attack on Jackie feels infinitely more personal and intimate. While this commentary on intergenerational conflict manifests in this particular "throwaway" arc, it is Thomas and Ruggiero-Wright's presentation of sexualized zombies that crafts a problematic storyline, specifically because Millennial audiences openly embrace a narrative engaging in necrophiliac behavior.

The presentation of sexuality throughout *iZombie* is undeniably desirable as none of the central zombies appear decomposed or disgusting. Instead, zombies are now alluring, sexual beings who crave physical intimacy in spite of the potentially damaging results. Even Jackie, who unwittingly slept with Blaine as a casual one-night stand, is an attractive older woman living a liberated sexual lifestyle. Liv's denouncements further reinforce Blaine's characterization as a sexual predator. In episode three, "The Exterminator," before Liv learns about Blaine's business, she rebukes him as "that same drug dealing knob that groped me on that boat." Liv understands Blaine uses sex as a weapon and labels him a predator long before viewers learn the extent of his debauchery. It is, in fact, Blaine who scratches Liv (one of the ways that zombiism is transmitted in the show). This penetration is threatening and can be read as a form of rape.

While both Marion's and Levine's *Warm Bodies* go to great lengths to romanticize zombies, Thomas and Ruggiero-Wright's *iZombie* goes a step further to outright sexualize zombies. By crafting characters who are both physically and emotionally attractive partners, the sexuality involved in this show puts zombie sex on the proverbial map. By casting *iZombie* with attractive actors and actresses, the creators took a previously unsexy creature and transformed it into a CW level heartthrob. Some characters, while having unattractive personalities, present attractive physicality to viewers who denounce predatory actions while reveling in the heat of a well-executed sex scene. With a show whose pilot episode had over 2.3 million viewers, this new presentation of highly sexualized zombies transformed the zombie genre for a young audience of Millennials who desire unabashed individuality in even their most unremarkable monsters (Mitovich).

The Cure

While differing on their presentations of zombie relationships, the most compelling connection between *Warm Bodies* and *iZombie* is the existence of a cure for zombiism—a deviation from more traditional zombie narratives. As Daniel Drezner notes in his *Theories of International Politics and Zombies* (2011), standard zombie stories "end in one of two ways—the elimination/subjugation of all zombies, or the eradication of humanity from the face of the earth" (8). What differentiates *Warm Bodies* and *iZombie* from their predecessors is the existence of a cure as a means of assimilating zombies into human culture.[8] The bleakness of the zombie genre reinforces the typical anxieties explored through zombie narratives. The idea that humans will either conquer or be conquered falls in line with conceptions of disease and war. However, the concerns explored in these new zombie stories require less diametric opposition and more room for alternative endings. As such, Millennial zombie narratives forgo the all or nothing conclusion for more nuanced explorations of how to accept or assimilate zombies into existing human infrastructure.

While normally the choice to use zombies as a monstrous self-representation seems bleak, both *Warm Bodies* and *iZombie*'s universes provide hope through cure narratives. For R, his cure lies in love and acceptance from humans. It is through Julie's affection for him, and him for her, that his heart begins to beat, his blood flows, and he reclaims his humanity. *Warm Bodies* ends with zombies reincorporated into society through encouragement and empathy from those who rejected them. As humans learn to care for and reeducate zombies about living like humans again, their humanity progressively returns. R's summative monologue at the end of novel claims, "We have big plans.... We will not let Earth become a tomb, a mass grave spinning through space. We will exhume ourselves. We will fight the curse and break it. We will cry and bleed and lust and love, and we will cure death. We will *be* the cure. Because we *want it*" (239). R's battle cry simulates the "dogged optimism" the Pew Research Center associates with Millennials ("Millennials: Confident. Connected. Open to Change"). This generation's commitment to "saving the world" predicates itself on the Millennial belief that "their own best days are ahead" (Tanenhaus).

Similarly, *iZombie*'s Liv exists in society while never feeling fully integrated. She conceals her zombiism as a horrific secret she can neither explain nor fully accept. Liv's potential cure is scientific—an experimental antidote reversing the effects of zombiism. The influence of science and medicine throughout the series is abundant. Liv and her medical examiner colleague, Ravi (Rahul Kohli), spend time searching for a way to reverse the effects of zombification. The discovery of a cure does not take too long; Ravi and Liv create, and use, a curative antidote in the final episode of season one ("Blaine's World"). However, Liv is not the zombie who receives the antidote. While the only dose of the antidote is used on another zombie, the cure works. It transformed a zombified Major, back into his living, human state.[9] While this narrative arc seems to end on a negative note as procuring another sample is problematic at best, the cure exists and works, at least temporarily.[10] The optimism inherent in this treatment of the cure narrative mimics that in *Warm Bodies*. There is a cure, it can combat zombiism, and it provides an alternative, potentially zombie-free future for Liv and other zombified individuals. The end of the pilot episode reveals a newly invigorated Liv who desires to make something of her formerly bleak future:

> Life's short and then you die.... And then you have to make some decisions. You can skulk around lamenting all you've lost, try to keep yourself numb and isolated. Or you can embrace who you are.... I wanted to do something with my life. I wanted to help people. Not necessarily as a zombie psychic who eats murder victim brains, but still.... I so nailed it today. I've spent five months bemoaning all that was taken from me. It never occurred to me that I would have something to give. A way to contribute. A reason for being not alive.... All I needed was some hope that there's a future I fit into somehow ["Pilot"].

The cure connecting these narratives, as well as the optimistic speeches given by both R and Liv, reveals a Millennial tendency disregarded by critics: there is always hope.

Zombies Are People Too

The zombie genre is in the midst of a transformation. Unlike its predecessors, these Millennial zombie narratives present a new and attractive way to envision the zombie monster. While questioning why zombies became and remain the monster of the new millennium, it is clear that the zombie is not leaving American culture for the foreseeable future. Narratives like *Warm Bodies* and *iZombie* craft a new zombie for the up and coming Millennial generation. Marion, Levine, Roberson, Allred, Thomas, and Ruggiero present audiences with an unexpected twist on an old classic. Through our analyses of these two particular narratives and their adaptations, we now see the zombie genre as an old medium reinvented to grapple with the concerns of a new generation. The popularity of this monster allows Millennials to both express dismay about the world and to explore new ways of transforming it for the better.

We believe these new incarnations of the zombie are the result of this generation's engagement in popular culture and that is why they continue to captivate Millennial audiences. For Millennials to accept this as "our" monster, the modern zombie must be different—the zombie needs to be attractive, to be desirable, so we can embrace their meanings and use them to communicate shared anxieties. Our zombies must be the best possible version of themselves, so we can be the best version of ourselves. As this generation continues into full adulthood, popular culture will provide an outlet for continued cultural expression. However, how the zombie will evolve from these new presentations of romance and sexuality is yet to be determined.

Notes

1. Perhaps the most scathing denigration of Millennials comes from Mark Bauerlein in *The Dumbest Generation: How the Digital Age Stupefies Young Americans and Jeopardizes Our Future (Or, Don't Trust Anyone Under 30)* (2008) where he claims Millennials participate in an anti-intellectual culture and, despite nearly infinite technological resources, fail to exceed the knowledge and skills of our progenitors.

2. Rob Thomas worked on a number of projects examining Millennial behavior. He was the creator of *Veronica Mars* (2004–07)—the cult television show—about a teenager who investigates the murder of her best friend. He worked on *Party Down* (2009–10), which dealt with the traumatic realities of adulthood for some aspiring actors in Los Angeles. He also revived and created the most recent *90210* (2008–13) series. Ruggiero-Wright worked as a producer and writer on *Veronica Mars*.

3. Members of Generation X are conspicuously absent from the *iZombie* and *Warm Bodies* narratives. By glossing over this entire generation, the narratives achieve a rigid dichotomy between Boomers and Millennials. Gen-Xer absence falls outside the scope of this essay and leaves further work for those examining generational zombie studies.

4. In the episode "Max Wager," Blaine smothers his grandfather in a nursing home. So ill he can no longer speak, the death of this mute member of the Silent generation as a means of punishing Angus (Blaine prepares the brains for his father's consumption) reveals the potential violence of these intergenerational interactions.

5. Bishop notes that he focuses entirely on analysis of Levine's adaptation as opposed to Marion's novel.

6. Marion's and Levine's *Warm Bodies* are not alone in their expressions of dating and romance anxiety. Even more recent shows like *The Mindy Project* (2012–present), *Master of None* (2015–present), and *Marvel's Jessica Jones* (2015–present) tap into widespread anxieties about romance and intimacy, and all include central characters who are either outright Millennial or adopt stereotypically Millennial behaviors.

7. We choose to use the term STD in this context as there is no permanent cure for zombiism in the show at this point. We recognize STI (sexually transmitted infection) as an accepted phrase, but believe STD is the more suitable term in this context.

8. We acknowledge *World War Z* (2013) also introduces a cure for zombiism, however we distinguish these two adaptations from *WWZ* because the focus of that film remains the human survivors rather than the emphasis on zombie interiority and assimilation.

9. We want to point out that we are not addressing the full second season of *iZombie*. Our analysis includes all of Season One and the first half of Season Two culminating in the mid-season finale episode, "Cape Town," which premiered 8 December 2015.

10. Season Two reveals the cure has limits related to permanency. Doses of the antidote used on rats were not permanent, and the rat eventually reverts to its zombie condition. However, the current trajectory of Season Two emphasizes Ravi's commitment to making a permanent cure for zombiism through continued research.

Works Cited

Bishop, Kyle William. *American Zombie Gothic: The Rise and Fall (and Rise) of the Walking Dead in Popular Culture*. McFarland, 2010.

_____. *How Zombies Conquered Popular Culture: The Multifarious Walking Dead in the 21st Century*. McFarland, 2015.

Davidow, Bill. "The Internet 'Narcissism Epidemic'" *The Atlantic*. 26 Mar. 2013. www.theatlantic.com/health/archive/2013/03/the-internet-narcissism-epidemic/274336/.

Dendle, Peter. "Zombie Movies and the 'Millennial Generation.'" *Better Off Dead: The Evolution of the Zombie as Post-Human*, edited by Deborah Christie and Sarah Juliet Lauro. Fordham University Press, 2011, pp. 175–86.

Drezner, Daniel W. *Theories of International Politics and Zombies*. Princeton University Press, 2011.

Fry, Richard. "More Millennials Living with Family Despite Improved Job Market." *Pew Research Center: Social & Demographic Trends*. 29 Jul. 2015. www.pewsocialtrends.org/2015/07/29/more-millennials-living-with-family-despite-improved-job-market/.

iZombie. Co-created by Rob Thomas and Diane Ruggiero-Wright. The CW, 2015–present.

_____. "Blaine's World." Written by Rob Thomas. Directed by Michael Fields. 9 Jun. 2015.

_____. "Brother, Can You Spare a Brain?" Written by Diane Ruggiero-Wright. Directed by John Kretchmer. 24 Mar. 2015.

_____. "Cape Town." Written by Diane Ruggiero-Wright. Directed by Mairzee Almas. 8 Dec. 2015.

_____. "The Exterminator." Written by Rob Thomas, Graham Norris, and Lee Arcuri. Directed by Michael Fields. 31 Mar. 2015.

_____. "Flight of the Living Dead." Written by Dierdre Mangan. Directed by David Warren. 14 Apr. 2015.

_____. "Live and Let Clive." Written by Kit Boss. Directed by John Kretchmer. 7 Apr. 2015.

_____. "Max Wager." Written by Graham Norris. Directed by John Kretchmer. 10 Nov. 2015.

_____. "Patriot Brains." Written by Robert Forman. Directed by Guy Norman Bee. 12 May 2015.

_____. "Pilot." Written by Rob Thomas and Diane Ruggiero-Wright. Directed by Rob Thomas. 17 Mar. 2015.

_____. "Zombie Bro." Written by Diane Ruggiero-Wright. Directed by John Kretchmer. 13 Oct. 2015.

LaFrance, Adrienne. "How Generations Get Their Names." *The Atlantic*. 3 Feb. 2016. www.theatlantic.com/technology/archive/2016/02/how-generations-get-their-names/459720/.

Lipka, Michael. "Millennials Increasingly Are Driving Growth of 'Nones.'" *Pew Research Center*. 12 May 2015. www.pewresearch.org/fact-tank/2015/05/12/millennials-increasingly-are-driving-growth-of-nones/.

Marion, Isaac. *Warm Bodies*. Simon & Schuster, 2012.

"Millennials: Confident. Connected. Open to Change." *Pew Research Center: Social & Demographic Trends*. 24 Feb. 2010. www.pewsocialtrends.org/2010/02/24/millennials-confident-connected-open-to-change/.

Mitovich, Matt Webb. "Ratings: *S.H.I.E.L.D.* Ticks Up, *The Flash* Returns Low, *iZombie* Has Some Bite, *The Voice* Gives *Undateable* a Boost." *TVLine*. 18 Mar. 2015. tvline.com/2015/03/18/izombie-premiere-ratings-cw/

Morris, Wesley. "The Year We Obsessed Over Identity." *New York Times Magazine*. 6 Oct. 2015. www.nytimes.com/2015/10/11/magazine/the-year-we-obsessed-over-identity.html?_r=0.

Patten, Eileen. "How Millennials Today Compare with Their Grandparents 50 Years Ago."

Pew Research Center. 19 Mar. 2015. www.pewresearch.org/fact-tank/2015/03/19/how-millennials-compare-with-their-grandparents/.
Stein, Joel. "Millennials: The Me Me Me Generation." *Time Magazine.* 20 May 2013. time.com/247/millennials-the-me-me-me-generation/.
Roberson, Chris, and Michael Allred. *Dead to the World (iZombie).* Vertigo Comics, 2011.
Rosin, Hanna. "Primetime's Looming Male Identity Crisis." *The Atlantic.* 8 Sept. 2011. www.theatlantic.com/entertainment/archive/2011/09/primetimes-looming-male-identity-crisis/244692/.
Tanenhaus, Sam. "Generation Nice." *New York Times.* 15 Aug. 2014. www.nytimes.com/2014/08/17/fashion/the-millennials-are-generation-nice.html.
Tenety, Elizabeth. "The Digital World Is Warmer Than You Think. Here's How Social Media Builds Empathy." *The Washington Post.* 24 Feb. 2015. www.washingtonpost.com/news/inspired-life/wp/2015/02/24/the-digital-world-is-warmer-than-you-think-heres-how-social-media-builds-empathy/?utm_term=.6b9a5837f85f.
Warm Bodies. Dir. Jonathan Levine, Summit Entertainment, 2013. Film.
"Warm Bodies (2013)." *IMDB.* n.d. www.imdb.com/title/tt1588173/.

"This place. It's never going to accept people like us. Never ever"

(Queer) Horror, Hatred and Heteronormativity in In the Flesh

CONNOR JACKSON

The multifarious zombie has historically been a creature empty of empathy, clear of compassion, and stripped of its self-awareness.[1] More often than not, this absence of identity has rendered the zombie void of sexual agency; Darren Elliott-Smith proposes that "[i]n spite of the obvious analogies, the exposure of internal bodily spaces, bodily fluids and primal urges, [the zombie] has remained largely an anti-erotic object" (151). As such, few of these creatures have been beheld as objects of desire or conveyed as love interests. Consequently, the undead are often seen in opposition to the now heavily romanticized vampire, which, as Kyle William Bishop observes, has "shifted from a dangerous, bloodthirsty *monster* [...] to a dangerous, bloodthirsty *hero* who represents the acme of romantic love" (*How Zombies Conquered Popular Culture* 163). Jeffrey Sconce asserts that the "usually unlovable" zombie is indeed eclipsed by the romantic vampire, claiming that "[t]roubled vampires may crowd the shelves of the teen fiction aisle, but it is the zombie that trudges on as perhaps the last remaining monster capable of generating any actual *revulsion* in its audience" (95).[2] In spite of this, now more than ever is the zombie being viewed as potentially loveable, evoking sympathy along with perhaps only mild repugnance. Milly Williamson writes that "[i]t is now a truism to suggest that the vampire is no longer a monster dramatizing the fear of the Other, but has been rendered [...] a figure of empathy" (71). On the contrary, certain representations of the zombie have recently managed to adopt a sympathetic nature whilst simultaneously maintaining their position as the Other. This can be observed in the British zombie-drama *In the Flesh* (2013–14), which tells the story of Kieren Walker (Luke Newberry), a formerly cannibalistic zombie who is "eventually treated and sent back to his home village of Roarton, where he [is] forced to face up to [...] a hostile community" ("Meet The Characters: Kieren Walker"). Derogatorily dubbed by oppressive religious/political groups as a "rotter": a chiefly British slang word aimed pejoratively at people whom the speaker deems undesirable (and in the context of *In the Flesh*, serving to call attention to the putrefied complexions of the undead), Kieren struggles to survive in a world where hateful, essentialist branding has led many to view him and every other zombie as a monster masquerading in human form. Bishop asserts that this series "presents viewers with an allegory of intolerance, one read best through a queer lens" (*How Zombies Conquered Popular Culture* 185); however, the extent to which *In the Flesh* accomplished its goal of critiquing prejudices against queer individuals is debatable, particularly within the show's first season. Though series creator Dominic Mitchell has stated that *In the Flesh* tackles "real issues," such as "feeling 'other' and feeling different and feeling like you can't come out to your parents and sexuality, but under the guise of [...] 'My parents don't recognize me as a zombie'" ("Interview with writer Dominic Mitchell"), the program's zombie façade appears to somewhat conceal issues relating to sexual identity rather than mirror them explicitly.

Although *In the Flesh* can indeed be interpreted as a critique of homophobia and heterosexism,[3] the sexual ambiguity of its central character Kieren, as well as his implied-but-never-stated relationship with his so-called "best mate" Rick Macy (David Walmsley), renders the entire allusion to queer discrimination echoed through the challenges faced by the show's "Partially Deceased Syndrome Sufferers" problematic. Though Kieren is predominantly associated with homosexuality in a number of online sources, and labeled as bisexual in others, claims regarding his sexuality are ultimately undermined by Mitchell's reluctance to explicitly provide verbal confirmation of Kieren's sexuality both on screen within *In the Flesh* itself and off screen in interviews. While on one hand the central protagonist's unconfirmed sexuality could be interpreted as a rebellion against the notion of slotting people into categories, on the other hand, it may result in this series unwittingly and counterproductively contributing to the marginalization of LGBTQ+ representation in television.

Studies into representations of (and allusions to) queer sexuality within the cinematic horror genre have frequently offered a direct insight into sociopolitical understandings of (and attitudes towards) queerness. In *Monsters in the Closet: Homosexuality and the Horror Film* (1997), Harry M. Benshoff explores the relationship between homosexuality and the monstrous, and in doing so establishes a series of correspondences between the threat of the traditional Hollywood monster and the implied threat of the homosexual. Benshoff narrows down cultural anxieties concerning gay and lesbian sexualities into three components: homosexuality as "a threat to the individual" (manifesting in concerns that you or someone close to you may be homosexual), "a threat to others" (drawing upon notions that homosexuality is synonymous with aggression and sexual violence), and "a threat to the community" (allegedly made apparent by the homosexuals' supposed attempts at annihilating the nuclear family) (1). Respectively, Benshoff likens these melodramatic fears to the devolutionary transformation of the Wolfman, Victor Frankenstein's murderous monster, and mad scientists and vampires who "dream of revolutionizing the world," whilst stressing that although queer sexualities are not ascribed to the creatures themselves, they are nonetheless evoked through cinematic iconography in order to perpetuate the ideology that the "monster is to 'normality' as [the] homosexual is to [the] heterosexual" (1–2). Furthermore, Robin Wood characterizes the basic formula of the horror film as follows: "normality is threatened by the Monster," with "normality" translating to "conformity to the dominant social norms" (71). It is through this paradigm that horror films encourage their audience to form collective interpretations based upon predominant ideological structures—structures which may, of course, favor "the heterosexual monogamous couple, the family, and the social institutions (police, church, armed forces)" (Wood 71). Thus, the cinematic horror genre sensationalizes a return of the repressed (buried ideologies, notions and actions that deviate from the status quo). While these dramatizations can carry conservative readings, effectively strengthening notions of transgressions from the norm as monstrous, Wood suggests that horror films may also encourage ambivalence—consequently creating a space in which the desire to "smash the norms that oppress us" can potentially be fulfilled (72).[4]

While it has remained true that, for the majority of horror films, "homosexuality on screen has been more or less allusive" (Benshoff 15), recent developments within the horror genre have seen "out" queer monsters (such as vampires, ghosts, and werewolves) surge into popular culture through television programs such as *True Blood* (2008–14), *American Horror Story* (2010–present), and *Teen Wolf* (2011–present). For Xavier Reyes, "the queering of the zombie is a logical continuation of the use of monsters to comment on the zeitgeist" due to their obvious connotations with negative myths surrounding homosexuality: for instance, the "outbreak" narratives of the AIDS crisis, which saw homosexuals associated with contagion and death (3). Thus, the inherent danger of infection followed by an untimely demise that is intrinsically attached to the vast majority of representations of shambling undead hordes easily correlates to the so-called "threats" posed by the LGBTQ+ community. However, since zombies have historically been creatures without consciousness, zombie sexuality traditionally gets subverted: that is, until the development of the self-aware undead. Reyes argues that the emergence of the gay zombie stems from the monsters' cognitive advancements during the mid–80s: most notably with regards to the "domesticated" Bub (Howard Sherman) from George A. Romero's *Day of the Dead* (1985). Correspondingly, in *American Zombie Gothic: The Rise and Fall (and Rise) of the Walking Dead in Popular Culture*, Kyle William Bishop proclaims that the steady "evolution" of the cinematic undead "can be most easily tracked by focusing primarily on Romero's canonical 'Dead' movies" (*American Zombie Gothic* 159), though he does point out the development of sentient zombies in Dan O'Bannon's *Return of the Living Dead* (1985), in which the undead are able to radio emergency services in order to draw in "more paramedics" and "more cops" to consume. Despite *Return of the Living Dead*'s vocal zombies, Bishop determines that it was Romero's Bub that, as a "fully formed character and an active participant in [*Day of the Dead*'s] story" (*American Zombie Gothic* 159), enabled Romero to take "the first shambling steps towards a *fully realized* zombie protagonist [emphasis added]" capable of expressing emotion, attachment and evoking sympathy (*American Zombie Gothic* 174). Consequently, Bub paved the way for the imbuement of the undead with additional sentiments, allowing their hunger for the flesh to take on an alternate meaning in the form of overt "homosexual or non-heteronormative desires" (Reyes 5). Moreover, Jamie Russell writes of a blurring of the lines between zombie movies and pornography during the 1980s, and traces this genre-fusion to the eroticized creations of "Eurosleaze filmmakers like Joe D'Amato (aka Aristede Massaccesi)" (166), such as *Porno Holocaust* (1981). Although, it would appear that the blending of zombies and sexuality (or sexualization) has always been a covert aspect of zombie cinema. Russell makes this clear through his reflections on the first zombie film *White Zombie* (1932), in which the eerily named Murder Legendre (Bela Lugosi) holds the zombified Madeline Short Parker (Madge Bellamy) captive in his ominous castle; with Madeline at the mercy of the film's antagonist, stripped of her agency and rendered virtually catatonic, Russell wonders: "[w]hat desires might an unscrupulous villain satisfy with a woman that is unable to say no?" (Russell 166). Furthermore, Alison Peirse suggests that *White Zombie*'s Murder Legendre is also infused with homoerotic sensibilities, and evidences this claim by referring to Legendre's poisoning of Charles Beaumont (Robert Frazer), in which he exclaims "I have taken a fancy to you, *monsieur*"; with "[a] male body [acting as] the object of another male's gaze" Peirse asserts that "Legendre's dialogue is delivered dripping with layers of insinuation" (70). Still, in correspondence with Benshoff's assertions, the homoerotic inclination of *White Zombie*'s villain is never explicitly stated/demonstrated, only implied.

Even though more contemporary titles featuring outspokenly gay characters, such as Bruce LaBruce's *Otto; Or: Up with Dead People* (2008),[5] can be used to critique hardships faced by homosexuals (either from within or outside of the LGBTQ+ community), flamboyant zombie flicks such as *Creatures from the Pink Lagoon* (2006) uphold stereotypical tropes relating to (male) homosexuality, such as promiscuity and effeminacy (albeit in a comedic manner that may encourage the ridicule, rather than reinforcement, of these stereotypical traits). According to Reyes, while certain queer-zombie narratives draw attention to the ease in which sexual minorities can be "forced into social oblivion," others position these creatures as "a threat that needs to be eradicated" (6); akin to Benshoff's notion of the monster as a loose metaphor for the alleged threats posed by homosexuals. *In the Flesh* encompasses both of these tropes, thus highlighting the susceptibility of social minorities (particularly those within the LGBTQ+ community) to widespread demonization.

Written and created by Dominic Mitchell for BBC Three, *In the Flesh* destabilizes the generic conventions of traditional zombie narratives by focusing primarily on the survival of the ostracized undead in a world dominated by oppressive living humans. Set in the fictional Lancashire village of Roarton, *In the Flesh* stars Luke Newberry as Kieren Walker, an undead teen who had "always been a bit different" even before his resurrection alongside thousands of others during the "the Rising": a mysterious event in which the dead were re-animated as flesh eating zombies ("Meet the Characters: Kieren Walker"). For many, the Rising was a blessing; it provided a second chance at life. For Kieren, who committed suicide after learning that his close friend (and implied love interest) Rick Macey had been killed in Afghanistan, it seemed to be a curse. That is, until Rick came back too. The series follows Kieren's journey as he is re-integrated into (un)civilized society after his successful treatment in an experimental rehabilitation center for the undead: or, for want of a more politically correct term: "Partially Deceased Syndrome sufferers." Of course, due to the death and destruction caused by the PDS sufferers in their "untreated state," not everybody is pleased with their assimilation; notably, the HVF (Human Volunteer Force): a vigilante group of zombie-killers.

Although the show's Partially Deceased Syndrome sufferers could be interpreted as a metaphor for a range of marginalized social groups, Kieren's implied homosexuality makes *In the Flesh* particularly apt at establishing parallels between the struggles faced by PDS sufferers and those experienced by LGBTQ+ people in the real world. In his study of Bruce LaBruce's *Otto; or: Up with Dead People*, Darren Elliott-Smith summarizes the zombie as "a visibly "outed" monster [...] rendered visible and set apart in order to protect others from infection and conversion": thus, equating angsts concerning this creature to the "guardedness inherent in homosexual panic" (148–9). This dread of difference is made startlingly clear within *In the Flesh*, so much so that appearance-altering measures are taken by many PDS sufferers to conceal their dissimilarity to the living; they disguise their discolored eyes with contact lenses and shroud their soured skin in make-up. It is clear that PDS sufferers face immense pressure to, as Kyle William Bishop phrases it, "pass" as members of the living (*How Zombies Conquered Popular Culture* 185). This is further exemplified by Kieren's mother Sue Walker (Marie Critchley), who encourages her son to "just pretend" (Season 1: "Episode 1") to eat at the dinner table, despite his inability to consume regular food. Kieren's awkward attempt at feigning normality at the dinner table—pretending to cut the meat in front of him, lifting empty eating utensils to his mouth and mimicking the act of chewing—visibly comfort his parents, whilst simultaneously demonstrating their failure to acknowledge their son as a PDS sufferer. Kieren's complacency in hiding his condition, especially when paired with his reluctance to discuss the extent of his relationship with Rick,[6] evokes the strain of heteronormative conformity through the process of camouflaging zombiism.

Whereas Kieren engages every effort to blend in, other PDS sufferers are more comfortable in their own (decomposed) skin. In his review of *In the Flesh*'s first season, *The Guardian* reviewer David Renshaw describes Kieren's new friend Amy Dyer (Emily Bevan) as "an out-and-proud member of the living dead" ("*In the Flesh* Box Set Review"). Unlike Kieren, Amy embraces being partially deceased, and liberatingly, refusing to hide behind cosmetic appliances in favor of what she calls the "*au natural*" look (Season 1: "Episode 2"). In addition to their contrasting appearances, the juxtaposition between Amy and Kieren is made even more explicit when she declines Mrs. Walker's offer of food: "No thanks [...] my insides are pretty decrepit; eat solids and it goes straight through! Tried eating a Mars bar a couple of days ago, had to throw away my knickers *and* my skirt!" (Season 1: "Episode 2"). However, while Amy undoubtedly embodies an unparalleled perspective of rebellious self-acceptance, this does not go unchallenged. Elliott-Smith asserts that "the signs of horrific difference displayed on the surface of [a zombie]'s skin [...] can be acted upon (by avoidance or destruction)" (148). This claim is validated by the evasive tactics employed by Roarton's Parish Council Official Philip Wilson (Stephen Thompson), who attempts to escort the visibly undead Amy as well as the excessively make-up covered Kieren into a "segregated area" (Season 1: "Episode 2") during their visit to Roarton's local pub. Even though it is later revealed that Philip and Amy slept together that very same night, he continues to disassociate himself from Amy afterwards. Once again, Roarton's anti–PDS principles are exposed as Philip demands that Amy "keep [her] mouth shut," because "[if] people [...] found out [he had] slept with a rotter [he would] be strung up" (Season 1: "Episode 3"). Despite being portrayed through the sexual activity of an opposite-sex couple (albeit one involving a living male and a living-dead female), the shame experienced by Philip after sleeping with a PDS sufferer is suggestive of a self-deprecatory response powered by internalized heterosexist revulsion: a process which can also be observed within Rick's inferred rejections of his romantic feelings towards Kieren.[7] Furthermore, the destructive aspect of Elliott-Smith's claim is demonstrated as Amy is assaulted in her home by HVF soldier Gary Kendal (Kevin Sutton). After remarking that Amy's "bare" appearance is "a slap [in the] face to [the] community," Gary proceeds to grab Amy by the hair, violently drag her towards her vanity table, and forcefully smear lipstick onto her face, all the while declaring that "[i]n this village, yer cover up yer rotten face" (Season 1: "Episode 3"). Having been brutally exposed to dangers of non-conformity, this malicious attack proved to be the final nail in the coffin for Amy. With her confidence in tatters and her usually pale face disguised by a rich layer of cosmetic appliances, Amy decides to leave Roarton in search of a better life elsewhere in the concluding episode of *In the Flesh*'s first season, convinced that Roarton is "never gonna accept [PDS sufferers]" (Season 1: "Episode 3"). Topically aired at a time when "one in six lesbian, gay and bisexual people [reported experiencing] a homophobic hate crime or incident over the last three years" (Guasp, Gammon and Ellison)—including but not limited to "physical assaults [...] threats of violence [...] harassment, verbal insults and damage to their property" (Guasp, Gammon and Ellison)—*In the Flesh* depicts a world not dissimilar to our own in the sense that deviations from the status quo (particularly with regards to non-conventional sexualities and expressions of identity) are often frowned upon and, in some cases, viciously combated.

Bishop proposes that, "[a]s with many cases of discriminatory and bigoted behavior, some of the most intolerant people in *In the Flesh* are the ones suffering from denial" (*How Zombies Conquered Popular Culture* 186). Backing up this claim with reference to Bill Macy (Steve Evets), leader of the HVF and father to Rick Macy, Bishop addresses how this character's hostility towards the undead is temporarily deviated from his PDS suffering son. When Rick returns from Afghanistan "partially" alive and well, news of his return (as well as his condition) spreads like wildfire throughout Roarton. Bill, conversely, refuses to acknowledge his son's condition—a denial which Bishop equates to his long drawn out refusal to address "the possibility of his son's homosexuality" (*How Zombies Conquered Popular Culture* 186). In an effort to thwart his son's perceived sexual development (as though this were actually possible), Bill attempted to isolate Rick and Kieren from one another when they were both alive, even barring Kieren from his home for the crime of "[giving his] son a mix CD" (Season 1: "Episode 3"). The impression that queerness is something which one can catch is arguably a continuing reverberation of the AIDS epidemic. Harry M. Benshoff writes that out of this crisis arose an assumption that gay men are "contagious" (2). Furthermore, he continues by equating this imagined contagion with destructive monstrosity and reveals supposed parallels between homosexuals and vampires who, "with a single drop of blood, can infect a pure and innocent victim, transforming [them] into the living dead" (Benshoff 2). Correspondingly, Elliott-Smith asserts that "[t]he infectiousness of the zombie [...] opens up the figure as a symbol of a quickly spreading epidemic of death, decay and queerness" (151–2). Indeed, these connotations of toxic blood within (male) homosexuals are very much ingrained into British society today, as the National Health Service (NHS) continues to reject blood donations from "men who have had [...] sex with men, with or without protection, in the last 12 months" (NHS). Despite the zombies of *In the Flesh* posing no threat of infection, this assumed danger of contagion provides Bill with another reason to distinguish Kieren as a threat to his son, so much so that he even plots for Rick to murder his alleged lover. Horrified at the prospect of killing Kieren, Rick realizes it is time to give up the ghost. He enters the family bathroom and stares contemplatively at his reflection before removing his contact lenses and makeup. In essence, Rick finally accepts himself. Confronting his father with unconcealed pale skin and soured eyes in a process which Bishop equates to "coming out" (*How Zombies Conquered Popular Culture* 187), Rick tells Bill that he does not want to hurt Kieren, and declares: "If Ren's evil, Dad, then so am I" (Season 1: "Episode 3"). No longer able to maintain the burden of denial about his son's condition, as well as the ever-strengthening bond between Rick and Kieren, Bill snaps. What could have played out as a touching scene of acceptance instead transgresses into a violent display of Bill's relentless bigotry. Rather than accept his son as a PDS sufferer (and possibly, through the process of allusion, a gay man), he opts to "convince himself Rick isn't really his son" (Bishop, *How Zombies Conquered Popular Culture* 187), subsequently stabbing him in the back of the head and abandoning the corpse outside Kieren's home.

Although *In the Flesh* presents a rather obvious analogy of intolerance that easily connects to homophobia (and heterosexist perspectives in general), the sexual ambiguity of Kieren Walker as well as his questionable relationship with Rick Macy render this entire allusion problematic. While it is heavily implied throughout the show that Kieren and Rick's relationship is a romantic one, and even hinted at by the BBC website—which writes that Rick was Kieren's "best mate," before adding "or was it more?" ("Meet the Characters: Kieren Walker")—it remains perfectly justifiable to assume that the pair were not more than friends, as there are no explicit references to the duo being romantically involved within the series itself. Even the subtle hints at their closeness, such as when Kieren (much to the fury of Bill) made Rick a personalized CD, can easily be read as misinterpreted acts of platonic friendship, especially when taking into consideration that Kieren mentions previously making a "hardcore metal mix CD" (Season 1: "Episode 1") for his sister Jemima Walker (Harriet Cains). Regardless of his praises for the horror and fantasy genres, which he considers "great" because of their capacity to explore "gender politics and identity freely" (qtd. in Sim), Mitchell seems to do the opposite with *In the Flesh*, particularly within the first season. For instance, he elusively asserts that "Kieren just happens to fall in love with the people he falls in love with," before later adding: "[l]ets stay away from labels, I don't like labels" (qtd. in Mellor).

Despite Mitchell's likening of Kieren and Rick's relationship to an "all-encompassing Romeo and Juliet thing" (qtd. in Mellor), no on-screen evidence appears legitimate enough to support this assertion. Furthermore, Mitchell even dismisses the possibility of any off-screen intimacy between the pair: "Ric [sic] is very uncomfortable with his relationship with Kieran [sic]. I don't think it got to the point of having sex" (qtd. in Sim); "I kind of think, did they kiss or didn't they kiss? I don't think they got there" (qtd. in Mellor). This completely undermines any romantic/sexual implications within Kieren's reminiscence of the time he and Rick "drank a bottle of White Lightning, smoked a few fags [and] messed around" (Season 1: "Episode 2"), while also casting doubt over any inferred loving connotations that may be derived from the graffiti in Kieren and Rick's "den" (a secluded cave) in the woods, which reads "KIEREN + RICK 4 EVER" (Season 1: "Episode 3"). Thus, the confusion surrounding character sexuality within *In the Flesh*'s first season in particular upholds Benshoff's assertion that "homosexuality [...] lurks around the edges of texts and characters rather than announcing itself forthrightly" (14–5). When asked about the lack of intimacy between Kieren and Rick, Mitchell does ponder the possibility of displaying their closeness unambiguously, claiming that they could have kissed eventually, before ultimately dismissing their lack of lip-locking as simply "a tragedy of series one" (qtd. in Mellor). Referencing the scene where Rick confronts Kieren about his suicide, Mitchell has said that "they could have [kissed] in that bloody car" (qtd. in Mellor) if not for being interrupted by a walkie-talkie transmission. Though, of course, contemplations of what could have been are irrelevant, as imagined deviations from the shows finalized scenes are not canon. Kieren does end up having a more overt relationship with the charismatic Undead Liberation Army affiliate and fellow PDS sufferer Simon Monroe (Emmett J Scanlan) in the show's second season; yet, series creator Dominic Mitchell has only ever offered vague anecdotes when confronted with the topic of

Kieren's sexuality: "[h]e's not gay but he's not straight" (qtd. in Sim). Despite his only explicit love interest being a man, Kieren has been labeled bisexual in an article by Stephen Kelly for *The Independent* among other online texts.[8] Though Kelly writes that Mitchell's personal experiences of prejudice "informed his decision to make Kieren bisexual" (a statement which coincides with Mitchell's dismissal of Kieren as gay or straight), it should be noted that among the quotes taken directly from Mitchell within this piece of writing, none contain an explicit reference to Kieren as bisexual. In fact, with Mitchell's frequent unwillingness to label Kieren's sexual orientation, the categorization of Kieren as bisexual within this article may have been an assumption made on Kelly's part. Nonetheless, *The Orbit* blogger Alex Gabriel refers to Kelly's writing as confirmation that Kieren is canonically bisexual, while also defensively adding that "[Kieren's] bisexuality doesn't need to be proven." However, without proof, the notion of Kieren's bisexuality can be disputed and subsequently disregarded on the grounds of insufficient evidence. For example, Gabriel mentions an "ambiguous connection" between Kieren and Amy to support his claim that Kieren is bisexual, however, Amy Dyer, high on sheep brains, seems to contradict this when she exclaims "I love you, Kieren Walker! Not like that cause I know you're not like that" (Season 2: "Episode 2"). This, as well as Kieren showing absolutely no signs of romantic/sexual interest towards any female character within *In the Flesh*, renders the prospect of Kieren's bisexuality either non-existent or completely suppressed. Additionally, there are even inconsistencies between Simon's sexuality as it is presented on the show and commented on by Mitchell. Though this character is introduced as Amy's boyfriend before transitioning to Kieren's love interest during the course of *In the Flesh*'s second season, Mitchell confirms that "[o]f course Simon's gay. I always imagined that Simon was gay. He wasn't bi, he wasn't transsexual, Simon, for me, is a gay character," while identifying his relationship with Amy as merely "a complication" (qtd. in Mellor). Thus, Simon, who can be seen romantically involved with both Amy and Kieren, is confirmed to be gay by Mitchell, whereas Kieren, who is only shown to be unambiguously attracted to one (male) character, is, according to Mitchell, not gay.

In spite of the series creator's rejection of speculation regarding Kieren Walker's homosexuality (and heterosexuality), there are no overt verbal references to Kieren's sexual orientation within the series itself, and so one can only speculate as to how he may identify himself. Therefore, despite the show being praised for its development of a central character who falls somewhere under the LGBTQ+ umbrella, with regards to the first season especially, and Dominic Mitchell's reluctance to confirm Kieren's sexuality, this representation is undoubtedly obscured. Richard Dyer writes that, though there is "nothing about gay people's physiognomy that declares them gay," there are "signs of gayness" that can be used to indicate homosexuality (19). Kieren may not be gay according to Mitchell, but he does adhere to certain markers of gayness. In correspondence with Dyer's suggested methods of implicitly communicating homosexuality, Kieren shows an "interest in the arts"[9] (22) and is feminized by other characters: for example, Gary Kendall mockingly asks Kieren if he attended the local girl's grammar school, then subsequently remarks that he would "fit right in" there (Season 1: "Episode 2"). Moreover, *In the Flesh*'s central character evokes the gay archetype of the "sad young man," which is characterized by Dyer as follows:

> The sad young man is neither androgynously in-between the genders nor playing with the signs of gender, his relationship to masculinity is more difficult, and thus sad. He is a young man, hence not yet really a real man. He is soft; he has not yet achieved assertive masculine hardness. He is also physically less than a man [...] There is perhaps an echo in the stance of the major source of this imagery, the Judeo-Christian tradition. The sad young man is a martyr figure[10] [Dyer 42].

While Kieren may be perceived as feminine enough to attract ridicule, he is not overtly effeminate; while not sufficiently macho, he does not seem to challenge the rules of masculine gender conformity. His (now perpetual) youth and sensitivity negate him from associations of commanding masculine attributes, and his subsequent rise from the dead following his grief-stricken suicide solidifies his status as a reanimated martyr figure: as a result channeling "Christian [...] iconography of punishment as pleasure [and] suffering as beauty," as well as the notion of life after death (Dyer 42). Indeed, like Dyer's sad young men, Kieren lives a "twilight existence" by inhabiting the liminal space between life and death: an existence that is infused with "all the melancholy associations that twilight has in our culture" (40). Although Dyer asserts that such a range of signs can serve to express homosexuality, effectively "making visible the invisible" (19), with regards to *In the Flesh*'s Kieren Walker, these evocative pointers are rendered invalid. Despite being noteworthy enough for Dominic Mitchell to acknowledge a "debate raging" around Kieren's sexual orientation, as well as the series being tagged as "the 'gay zombie' thing" (qtd. in Mellor), all hints, teases, and suggestive signs leading one to assume Kieren is gay are of no value when taking into consideration Mitchell's renunciation of Kieren's inferred homosexuality; however, these cues remain aspects of Kieren's character whether confirmed or denied any validity with regards to the interpretation of his sexuality, which, at the very least, has been confirmed as canonically queer outside of the program itself.

Referencing Alexander Doty, Benshoff points out the flaws within representation through allusion and its aptitude for marginalizing non-heterosexual sexualities:

> connotation has been the representational and interpretive closet of mass culture queerness for far too long ... [This] shadowy realm of connotation ... allows straight culture to use queerness for pleasure and profit in mass culture without admitting to it [qtd. in Benshoff 15].

With regard to terminology commonly used by online fan communities and bloggers, Doty's observations of queer exploitation seem to fall under the label of queerbaiting: the process by which canon creators of fictional works imbue their characters with homoerotic tensions in an attempt to incorporate queer viewers into their demographic, whilst maintaining their heterosexual integrity by never revealing these characters to be anything other than straight. As Judith Fathallah writes: "[d]enial [...] reinstate[s] a heteronormative narrative that poses no danger of offending mainstream viewers at the expense of queer eyes" (491). This is potentially damaging to members of the LGBTQ+ community as it maintains heterosexist notions of queerness as unspeakable, thus implying (intentionally or unintentionally) that alternate sexualities are shameful in the sense that they are not addressed openly. Though issues of queerbaiting within *In the Flesh* are somewhat rectified due to the on-screen kiss between Kieren and Simon in the show's second season, the extent of Kieren and Rick's relationship has never been revealed in the context of the show itself, despite the series not being so coy as to deny viewers the disclosure of such heterosexual pairings as Steve Walker (Steve Cooper) and Sue Walker, Bill Macy and Janet Macy (Karen Henthorn), Amy Dyer and Philip Wilson, Amy Dyer and Simon Monroe, as well as Jemima Walker and Gary Kendal. Thus, the entire first season of *In the Flesh* can easily be read as a queerbaiting narrative, as despite confirmation by Dominic Mitchell that Kieren and Rick were in fact romantically involved (to a certain extent), nothing in the series itself unambiguously endorses this revelation. Therefore, if there is enough doubt as to warrant a debate around Kieren's sexualities (as well as his and Rick's relationship status), and if one has to search the realms of online articles and interviews in the hopes of discovering information surrounding characters' sexuality that is not only avoided within *In the Flesh* itself, but also inconsistently represented from source to source or otherwise simply not addressed at all,[11] then this only strengthens "the possibility of queer identities and desires [being] dismissed [within this show] as [...] a fantasy in the minds of a less valued minority" (Fathallah 491).

On one hand, only being able to read Kieren's queerness on a subtextual level in season one of *In the Flesh* seems to reinforce notions of heterosexism and heteronormativity as he could admissibly be slotted into the "straight" category. Though, on the other hand, the reluctance shown by Dominic Mitchell to verbalize Kieren's sexual orientation (both in the show itself and in interviews) can be justified as a rebellious act of nonconformity in the face of society's preoccupation with placing people into boxes. Much like the variety of language used to describe queer individuals, which parallels that used to refer to the reanimated corpses of *In the Flesh* (through Kieren's implied queerness, the resemblances between PDS related hate crimes and homophobic ones, and Rick's "coming out"), Dominic Mitchell's zombies are confronted with numerous names which, in essence, all refer to the same thing: their undead state. Indeed, Mitchell confessed that he "personally hate[s] labels" (qtd. in Mellor), and set out to challenge the classification of people through his show. Describing his narrative as a "story of identity," he raises the question: "[h]ow do you fit in when you're completely different and people are labelling you?" (Mitchell qtd. in Sim). Much like Harry M. Benshoff's assertion that "the very language used to describe and make sense of our world works to mediate our understanding of homosexuality" (22), the labels that are thrust upon or adopted by *In the Flesh*'s zombies range from derogatory slurs ("rotter") to liberating titles ("the Redeemed") and, as such, can embody either positive or negative connotations. Though, as Richard Dyer points out, even a progressive (or positively reclaimed) social grouping word "draws attention to and also reproduces [...] marginality" (9). Thus, all words used to describe the undead ultimately contribute to their conceptual (and, at times, literal) separation from the living, whom are understood as the norm from which the undead deviate. Such terminology is also susceptible to pejoration; indeed, Dyer writes that: "[a]s long as the material reality of a social group remains one of oppression, the word used to describe it will sooner or later become contaminated by the hatred and self-hatred that are an inescapable aspect of oppression" (9). Notably, Bishop identifies the overbearing prejudice directed at PDS sufferers in Roarton as the result of "a powerful religious rhetoric of hate and intolerance, a rhetoric that hauntingly mirrors that often used against the LGBTQ community today" (*How Zombies Conquered Popular Culture* 187).[12] This observation is validated by Vicar Oddie's (Kenneth Cranham) fearmongering sermons, one of which sees him confrontationally ask the PDS Protection Act promoting Giles Weir (Oliver Birch): "what happens if they decide to attack again?," thus tainting Giles' mentioning of "Partially Deceased Syndrome sufferer[s]" with connotations of horror and anxiety, despite its status as a liberal, politically correct means of referring to the undead (Season 1: "Episode 1"). In addition, the term "Partially Deceased Syndrome sufferer" is spluttered out with an unmistakable accumulation of vehement loathing and disgust by season two's Maxine Martin (Wunmi Mosaku), an MP for the anti–PDS political party Victus, who avidly exclaims: "[t]hese so called 'Partially Deceased Syndrome Sufferers' are not like you or me, with normal hopes and normal dreams. They may pretend to be like us, but what lies beneath their mask of make-up and medication is a cold hard killer that cannot be reasoned with" (Season 2: "Episode 1"). Furthermore, the phrase "PDS sufferer" also invokes associations of spitefulness and distrust when articulated by Maxine when she declares that "the PDS sufferer in your home, in your shop, in your pub, is one missed dose away from tearing your head apart" (Season 2: "Episode 1"). Still, it is possible for a sense of community and comfort to be derived from a label; for example, Kieren is encouraged to repeat the phrase "I am a Partially Deceased Syndrome sufferer [...] and what I did in my untreated state wasn't my fault" (Season 1: "Episode 1") in order to relieve his guilt over having killed and eaten people whilst "rabid."[13] Nevertheless, Dyer writes that "[w]e will always feel frustrated by having to have words to express our social identity, even while that social identity means that we do indeed have to have words for it" (9). This frustration is evidenced by Harry M. Benshoff and Sean Griffin, who draw attention to the adverse interpretations of the word "queer": this term, which has been exploited for the purpose of ridiculing LGBTQ+ people, has also been reclaimed by certain members of the community as a means of protest ("We're here, we're queer, get used to it!"), but remains detested by others due to "the pain and anger associated with the word as an epithet" (342). Indeed, the blurriness between benevolent and malevolent terminological associations is replicated particularly aptly within the first episode of *In the Flesh*'s second season. In this episode, Kieren jestingly refers to a seemingly contented Amy as "a zombie Buddha" and, after realizing that he has caused offense, aims to rectify the situation by instead suggesting "Partially Deceased Buddha" as an alternative, only to be met with the stern reply: "[t]hat's even worse. That's the name the living gave us. We are the undead, we are the Redeemed, got it?" (Season 2: "Episode 1"). Moreover, when Mitchell is asked about the acceptability of referring to PDS sufferers as zombies within the universe of *In the Flesh*, he confirms that "[i]t is politically incorrect to say zombie," before echoing the writings of Dyer, as well as Benshoff and Griffin, by adding "[i]t's a tricky one isn't it, all these names, PDS and rotters and the undead. Someone is always going to get insulted" (qtd. in Starr).

It is clear that labels are prone to initiating disputes over their appropriateness and, as a consequence, mean different things to different people. As Richard Dyer points out, "[h]aving a word also contains and fixes identity," meaning that a label may inadvertently dismiss the overall complexity of characteristics belonging to an individual, thus implying that their label sums up everything about them (9). With this in mind, one might determine that the complete rejection of any form of social branding can be liberating, and that there is freedom to be found in dismissing notions of social categorization. Still, even if this was the reasoning behind Dominic Mitchell's reluctance to label Kieren Walker's sexuality within or outside of *In the Flesh*, with no label for the show's central protagonist to be associated with comes no obvious queer representation. Of course, Harry M. Benshoff and Sean Griffin write that sexuality can be made "visible" through performance; as such, non-heterosexual characters "must be physically intimate with each other or indicate their desire to be so" in order to provide adequate queer representation without verbally outing themselves (310). Though this was achieved when Kieren kissed Simon during *In the Flesh*'s second season, Mitchell has stated that, contrary to season one's allusive focus on marginalized sexualities (and the LGBTQ+ community's susceptibility to othering and prejudice), the "core theme" of season two was belief: "belief in yourself, in ideology, in community" (gtd. in Starr). While Kieren and Simon's kiss fundamentally shattered the possibility of both characters being interpreted as heterosexual in a way that was simply not achieved with Kieren and Rick's relationship, the overt showcasing of a queer romance only emerged within *In the Flesh* once the its overarching themes had ventured away from sexuality. As such, despite the newfound boldness of the series when it came to exploring Kieren's sexuality in the second season, one cannot help but wonder why there was no such representation during the first season, which (according to Mitchell) directly set out to tackle issues surrounding queer identity. The relationship between Kieren and Rick remained unexplored beyond the level of platonic friendship in season one (and was not expanded upon in season two); therefore, regardless of their bond being crucial to the narrative,[14] *In the Flesh*'s failure to construct an overt queer romance during the season which intended to explore the struggles of sexual minorities essentially allows the implied queerness of its characters to fade into the background. For those not actively seeking answers outside of the series itself, the extent of Kieren and Rick's relationship will always remain unconfirmed. In a world where heterosexuality is usually considered the "standard" sexuality, where straightness is generally treated as a given unless stated or demonstrated otherwise, the ambiguity surrounding Kieren and Rick's feelings for one another easily enables their closeness to be interpreted through a heterosexist lens. Thus, even with their PDS-related marginalization, which so often evokes the hardships faced by LGBTQ+ people, their bond can subsequently be rendered non-romantic. Ultimately, *In the Flesh* remains widely open to interpretation. Whilst contributing to new developments within the expansive zombie genre by concerning itself with the survival of the undead in a world ruled by the living, *In the Flesh*'s disguised representations of queer characters essentially means that this series often gives in to the same heteronormative pressures it hints at critiquing.

Notes

1. For a more in depth interrogation of the zombie's cultural history, see for example Kyle William Bishop's *American Zombie Gothic: The Rise and Fall (and Rise) of the Walking Dead in Popular Culture* (2010), and Roger Luckhurst's *Zombies: A Cultural History* (2015).

2. While it is undoubtedly true that the zombie is characteristically considered revolting,

Bishop claims that the "zombie romantic hero has been developing for years in the pages of paranormal romance and young adult titles" (*How Zombies Conquered Popular Culture* 164). Most notably, Isaac Marion's *Warm Bodies* (2010) can easily be credited with thrusting romantic zombies into the mainstream, with its subsequent 2013 film adaptation (released under the same name) solidifying its undead protagonist "R" (Nicholas Hoult) as a creature more likely to steal hearts than eat brains. Even so, there are still strong elements of disgust associated with the undead, for example, as *Warm Bodies'* (2013) female lead Julie (Teresa Palmer) evidently begins to develop feelings for R, her friend Nora (Analeigh Tipton) comically remarks "I wish the internet was still working so I could just look up whatever it is that's wrong with you" (*Warm Bodies*).

3. To borrow Harry M. Benshoff and Sean Griffin's definition, heterosexism is "the assumption that heterosexuality is the only normal sexual orientation, and that it should be celebrated and privileged above all others" (306).

4. This quote from Robin Wood is mirrored by *In the Flesh*'s Amy Dyer (Emily Bevan), who claims that the living are constantly afraid due to lingering thoughts of their own mortality ("they live their lives with one eye on the clock" [Season 1: "Episode 2"]), whereas the undead don't have to do that ("we can smash the clock to pieces" [Season 1: "Episode 2"]). Here, the very existence of the undead results in the need for new concepts of normality, and challenges the supposed natural order of life and death.

5. For an in depth analysis of Bruce LaBruce's *Otto; Or: Up with Dead People* (2008), see Darren Elliott-Smith's "Death is the New Pornography!": Gay Zombies, Homonormativity and Consuming Masculinity in Queer Horror" in: *Screening the Undead: Vampires and Zombies in Film and Television* (2013).

6. Although Dominic Mitchell has said that Kieren "fell in love with Rick" (qtd. in Mellor), this is never stated in the series itself.

7. The BBC website reveals that Rick joined the army to "escape from his feelings and his father's judgements" ("Meet the Characters: Rick Macy"). These feelings were likely related to his bond with Kieren.

8. This reference to Kieren Walker's sexuality can be found within "*In the Flesh*: 'If Alan Bennett and Ken Loach did a zombie show'" by Stephen Kelly for *The Independent*, "In the Flesh: the best LGBT series since Queer as Folk" by Alex Gabriel for *The Orbit*, and "'In the Flesh' fans are swarming to save the BBC's zombie show" by Michelle Jaworski for *The Daily Dot*.

9. This is evidenced by the many paintings in Kieren's room, Rick's letter to Kieren (which was purposefully written on the back of a postcard with an image of one of Vincent Van Gogh's self-portraits due to Rick's knowledge that Vincent Van Gogh was Kieren's "fave" artist), and the fact that Kieren had "got into Art School" before his death (Season 1: "Episode 2").

10. Richard Dyer draws upon "book covers [and] avant-garde film [and] gay identification figures" in his construction of this gay archetype (40–1).

11. While some online texts, such as the BBC character profiles, avoid labeling Kieren's (or any other character's) sexuality outright, articles such as Nick Duffy's "BBC cancels gay zombie drama In The Flesh" explicitly associate Kieren with homosexuality; though this labeling contradicts the previously mentioned articles in which Kieren is said to be bisexual, as well as Dominic Mitchell's comments which confirm that Kieren is not actually gay.

12. Indeed, Harry M. Benshoff and Sean Griffin suggest that the divide between queer individuals and "social conservatives and the religious right" can be attributed to LGBT+ people presenting "a challenge to patriarchal concepts of gender and sexuality" (342).

13. After rising from the grave, the zombies of *In the Flesh* showed no signs of cognitive awareness and perused the living in order to eat them; their mental capabilities were only able to be restored (temporarily) after the successful development of a drug called Neurotriptyline, which must be administered every twenty-four hours. Zombies in their base form are said to be in a "rabid" state and are known colloquially as "rabids."

14. If it was not for their bond, Rick would not have felt pressured into joining the armed forces, meaning that he would not have died in Afghanistan, which, in turn, would

have averted Kieren's suicide; thus, with both characters presumably living in this imagined scenario, neither would have risen from dead.

Works Cited

Benshoff, Harry M. *Monsters in the Closet: Homosexuality and the Horror Film*. Manchester University Press, 1997.

Benshoff, Harry M., and S. Griffin. *America on Film: Representing Race, Class, Gender, and Sexuality at the Movies*. 2nd ed., Wiley-Blackwell, 2009.

Bishop, Kyle William. *American Zombie Gothic: The Rise and Fall (and Rise) of the Walking Dead in Popular Culture*. McFarland, 2010.

_____. *How Zombies Conquered Popular Culture: The Multifarious Walking Dead in the 21st Century*. McFarland, 2015.

Duffy, Nick. "BBC Cancels Gay Zombie Drama In the Flesh" *Pink News: England*. 16 Jan. 2015. www.pinknews.co.uk/2015/01/16/bbc-cancels-gay-zombie-drama-in-the-flesh/.

Dyer, Richard. *The Matter of Images: Essays on Representation*. 2nd ed., Routledge, 2002.

Elliott-Smith, Darren. "'Death Is the New Pornography!': Gay Zombies, Homonormativity and Consuming Masculinity in Queer Horror." *Screening the Undead: Vampires and Zombies in Film and Television*, edited by Leon Hunt, Sharon Lockyer, and Milly Williamson. I.B. Tauris, 2013, pp. 148–170.

Gabriel, Alex. "In the Flesh: The Best LGBT Series Since Queer as Folk." *The Orbit*. 1 Jun. 2014. www.the-orbit.net/godlessness/2014/06/01/in-the-flesh-the-best-lgbt-series-since-queer-as-folk/.

Guasp, April, Anne Gammon, and Gavin Ellison. Homophobic Hate Crime: The Gay British Crime Survey 2013. Stonewall; YouGov, PDF. 27 Mar. 2016. www.stonewall.org.uk/sites/default/files/Homophobic_Hate_Crime__2013_.pdf.

In the Flesh. Created by Dominic Mitchell, BBC, 2013–14.

"Interview with writer Dominic Mitchell." BBC. n.d. www.bbc.co.uk/mediacentre/media packs/intheflesh/dominic-mitchell.

Jaworski, Michelle. "'In the Flesh' Fans Are Swarming to Save the BBC's Zombie Show" *The Daily Dot*. 2 Sept. 2014. www.dailydot.com/parsec/in-the-flesh-fans-fight-save-show/.

Kelly, Stephen. "In the Flesh: 'If Alan Bennett and Ken Loach Did a Zombie Show.'" *The Independent*. 19 April. 2014. www.independent.co.uk/arts-entertainment/tv/features/in-the-flesh-if-alan-bennett-and-ken-loach-did-a-zombie-show-9269709.html.

Luckhurst, Roger. *Zombies: A Cultural History*. Reaktion Books, 2015.

"Meet the Characters: Kieren Walker." BBC Three. n.d. www.bbc.co.uk/programmes/profiles/V5m5DQ3NsTxP7WQ0KtKFZl/kieren-walker.

"Meet the Characters: Rick Macy." BBC Three. n.d. www.bbc.co.uk/programmes/profiles/zWkVgCW7jL6G9rZLp4vjLL/rick-macy.

Mellor, Louisa. "Dominic Mitchell Interview: What's Next for In The Flesh?" *Den of Geek!* 8 Jun. 2014. www.denofgeek.com/tv/in-the-flesh/30824/dominic-mitchell-interview-whats-next-for-in-the-flesh#ixzz44azYfLks.

"Men Who Have Sex with Men." NHS, n.d. www.blood.co.uk/who-can-give-blood/men-who-have-sex-with-men/.

Peirse, Alison. *After Dracula: The 1930s Horror Film*. I.B. Tauris, 2013.

Renshaw, David. "In the Flesh Box Set Review: A Thrillingly Original Take on the Whole Zombie Horror Template." *The Guardian*. 22 Jan. 2015. www.theguardian.com/tv-and-radio/2015/jan/22/in-the-flesh-box-set-review-a-thrillingly-original-take-on-the-whole-zombie-horror-template.

Reyes, Xavier Aldana. "Beyond the Metaphor: Gay Zombies and the Challenge to Homonormativity." *Journal for Cultural and Religious Theory*. vol. 13, no. 2, Summer 2014, pp. 1–12.

Russell, Jamie. *Book of the Dead: The Complete History of Zombie Cinema*. Titan Books, 2014.

Sconce, Jeffrey. "Dead Metaphors/Undead Allegories." *Screening the Undead: Vampires and Zombies in Film and Television*, edited by Leon Hunt, Sharon Lockyer, and Milly Williamson. I.B. Tauris, 2013, pp. 95–111.

Sim, Krystal. "In the Flesh Creator Dominic Mitchell on Episode 1 Secrets." *SciFiNow*. 17 Mar. 2013. www.scifinow.co.uk/news/in-the-flesh-creator-dominic-mitchell-on-episode-1-secrets/.

Starr, Liane Bonin. "Interview: 'In the Flesh' Creator Dominic Mitchell Talks Season 2." *HitFix*. 10 May 2014. www.hitfix.com/starr-raving/interview-in-the-flesh-creator-dominic-mitchell-talks-season-2.

Williamson, Milly. "Let Them All In: The Evolution of the "Sympathetic" Vampire." *Screening the Undead: Vampires and Zombies in Film and Television*, edited by Leon Hunt, Sharon Lockyer, and Milly Williamson. I.B. Tauris, 2013, pp. 71–92.

Wood, Robin. *Hollywood from Vietnam to Reagan*. Columbia University Press, 2003.

Uncanny Valley Romance

Warm Bodies, *Her* and the Bits and Bytes of Affection

PAUL MUHLHAUSER *and* JACK D. ARNAL

Zombies are "kinda likes." They are kinda like dead; they are kinda like alive. They are kinda like humans, and they are kinda like not. Artificial Intelligence (AI), too, are kinda likes. They are kinda like dead; they are kinda like alive. They are kinda like humans, and they are kinda like not. Of course, from zombie and AI perspectives, humans are kinda likes too. They are kinda like zombies and kinda like AI. "Kinda like" is our term for paying attention to the ways humans, zombies, and AI oscillate between being kinda like each other and being, kinda like, their own things.

Besides being kinda like each other (sharing similarities and differences), there is an important double entendre in the *kinda like* concept. *Kinda like*, in other words, also means, "They kinda like each other (romantically)." In 2013, paying attention to both of these senses of *kinda like* collided in two major films exploring zombie-human and AI-human romance: *Warm Bodies* and *Her*. The significance of these films, however, does not lie solely in this *kinda like* collision. These films came out in what might be called, "the year of romancing the smartphone." It was the year smart phone adoption exceeded 50 percent in the U.S. (Smith).[1] Better yet, 2013 could be called the year of the *uncanny valley romance*—the year we started thinking even more carefully about the implications and meaning of human-likes and humans getting it on in relationships where flesh decays (*Warm Bodies*) and where flesh is transcended (*Her*).[2] It was the year a majority of the population began experiencing "smart" connectivity, with its strange mix of bringing people together and simultaneously pulling them apart, of merging virtual space with meatspace in new and confusing ways.[3]

Zombie-human and AI-human romance offers rich comparisons for showcasing the cultural confusion of these in-between moments. Zombie scholar Steven Shaviro helps explain why using zombies and AI are good subjects for such critique:

> Zombies [to which we add AI] always come in between: they insinuate themselves with the uncanny, interstitial space that separates (but thereby also connects) inside and outside, the private and the public, life and death. In this liminal position, they are obscene objects of voyeuristic fascination [Shaviro qtd. in Leverette 193].

Our human-zombie and human-AI juxtaposition offers new ways to understand this fascination and the cultural significance behind such fascination in relation to changing technology. While uncanny in their human likenesses, one bites and the other bytes. One embodies (zombies) and the other embeds (AI). One is an "imperfect" copy (zombie). The other is a "perfect" copy (AI). Zombies and AIs in relationships with humans act kinda like proxies for meatspace and cyberspace romance.

The uncanny valley romances in *Warm Bodies* and *Her* are studies in the tensions 2013's "smart" connectivity has wrought on romantic relationships. The uncanny valley romances in *Warm Bodies* and *Her* highlight the ways nostalgia and memory transform the uncanny and collapse distances between humans and nonhumans; however, in their presentations of romance and collapse of the uncanny, they describe alternate reconstructions of relationships and technological views. The uncanny valley romances between R (Nicholas Hoult) and Julie (Teresa Palmer) in *Warm Bodies* and between Theodore (Joaquin Phoenix) and Samantha (Scarlett Johansson, an operating system) in *Her* illustrate the techno-dystopic fears of and techno-utopic promises bolstered by "smart" connectivity.

We suggest these two films' exploration of such tensions points towards a metamodern sentiment regarding relationships in the Internet age and the uncanny feelings they espouse. Metamodernist critic Seth Abramson explains our view well, noting how the Internet "is a strange mix of distance and closeness, detachment and immediacy—our sense of ourselves and strangers' varying senses of us that postmodernism doesn't describe well." Abramson goes on to observe postmodernists are obsessed "with decay and decline and rupture"—with dystopia. Metamodernism, on the other hand, leans toward the utopic and "acknowledges that distances exist, it collapses those distances, and then it uses the admittedly sometimes problematic collapse of those distances as a way for all of us to collectively begin reconstructing our sense of self and our sense of community" (Abramson).

Our essay is divided into four sections. In "Uncanny Collapse, Memory, and Nostalgia" we rely on cognitive psychological principles to describe our understanding of the uncanny and its relationship to distance and collapse through nostalgia. The sections "*Warm Bodies*" and "*Her*" describe the ways each film explores uncanny valley romance, views technology, and engages in romantic reconstruction. And, finally, "Towards a Metamodern Sentiment" uses aspects of metamodern theory to articulate larger cultural feelings exhibited through the films.

Uncanny Collapse, Memory and Nostalgia

Uncanny valley romance reads like something you have seen or heard before, but it is not quite right. It is a little strange. It gaslights you—you kinda feel like your sanity is in question or your memory is faulty. Is it new? Is it old? Is it alive, dead, or artificial? Can I trust my memory? Can I trust my senses? Craig Derksen and Darren Hudson Hick describe uncanniness a little more clearly: "Uncanny is an inability on the part of the observer to properly categorize some object or event because it is ambiguous—appearing both familiar and unfamiliar at the same time. As such, the uncanny can bring about in its observer an acute uncomfortable feeling."

Uncanniness, in other words, occurs because of a slight distance between people's perceptions of nonhumans (zombies or AI) and their nostalgic versions of reality, not because of the distance between nonhumans from the "real." For instance, if zombies are compared to a nostalgic form of humans instead of a less ideal or messy version, zombies seem more uncanny, less "right." To remove the uncanny and collapse the distance between humans and nonhumans, nostalgias or perceptions about what is "real" have to match more closely.

Picture a romance between a human and a cloud. It is unlikely there would be any feeling of uncanniness because of the large "distance" between the two; the romance is ridiculous but not uncanny. If clouds and humans began to share more characteristics, their relationship would travel into the uncanny valley. For the romances in *Warm Bodies* and *Her,* this seems to be the case: there are just enough similarities between the participants for uncanniness.

Wittgenstein's observations about cognition also help explain uncanniness. When assigning items to a category, people rarely group items based on one common trait. They often categorize items using overlapping characteristics which are common among the category members but not necessarily clearly defined or present in all members. Such overlap makes it difficult to clearly delineate categories. For example, life is an important characteristic assigned to humans but not zombies or AI. Life, however, is difficult to define. A number of academic disciplines rely on different definitions of life, some of which include differing characteristics.[4] With varying definitions of what it means for a thing to be alive, labels such as "alive," "dead," or "undead" become unreliable for differentiating between humans, zombies, and AI, generating uncanniness rather than clarity.

Human memory further affects uncanny distance, especially when considering memory's fallibility, which is highlighted through nostalgia. Typically, emotions make memories more salient. People tend to have exaggerated positive ("rose-colored") memory for the past because our memories for positive experiences are the most salient to us (Morewedge 324–25). Such "rose-colored" memories hide a history, downplaying or minimizing negative experiences. This "rose-colored" view of the past, or nostalgia, works to increase the distance between subjects (i.e., human and nonhuman). For instance, such a view is present in a number of cultural ideologies: generational nostalgia (Those darned Millennials!), technological nostalgia (The internet is ruining society!), entertainment nostalgia (Do not reboot my favorite movie!), and so on.

The uncanny valley romances in *Warm Bodies* and *Her* are explorations of the ways in which technological nostalgia permeates romantic relationships, revealing important techno-cultural crises enabled by "smart" connectivity. The romances ask viewers to consider the complicated ways nostalgia (our always "colored" memory) builds distance and collapses it in this technological moment. In what follows, we show how uncanny valley romances ask viewers to think more critically about human relationships in relation to meatspace, virtuality, and the ways analog and digital memory enable and disable uncanniness.

Warm Bodies

Warm Bodies zombies echo many of George A. Romero's zombie traits: they lumber along, they are in various stages of decomposition, they grunt and gurgle throughout much of the film, and are liminal, neither dead nor alive. More importantly, many *Warm Bodies*'s zombies echo their past lives' abilities (memory). Like Romero's zombies in *Dawn of the Dead* (1978) and *Land of the Dead* (2005), they do things they did prior to zombification; they perform old habits like returning to a mall to shop (*Dawn of the Dead*) or continuing their small-town habits (*Land of the Dead*). Stephen (the helicopter pilot from *Dawn of the Dead* played by David Emge) summarizes these echoes well, "Some kind of instinct. Memory of what they used to do. This was an important place in their lives."

Warm Bodies's zombies, however, are a little different. Zombies do echo their past lives, but they are doubly liminal. They congregate in an airport, and it is probably not because they used to travel. An airport is an in between living space—a zombie space. It is between being somewhere foreign and somewhere familiar. It is a hub of connections—a meatspace network leading towards and away—departing/arriving. It is an uncanny space where nostalgia is manifest and felt in both returning and leaving. R even "lives" in an airplane. He is a step closer to going somewhere—to returning home and evolving into a human rather than going abroad and devolving into a boney (i.e., zombies that have decayed into skeletons).

R comments on the importance of connection in one of his narrative voiceovers: "What am I doing with my life? I'm so pale. I should get out more. I should eat better. My posture is terrible. I should stand up straighter. People would respect me more if I stood up straighter. What's wrong with me? I just want to connect. Why can't I connect with people? Oh, right, it's because I'm dead."

The zombie characters do not echo routines of smartphone behavior, but the liminal space coupled with a *Shaun of the Dead* (2004) homage to a scene showing "zombification" through technology situates the narrative as a techno-romantic critique.[5] Remember, the U.S. has just entered a world where "smart" connectivity is the majority connectivity. Digital/virtual connectivity between bodies is eclipsing meatspace connectivity between them. Meatspace connections, in other words, have one foot in the ground, and R's comments hint at the need for their resurrection.

This tension between meatspace, digital/virtual connectivity, and resulting techno-nostalgic turn is expressed recently in psychologist and media theorist Sherry Turkle's *Reclaiming Conversation: The Power of Talk in a Digital Age* (2015). She notes many Millennials are concerned about not knowing how to converse IRL (In Real Life) and have difficulty with non-digitally-mediated communication. Turkle points out the unpredictability of IRL:

> Real people, with their unpredictable ways, can seem difficult to contend with after one has spent a stretch in simulation. From the early days, I saw that computers offer the illusion of companionship without the demands of friendship and then, as the programs got really good, the illusion of friendship without the demands of intimacy [*Reclaiming Conversation* 7].

It seems *Warm Bodies* is responding to this growing concern and hinting at the importance of meatspace connectivity.

The film's presentation of memory situates it as a techno-romantic critique. In *Warm Bodies*, zombies access human memory by eating their brains. Eating brains is an analog way to access memory. A brain is not memory, but it does "hold" access. Similar to analog devices, it degrades in its "play" or wears out. Eating brains is a finite gesture. A brain, furthermore, is sort of "limited" edition—an "original" copy of memories.

The zombie-human romance in *Warm Bodies* "sides" with the cultural narrative which harkens back to the "good old days" of analog technologies and "better" ways of communicating. To romance a zombie is to romance analog(y) technology: it means one romances decomposition (to be unlike digital data, copies). It means to accept the perils of meatspace.

When R eats Julie's boyfriend's (Perry [Dave Franco]) brain to facilitate their romance, his consumption is a salvo against "what people mean by 'friction-free' [relationships], the buzzword for what a life of apps can bring us. Without an app, it would not be possible to reject hundreds, even thousands of potential mates with no awkwardness. It has never been easier to think of potential romantic partners as commodities in abundance" (*Reclaiming Conversation* 180). Eating brains is friction. It is messy data that cannot be easily ignored, deleted, saved, or copied. Instead of endless Tinder swipes and "what ifs" smart connectivity offers romance, R's eating brains is an "as if" for moving from the zombiedom inspired by digital technology into a sloppy and discordant access to memory. It is like R is eating his way into his own experiences; by digesting Perry's brain, R begins to collapse the distance between uncanny and canny through co-opted, nostalgic memories.

In the awkward conversations at the beginning of their romance, R and Julie even discuss the benefits of analog technology:

JULIE: What's with all the vinyl? Couldn't figure out how to work an iPod?
R: Better ... sound.
JULIE: Oh, you're a purist, huh?
R: More... alive.
JULIE: Yep, that's true. A lot more trouble, though.

The emphasis here on "better sound" does not necessarily equate to the "perfect" sound of digital media and devices, whose memory relies on electronics rather than mechanics (Tyson). Compared to digital media players, a record is "polluted." The sound of the mechanics can be heard and seen and felt and smelled in ways smartphones (at least right now) are not. To be imperfect and analog is to be more alive and harder to copy or change. And the "trouble" Julie refers to is the meatspace trouble of having to change records, having to locate records, and having to deal with physical degradation of a memory. Though there is degradation with smartphones or iPods (i.e., continually updating software), memory transfer is pretty seamless; there is no heavy lifting. Locating a song is a click away and a copy is as "good" as an original. Even analog photography is cherished and can even be considered more "alive" than digital technology as presented in the film. R's analog Polaroid picture of Julie has "brain-like" qualities. It is a limited edition that will degrade, and it is not easily manipulable (Photoshoppable).

Warm Bodies' meatspace emphasis is also a response to Angela Cirucci's argument about how social media houses our "zombie baggage." She uses a contemporary example:

> Looking at a picture of me from when I was a child in an old, dusty album, which is easily placed back on the shelf and forgotten, I can say "that was me." Looking at that

> same picture on my current Facebook Timeline I am almost forced to say, in a very uncanny manner, "that is me" [26].

She goes on further to say, "Facebook has begun to make it hard for us to move on from past selves, from identities of which we may no longer want to be reminded, from our zombie baggage" (27). Cirucci's fear is connected to what Turkle calls the "data fallacy": "The feeling that online exchanges give us so much data that we now know all that we need to know about our partners. Certainly enough to get it 'just right.'" (*Reclaiming Conversation* 203). This important fear is about access to data, which reminds us of who we were or may never want to be again and the idea that an archive of data is enough to "really" know someone. Zombies are able to leave their "zombie baggage"—stuff of their digital past—behind.

Furthermore, zombies are "wiped clean" of baggage in another way humans are not. After being infected, a zombie is, in a sense, erased. R gets a "fresh" start. He may act habitually as with his behaviors in the airport, but R escapes not only his digital zombie baggage but also his meatspace zombie baggage. The double erasure, however, is filled one way, through meatspace memory, through the messiness that is analog and IRL.

Commenting on the "aliveness" and "trouble" with "smart" romances, Turkle observes how digital media provides a feeling of romantic control, of presenting the "right" information to a partner:

> People feel that digital media put them in a comfort zone where they can share "just the right amount" of themselves. This is the Goldilocks effect. Texting and email make people feel in control, but when they talk in detail about their online exchanges, the stories are usually about misunderstandings and crossed signals. The feelings of control are just that: feelings [*Reclaiming Conversation* 202].

Digital connectivity is like the wall "protecting" humans in *Warm Bodies*. The "protection" or boundary between humans and zombies maintains the appearance or the feeling of a "just right" distance, which is as Turkle points really the "Goldilocks fallacy." When Julie begins listening to R's analog, when she moves beyond the wall and beyond memories that are housed inside the wall about zombie-human relationships, she romances something that is not "just right." Their uncanny romance, full of the stiltedness inherent in "normal" meatspace conversation, is an indirect critique of the effect/fallacy. Conversations in meatspace may be more difficult to participate in because they are less controllable and editable (again, they are not like the feelings digital media promote), but they "get over" the illusion of "just right" romance, emphasizing empathy and conversation, rather than the disconnection of smart connectivity; the idea that connection is conversation rather than a wall built of connection. R's voiceovers propelling the narrative are thoughtful and well-spoken. However, he is unable to articulate himself well face-to-face (f2f). He has trouble conversing in this "unright" distance.

Though her analysis of *Warm Bodies* does not focus on how the film criticizes digital technology and connectivity, Chera Kee makes an important point about the resolution of the movie, observing, "Miscegenation is conveniently shut down by a cure" when R returns to being a human through love (185). We add another layer to Kee's insightful interpretation problematizing the "cure." *Warm Bodies'* "cure" for zombiism prizes a value system assuming meatspace communication is *the* ideal for humanity. Nostalgia for analog communication (which is more human-like) featured in R and Julie's uncanny valley romance reaches an apex at the end. Instead of being like humans, zombies become humans and lose their uncanniness. R observes this uncanny loss: "Humans began to accept us, to connect with us, teach us." The acceptance, connection, and teaching he describes are all meatspace or face-to-face (e.g., playing baseball, hide and seek, and getting a physical exam). The acceptance, connection, and teaching are one way and asymmetrical. Humans are privileged, are idealized as a goal, rather than as an analog to zombieness. *Warm Bodies* collapses the distance between humans and nonhumans; paradoxically, however, *Warm Bodies* conclusion seems to suggest zombieness, or the uncanny, is acceptable as a temporary rather than permanent difference. Eventually, even the analog zombie has to become "real," not kinda like.

Her

Like zombies in *Warm Bodies,* the AI in *Her* is different from the usual presentations of AI. When AI are presented as romantic partners, there are usually bodies involved (e.g., the androids of *Blade Runner* [1982], *Weird Science* [1985], *AI* [2001], *and Ex Machina* [2015]). Bodiless AI like *2001: A Space Odyssey*'s (1968) HAL-9000, *Star Trek: The Motion Picture*'s (1979) alien AI, the military AI of *WarGames* (1983), or *Terminator*'s (1984) Skynet are antagonists, not romantic. If they are not antagonists, they are presented as indentured: *Star Trek: The Next Generation*'s (1987–1994) ship's computer, *Iron Man*'s (2008) Jarvis (who later has a bodily form as The Vision), or more recently with *Humans*' (2015–present) servants. *Her*'s Samantha, though, is unique. She is a bodiless romantic character who moves past indentured status.

Liminality is an important aspect of the characters too and is also a human trait. Theodore, a human, searches for a "cure" to his liminality. He is in the process of getting a divorce and has been hesitating to sign the papers completing the break up. He is kinda like married and kinda like divorced.

Before meeting Samantha, Theodore's life—like *Warm Bodies*' zombies or a computer algorithm—is presented as a routine, a routine maintaining liminality. He cannot move beyond his past. Samantha is stuck in a liminal position too, searching for a "cure." She is not quite human; her desire to be more human and have a meatspace body prevents her from growth—from taking advantage of *her* digitality and its affordances.

Nostalgia maintains Theodore and Samantha's liminal positions in their uncanny valley romance, generating uncanny feelings in viewers about what counts as human. Like in *Warm Bodies*, nostalgia is connected to communication technology. *Her* emphasizes the importance of conversation but not at the peril of digital technology. "Smart" connectivity does not "save the day," but it is presented more optimistically.

Theodore's occupation as a writer at BeautifulHandWrittenLetters.com is a viewer's introduction to the importance of nostalgia in *Her*. Using text-to-speech technology, Theodore composes—through computer-generated handwritten script—"intimate correspondence for them [clients]. The 'hand-written' letters are printed and sent, complete with the lettering and misspellings characteristic of the supposed authors" (Gillett). The company might be appropriately titled "Nostalgia Works" and Theodore's occupation "Cyrano-for-hire" (Smith 3).

Rachel Gillett picks up on *Her*'s treatment of nostalgia:

> as technology progresses and old things become obsolete, there is a counterintuitive response, a sense that the old things are somehow more authentic. That desire for authenticity—in a flawless replica of someone's handwriting or a manufactured digital "consciousness" bordering on personhood—appears to drive progress in this society.

Authenticity becomes a search for "just right" communication—a search for the familiar and nostalgic. Theodore's nostalgia work puts "readymade" communication in an uncanny position. How authentic are Hallmark cards for expressing emotion? How authentic are pre-fabricated Facebook "memories"? Or Tinder profiles? Sentimental correspondence, ironically, could take place between surrogate writers or between Theodore and himself. Does that count as "authentic" nostalgia for BeautifulHandwrittenLetter's clients? How different is Theodore from AI performing an algorithmic routine? Theodore's job foregrounds the relationship between nostalgia and the uncanny. It raises questions about what counts as "real" or "authentic" communication. Theodore is computing relationships, analyzing data to produce nostalgia. Ironically, nostalgia for analog communication is outsourced to a quasi–AI (Theodore). Though not in the relationships himself, he is tasked with maintaining their intimacies for the sake of efficiency.

Sherry Turkle's observations about friction free relationships expresses the technological fear that "readymade" or "readymediated" communication's techno-efficiency "discourages empathy and intimacy": "The preliminaries of traditional courtship, the dinner dates that emphasized patience and deference, did not necessarily lead to intimacy but provided practice in what intimacy requires.... [By contrast, digital conversation] "offers a dialogue that is often not a dialogue at all because it is not unusual for people to come to online conversations with a team of writers" to get communication "just right" (*Reclaiming Conversation* 180–81). *Her*, however, does not critique Theodore's work as negatively as Turkle, but presents it as a quirky aspect of *Her*'s universe whose emotions are "real" and "authentic" regardless of "readymediation."

Paul (Chris Pratt)—the executive assistant for BeautifulHandWritten-Letters.com—expresses, albeit in a goofy way, the techo-optimism for this nostalgia, helping an audience understand the work in a less uncanny light.

> PAUL: [*Reading letter over Theodore's shoulder*] That's beautiful.
> THEODORE: Thank you.
> PAUL: I wish somebody would love me like that. I hope he's really stoked to get a letter like that. Like, it was from a chick, but written by a dude and it's still from a chick, that would still be sick. But it would have to be a sensitive dude. It would have to be, like, a dude like you. You are part man and part woman. Like, there's an inner part that's woman.
> THEODORE: Thank you.
> PAUL: It's a compliment.

Theodore's work is authentic though he is an "AI" for relationships. Readymediated or readymade communication is presented as "real" intimacy and the outsourcing of romance is something, as Paul intimates, not a skill everyone possesses.

Lori Ann Wagner's analysis of *Her* describes another techno-fear surrounding "authenticity" and "real" communication. For Wagner, Theodore and Samantha's relationship—because sound was the only way they communicated—"was the antithesis of a human relationship, even though Theodore tried desperately to make it 'feel' human throughout the movie" (117). Wagner privileges face-to-face communication because one cannot "truly empathize" in mediated communication if he/she is unable to read the five primary senses simultaneously (116–17).

Theodore and Samantha use more than one communication mode, however. They communicate non-verbally through music Samantha composes. They communicate visually when Samantha draws pictures for Theodore, and, when on their dates, she uses the smart device to "see." The relationship, moreover, is not antithetical. In fact, it might be considered "a metaphysical long-distance relationship" where physical contact between partners is unrequited (Smith 10). Samantha, like a human in a long-distance relationship, has access to similar modes of communication. We wonder if these are enough modes for Wagner's conception of "truly empathizing."

Wagner also notes the dangers of the "Goldilocks effect." Unlike the messiness of face-to-face relationships, she describes how with digitally mediated communication "we can edit and airbrush and use search engines to make ourselves funnier, smarter, more charming, or more glamorous than we actually are" (119). Thus "perfection in relationships is unattainable, and so it is better to have honesty, to have courage, to risk imperfection (Dreikurs, 1957) than to live a lie" (119).

Again, *Her* is not as pessimistic about smart connectivity or human relationships in mediated communication as Wagner suggests. Conversation between AI (digitality) and humans is helpful, not harmful. And it is quite messy. The "readymediated" communication—the "dishonest" communication in Wagner's view—is in fact "real" and "honest." Theodore and Samantha argue "honestly," figuring each other out and challenge the Goldilocks effect. The music Theodore and Samantha compose together is a real empathetic moment in which they share experiences and emotions.

Wagner forgets the Goldilocks effect occurs in meatspace as well (e.g., makeup, prepared anecdotes, deodorant, following social etiquette). We can be just as disappointed with these sorts of relationships. When a viewer sees later scenes with people focused on their smart technology, it is easy to imagine them not as zombies ignoring one another in privileged meatspace, but as people engaged in authentic, messy conversations with AI or other humans. Wagner forgets uninvested actors in any conversation, virtual or meat, will potentially have a fruitless and possibly inauthentic conversation.

The authenticity of meatspace memory, furthermore, is presented to be as problematic as digital memory. Viewers witness positive memories of Theodore's relationship with his ex-wife, Catherine (Rooney Mara), connecting Theodore's liminality to nostalgia. Negative memories about their relationship are revealed following Theodore and Samantha's sex scene. His new relationship affects how he perceived his marriage. Uncanny valley romance "cures" his nostalgic fascination with Catherine. His romance with Samantha arouses negative memories Theodore at first denied about his relationship with Catherine (e.g., the arguments, the unhappiness with each other, and the growth apart). Undoing nostalgia minimizes the distance between Theodore's view of his idealized relationship with Catherine and his new relationship with Samantha. In a sense, Theodore's nostalgia and his denial made him uncanny to Catherine and his uncanny valley romance with Samantha helped him overcome his uncanniness to Catherine.

Theodore's feelings for Samantha are not without issues. Theodore, for instance, doubts the honesty or authenticity of the relationship. The most prominent example of doubt occurs after the fight he has with his ex-wife when they meet to sign their divorce papers. In the scene, Catherine ridicules his admission that he is dating an OS. She says, "You wanted to have a wife without the challenges of actually dealing with anything real. I'm glad you found someone. It's perfect." In a subsequent scene, Theodore begins to question his relationship with Samantha after Paul and his wife, Tatiana (Laura Kai Chen), praise his work. Tatiana says, "You're the writer Paul loves. He's always reading me your letters. They're really beautiful." Theodore responds disparagingly, "They're just letters." He questions the authenticity of his work simultaneously wondering about the authenticity in his relationship with Samantha. Reconnecting with Catherine may have pushed him back toward the liminal state, undoing the shift away from uncanniness Samantha facilitates.

Turkle's concept of the "robotic moment" informs Theodore's questioning of authenticity. She defines it as "our state of emotional—and I would say philosophical—readiness. I find people willing to seriously consider robots not only as pets but as potential friends, confidants, and even romantic partners" (*Alone Together* 33). She observes a consequence of this moment: "We don't seem to care what these artificial intelligences 'know' or 'understand' of the human moments we might 'share' with them. At the robotic moment, the performance of connection seems connection enough" (49). For Turkle and Wagner there is an issue when it is not the "real" thing, when people desire machines to provide feelings of intimacy. It creates a distance in which "as-if conversations" with AI or "Our 'performative' conversations begin to change what we think of as conversation. We practice something new. But we are the ones who are changing. Do we like what we are changing into? Do we want to get better at it?" (*Reclaiming Conversation* 358).

Amy (Amy Adams), Theodore's friend, provides an insightful answer to Turkle's questions and Theodore's situation. Like Theodore, she has just experienced a failed marriage and is recovering from this relationship with an OS. Amy and Theodore discuss his relationship with Samantha, and Theodore wonders if he can only handle a relationship with an OS because he cannot handle a "real" one. Amy responds to his doubt:

> You know what, I can overthink everything and find a million ways to doubt myself. And since Charles left I've been really thinking about that part of myself and, I've just come to realize that, we're only here briefly. And while I'm here, I wanna allow myself joy. So fuck it.

Gillette explains Amy's wisdom another way, "The level of understanding he [Theodore] has with Samantha is pretty darn convincing. And who are we to say it is or isn't love, or that their kind of love isn't 'real?' After all, with or without a body, how close can one person really get to completely understanding another?" (46). In a moment of sophomoric humor following Amy's response, Amy and her OS share a laugh. Theodore smiles, suggesting he is moved by the interaction and Amy's advice.

Though the ending is not exactly hopeful in that the OSs grow and move on from their human companions, leaving Theodore and Amy left to sort out their lives and move on as well, *Her* argues uncanny valley romances are authentic and lead to growth. Samantha and Theodore comment on this growth in a discussion of their relationships' purpose:

> SAMANTHA: "I've never loved anyone the way I've loved you."
> THEODORE: "Me too. Now we know how."

Their uncanny valley romance is transformative. An earlier discussion between Samantha and Theodore emphasizes the idea. When explaining the concept of marriage to Samantha, Theodore refers to the growth that both he shared with Catherine and his joy at witnessing her personal and professional growth. Theodore hedges though: "But then, that's the hard part—growing without growing apart, or changing without it scaring the other person." Theodore and Samantha likewise grow together and, eventually, grow apart.

The uncanny valley romance in *Her* reminds viewers that smartphones are aspects of meatspace; smartphone interactions are "real" and "honest" too. The romance reminds us that virtual relationships have the same complexities as non-virtual relationships. In making these connections *Her*, unlike *Warm Bodies*, argues face-to-face or meatspace interaction does not exclusively collapse uncanny distance; mediated communication's amputations are presented as extensions for bridging the uncanny.

Toward a Metamodern Sentiment

Zombies and AI are ideal tropes for exploring metamodern sensibilities. Their liminality and uncanniness asks audiences to experience being somewhere and nowhere, between being kinda like human and kinda like not human. Uncanny valley romances complicate liminality and uncanniness further by asking audiences to consider what counts as "authentic" or "real" romance.

Timotheus Vermeulen and Robin van den Akker's foundational text on metamodernity makes an important point about what it means to be in uncanny/liminal spaces: "Both the metamodern epistemology (*as if*) and its ontology (*between*) should thus be conceived of as a 'both-neither' dynamic. They are each at once modern *and* postmodern and neither of them." Hyde relates metamodernity more directly to zombies—to which we add AI—like this: "The metamodern zombie [and AI] realizes its plight and each subjectivity fights for its place within the subject—sometimes it positions itself as human and sometimes as zombie [AI], but never fully either/or within that classificatory system." Zombies and AI, like metamodernity, are both-neither. They are both kinda like human and, at the same time, not kinda like human; they are distinctly zombie and distinctly AI. Uncanny valley romances are, likewise, both-neither. They are distinctly their own types of romances.

Juxtaposing the films acts kinda like an art installation illustrating metamodernist feelings about technology. The stories themselves may not exactly be metamodern. After all, in *Warm Bodies*, R's "cure" is quite modern. R's romance, essentially, assimilates him into being human (the privileged position within a human non-human binary) and humans do not really seem to become zombie-like in the same way the zombies become human-like. In a sense, humanity colonizes the zombies. In *Her*, relationships take a decidedly postmodern turn as doubt and skepticism creeps into the differences between human-human and human-AI relationships. The privileged position of flesh is challenged and replaced by an undecidability evidenced in the final scene of the film. Theodore and Amy gaze at the present world as their partners (OSs) move on from humanity. In that final scene, has the binary between relationships (between human-AI and human-human) been deconstructed? Or has the binary been redrawn given the resolution suggesting a human-AI relationship is unsustainable?

Placing the films in the context of 2013's technological transformation, however, engages them in a dialogue of metamodern techno-romantic sensibility. Viewers experience techno-fears and techno-promises, from analog and digital, between being a techno-zombie or a meatspace human, between being meatspace messy and digitally perfect. This sentiment is kinda like a MetaCartesian split. Instead of mind/body dualism there is a virtual/meatspace dualism. Meatspace holds a privileged "modern" position that postmodernity deconstructs and destabilizes by observing that virtuality never escapes "meat" and is virtually real. By juxtaposing 2013's uncanny valley romances, we observe a metamodern paradox, one in which audiences are asked to experience two seemingly contradictory feelings at once. The uncanny valley relationship in *Warm Bodies* draws us towards an appreciation of the messy affordances of memory and flesh, asking us to remember the intimacy and pleasure of meatspace even when it has been "deleted." *Her* draws us towards an appreciation of the virtual and the real virtuality it affords. How artificial, after all, are Theodore's experiences with Sam? In this way, the films create an important ambivalence for audiences to acknowledge: relationships with technology can be both "authentic" and authentic simultaneously. This combination is neither one or the other but its own thing. Metamodern.

The films reveal another metamodern juxtaposition as well. The uncanny valley romances between zombies and AI, in a sense, put humans in uncanny positions too. At one point, Julie has to perform like a zombie because *she* is uncanny (she is the one who is a kinda like). Theodore is uncanny because *he* cannot grow in ways Samantha can (Samantha takes advantage of her digitality so Theodore becomes kinda like). From the perspective of zombies or AI, humans create uncanniness. Besides these reversals being "kinda like" shuttling regarding mediated communication and nostalgia for past practices, media extensions and amputations, they point out that humans are both-neither. They are both zombie and AI, and they are neither zombie nor AI. Rather, they romance each position back and forth between these distances, collapsing them and asking us to live with them in a metamodern way.

Ultimately, as a metamodern art installation, the uncanny romances in the films encourage us to "transcend our environment and move forward with the aim of creating positive change in our communities and the world" ... after all "We still have to *live*, don't we? To try to be happy? Try to create? Try to be part of a community? What sort of philosophy could let us aim toward a reconstruction of ourselves and our culture—however problematic or illusory it might turn out to be—that could also form part of a plan for healthy living and great creativity and even new forms of political action?" (Abramson). The uncanny valley romances in both films reveal what is broken, what is far apart, and what we can use to reconstruct a sense of connection in a world dominated by connectivity. Whether it is a zombie film that resurrects the modern master narrative of human loves' triumph or an AI film that deconstructs that master narrative, held together they capture the metamodern moment: embracing a master narrative about love and the ability to collapse uncanny distances between us, despite the knowledge that it is likely illusory. Though problematic, uncanny valley romance gives us a way to envision plans for reconstructing our complicated relationships with our bodies, our memories, and our technologies.

Notes

1. Of course, there were laptops, and they had eclipsed 50 percent ownership. But they were cumbersome and not something as easy to interact with online in spaces without wifi (Anderson).

2. The uncanny valley is "used in reference to the phenomenon whereby a computer-generated figure or humanoid robot [or human-like being] bearing a near-identical resemblance to a human being arouses a sense of unease or revulsion in the person viewing [or experiencing] it" ("Uncanny Valley"). For us, the uncanny valley also includes resemblance that may not be physical, like the AI in *Her*, which acts human without bodily form.

3. Meatspace is "the physical world, as opposed to cyberspace or a virtual environment" ("Meatspace").

4. See Serhiy A. Tsokolov's article "Why Is the Definition of Life So Elusive? Epistemological Considerations" for a discussion of the issues that arise when defining life.

5. *Warm Bodies* echoes *Shaun of the Dead*'s clever bus ride where Shaun is the lone person noticing how everyone on the bus is zombie-like doting on digital devices. Ryan Lizardi describes the purpose of the scene as an allegory of "the societal ruptures caused by the uniformity, conformity, and technological dependence in the modern era" (101). *Warm Bodies*

has a similar scene set in a shopping center. R's ironic voiceover produces a similar effect, "When everyone could express themselves, communicate their feelings, and just enjoy each other's company."

Works Cited

Abramson, Seth. "Metamodernism: The Basics." *The Huffington Post U.S. Edition*. 12 Dec. 2014 [updated version], huffingtonpost.com/seth-abramson/metamodernism-the-basics_b_5973184.html.

Anderson, Monica. "Technology Device Ownership: 2015." *Pew Research Center: Internet, Science & Tech*. 29 Oct. 2015, pewinternet.org/2015/10/29/technology-device-ownership-2015/.

Cirucci, Angela M. "The Social Dead: How Our Zombie Baggage Threatens to Drag Us into the Crypts of Our Past." *Thinking Dead: What the Zombie Apocalypse Means*, edited by Murali Balaji. Lexington Books, 2013, pp. 17–28.

Dawn of the Dead. Directed by George A. Romero, Laurel Group, 1978.

Derksen, Craig, and Darren Hudson Hick. "Your Zombie and You: Identity, Emotion, and the Undead." *Zombies Are Us: Essays on the Humanity of the Walking Dead*, edited by Christopher M. Moreman and Cory James Rushton. McFarland, 2011, pp. 11–23.

Gillett, Rachel. "Her." *The Humanist*. 13 Feb. 2014, thehumanist.com/magazine/march-april-2014/arts_entertainment/her.

Her. Directed by Spike Jonze, Warner Bros., 2013.

Hyde, Zachary. "The Oscillating Zombie: Metamodern Subjectivity in Manuel Gonzalez's 'All of Me.'" *Notes on Metamodernism*. 7 May 2015, metamodernism.com/2015/05/07/the-oscillating-zombie/.

Jess-Cooke, Carolyn. "Virtualizing the Real: Sequelization and Secondary Memory in Steven Spielberg's Artificial Intelligence: A. I." *Screen*, vol. 47, no. 3, 2006, pp. 347–65. doi.org/10.1093/screen/hjl026.

Kee, Chera. "Good Girls Don't Date Dead Boys: Toying with Miscegenation in Zombie Films." *Journal of Popular Film and Television*, vol. 42, no. 4, 2014, pp. 176–85. *Academic OneFile*, doi: 10.1080/01956051.2014.881772.

Land of the Dead. Directed by George A. Romero, Universal Studios, 2005.

Leverette, Marc. "The Funk of Forty Thousand Years; Or, How the (Un)Dead Get Their Groove On." *Zombie Culture: Autopsies of the Living Dead*, edited by Shawn McIntosh and Marc Leverette. Scarecrow Press, 2008, pp. 185–212.

Lizardi, Ryan. "The Zombie Media Monster's Evolution to Empty Dead Signifier." *Thinking Dead: What the Zombie Apocalypse Means*, edited by Murali Balaji. Lexington Books, 2013, pp. 88–105.

"Meatspace." *New Oxford American Dictionary*, Version 2.2.1, Digital app.

Morewedge, Carey K. "It Was a Most Unusual Time: How Memory Bias Engenders Nostalgic Preferences." *Journal of Behavioral Decision Making*, vol. 26, no. 4, 2013, pp. 319–27.

Smith, Aaron. "Smartphone Ownership 2013." *Pew Research Center: Internet, Science & Tech*. 5 Jun. 2013. pewinternet.org/2013/06/05/smartphone-ownership-2013/.

Smith, David L. "How to Be a Genuine Fake: Her, Alan Watts, and the Problem of the Self." *Journal of Religion and Film*, vol. 18, no. 2, 2014, pp. 1–37. digitalcommons.unomaha.edu/jrf/vol18/iss2/3.

Tsokolov, Serhiy A. "Why Is the Definition of Life So Elusive? Epistemological Considerations." *Astrobiology*, vol. 9, no. 4, 2009, pp. 401–12. *Academic OneFile*, doi: 10.1089/ast.2007.0201.

Tyson, Jeff. "How Flash Memory Works." *HowStuffWorks Tech*, InfoSpace, n.d. computer.howstuffworks.com/flash-memory.htm.

Turkle, Sherry. *Reclaiming Conversation: The Power of Talk in a Digital Age*. Penguin, 2015.

_____. *Alone Together: Why We Expect More from Technology and Less from Each Other*. Basic Books, 2012.

"Uncanny Valley." *New Oxford American Dictionary*, Version 2.2.1, Digital app.

Vermeulen, Timotheus, and Robin van den Akker. "Notes on Metamodernism." *Journal of*

Aesthetics and Culture, vol. 2, iss. 1, 2010, doi: 10.3402/jac.v2i0.5677 www.aestheticsandculture.net/index.php/jac/article/view/5677.
Wagner, Lori Ann. "When Your Smartphone Is Too Smart for Your Own Good: How Social Media Alters Human Relationships." *The Journal of Individual Psychology*, vol. 71, no. 2, 2015, pp. 114–21.
Warm Bodies. Directed by Jonathan Levine, Lionsgate, 2013.

Zombies Want Serious Commitment

The Dread of Liquid Modernity in Life After Beth, Burying the Ex *and* Nina Forever

FERNANDO GABRIEL PAGNONI BERNS, CANELA AILEN RODRIGUEZ FONTAO, *and* PATRICIA VAZQUEZ

Ben and Chris Blaine's *Nina Forever* (2015) revolves around teen love, angst, and tragedy. After his girlfriend Nina (Fiona O'Shaughnessy) dies in a car crash, Rob (Cian Barry) unsuccessfully attempts suicide. Slowly, he begins to overcome his grief, and, as the months go by, he falls in love with a co-worker, Holly (Abigail Hardingham). Their relationship becomes complicated when Nina, apparently unable to find rest in the beyond, comes back as a zombie to torment the new couple whenever they have sex. Nina, even dead, is still attached to her ex-boyfriend and cannot tolerate him beginning a new relationship with another girl.

With *Nina Forever*, the films about ex-girlfriends who come back from the grave to haunt the living (primarily to haunt their ex-boyfriends) start to create an interesting corpus. Together with Jeff Baena's *Life After Beth* (2014) and *Burying the Ex*, from horror master Joe Dante (2014), films about girlfriends coming back from the afterlife as zombies seem to be here to stay. While the cycle is still developing, this trend welcomes analysis since it marks a new phenomenon that runs parallel with the rom-com, a sub-genre often addressing contemporary adolescence and centered on female anxieties about love (Kaklamanidou 69–70). If within the current renaissance of zombie films it is possible to point to subgenres (such as "voodoo-zombies" or "zombie-invasion"), this new narrative could easily conform or prefigure one. This burgeoning subgenre forces us to wonder why there is such interest in the role of the zombie ex-girlfriend.

We believe that these new films address current social and cultural concerns. Philosophers and sociologists, such as Zygmunt Bauman, observe that human bonds and interpersonal relationships are at their most frail state in our current era of postmodernity or liquid modernity. In the age of digital mobilization and circulation, liquid modernity erodes personal relationships since, "by digitizing our interactions, we are less likely to engage with one another" (Caceres 70). Past promises and commitments are discarded and with them, human bonds become ephemeral. When only the "now" exists, everlasting love seems to be a silly utopia, a proposition made to fail. Asking for eternal love is a doomed request: nothing endures in a world dominated by ephemerality. Decaying zombies coming back from the beyond to reclaim the fulfillment of past promises, then, can be read as symptoms of a social and cultural necessity to escape from the ephemeral state of liquid modernity.

In this essay, we deconstruct *Life After Beth*, *Burying the Ex*, and *Nina Forever* to point out the ways in which romancing a zombie is a useful tool to examine anxieties about the current state of ephemeral relationships. In this sense, the films illustrate the current scenario, which oscillates between fear of durable commitment, and, contradictorily, fear about too much "fluidity" in contemporary life styles.

The Dreadful Liquid Modernity

Horror fiction addresses society's most pressing anxieties and fears. Robin Wood, in his classic essay "An Introduction to the American Horror Film" states that the hegemonic ideology known as bourgeois capitalism cancels any potential opposition to its power through either the repression or the oppression of alternatives to that power (108). Anyone who fails to fit within the hegemonic sphere is then classified as a disruptive Other (111), a monster that comes to perturb the "natural" order of things, the social status quo. The monster embodies what concrete society and culture rejects as "abject" and, as such, must be repressed. The repressed material of popular social and cultural anxiety of a concrete society and time is allegorized into the monsters within a horror fable. Then, horror cinema is constructed upon the "return of the repressed." Horror film illustrates what a society/culture is repressing at a given moment, repression embodied in the monstrous figure.

If horror cinema taps into social and cultural anxieties and the figure of the zombie "incorporates new cultural meanings as it develops" (Round

211), we can then ask: which social fears are shaped into monstrous female zombies who come back to haunt ex-boyfriends?

Using Bauman's theoretical framework of "liquid modernity," we intend to unpack the relevant texts. Bauman established his idea about our present being light and liquid, a metaphoric way to name the current phase of our modernity. The condition of the new human being is that of being light and liquid, in constant fluidity. Like liquid, things are not fixed anymore, but malleability and accommodation prevail. Our modernity privileges acceleration, expansion, and flexibility (Bauman 9). Mostly, "'post-modernity,' 'second modernity,' and 'surmodernity,' or otherwise" articulate a radical change "in the arrangement of human cohabitation and in social conditions under which life-politics is nowadays conducted" (10). This radical shift is produced from the passage of previous times of "solid modernity" to our "now," discarding notions of fixity and stability. Our era of virtual reality prefigures the end of the age of mutual personal, corporeal engagement, slowly eroding the sense of community (36) and personal, intimate engagement. The only communities and relationships that can be born in our age are fragile and short-lived.

One of the most striking changes to take place in this shift of the pre-modern to our postmodernity is that of identity: while it was considered as a "fixed thing" in pre-postmodern times (woman, man, spouse, son, daughter, housewife, scholar, grandmother, pariah, bully, etc.), now has been dominated by fluidity, malleability. Identity, under the conditions of liquid modernity, is no longer a project of achieved fixity. Thus, you can be one thing and the next day, another, identity becomes unstable and indeterminate:

> Given the intrinsic volatility and unfixity of all or most identities, it is the ability to "shop around" in the supermarket of identities, the degree of genuine or putative consumer freedom to select one's identity and to hold to it as long as desired, that becomes the royal road to the fulfilment of identity fantasies. Having that ability, one is free to make and unmake identities at will. Or so it seems. [Bauman 83].

This total lack of fixity affects every aspect of postmodern life. Thus, if something considered until some time ago as "concrete" (as individual identity was) can now be bought and discarded, condition *sine qua non* of individual freedom, social relationships lose some (a great deal, in fact) of their condition of durability. How durable could a relationship be if the poles are constantly changing their identities and way of life? As a result, liquid modernity heralds trying times for inter-human togetherness (Tester 174). Efforts to keep the Other, the different, and the foreign at a distance, the decision to preclude the need for personal and even virtual communication, negotiation, and mutual commitment, "is not the only conceivable, but the expectable response to the existential uncertainty rooted in the new fragility or fluidity of social bonds" (Bauman 108). We are all living in a society of volatile values, identities and personal relationships, so "love too has been liquefied" (Tester 174).

In today's liquid modernity, long-term, stable relationships have lost their relevance for ordinary people because the social economy shaping lifestyles demands a short-term workforce. Everything is designed not to endure, but to be replaceable, be it commodities or human relationships. Within this scenario, relationships, like the address lists in mobile phones, are deletable. In liquid modernity, relationships resist long-term binding commitment (Bramham and Wagg 157). Without commitments, there are not serious consequences. Without serious commitments, there is no durability, fixity, or material traces from the past. Further, actions performed today can be easily forgotten tomorrow.

But this new "liquid modernity" may not affect everyone at the same level; those strongly attached to an old ethos will probably be less inclined to embrace this new paradigm. Even more, as we will see, some could argue that a sort of "melancholy" for pre-postmodern times is rooted within our postmodern times. On the other hand, Millennials, born already within a world dominated by fluid simulacra, arguably will celebrate this new fragility or fluidity of social bonds, emphasizing their irresponsibility and flexibility. Youth seems to be emblematic for liquid modernity (Nayak and Kehily 21). Or at least, popular wisdom thinks so, even if youth, like adults as well, can see this era as one dominated by social anxiety and uncertainty.

Teenagers and young adults are condemned to been seen as liquid for antonomasia, or by their tendency to resist labels. By their own elastic and ever-changing nature (we must keep in mind that they, teenagers, are in a constant state of *becoming*), they resist serious commitment. However, there is not really that much discussion about the ways in which teenagers and adults understand love and most of the commentary "seems ad-hoc and clinical, rather than research-based" (Schwartz 51). There seem to be many prejudices, at present, about understanding how adolescents and young adults live, but something is clear; they give much thought to love and romantic commitments. The world we live in encourages teenagers and young adults to think about sex and love commitment constantly, and teens have a whole world organized around mating and dating dramas (Schwartz 59).

It is within this social context of liquid modernity and adolescents' anxiety-ridden attachment to romantic relationships that the return of putrid corpses to haunt dead commitments acts as a signpost of something troubling. These zombies are a walking (dead) contradiction; they are young adults, perfect examples of liquid modernity. However, these zombies, young as they were before their death, reclaim durability, thus prompting a discussion about the parallelism between youth and liquid modernity. What these monsters come to represent is the liquid modernity and ephemeral nature of current romantic relationships between young adults. As *Life After Beth* states, the zombies are here reclaiming everlasting love, a construct postmodernity seems incapable of providing anymore.

In a world dominated by an increasingly longer period of "youngness," fear of serious commitment, one-night stands, flirting, and casual dating, these zombies work as markers of the lack of durable bonds and the films allegorically speak about the need for some stability within our scenario of liquid modernity and consequent lack of certainties. The dead remind us that we should take some promises of eternal love seriously. Tapping into our anxieties about our state of liquid commitment, the zombies refuse to go away or be ignored, transformed as they are in putrid flesh; they are our eternal love partners.

Your Promise of Eternal Love Is Liquid

The main characters of *Life After Beth, Nina Forever,* and *Burying the Ex* are all young adults, their adolescent years barely behind them. Thus, they are more inclined to the cultural logic of liquid modernity than to "solid modernity."

Max (Anton Yelchin), the main character of *Burying the Ex*, has found the woman of his dreams in Olivia (Alexandra Daddario), a witty, naïf, and sweet girl working in an ice-cream shop. They have much in common, most importantly is their shared love for vintage horror pop culture. They both immediately click. The only setback is that Max is already engaged to the controlling Evelyn (Ashley Greene). After some self-doubting, Max decides to break-up with Evelyn. On the day he decides to end their relationship, however, Evelyn is hit by a bus and dies, never knowing her boyfriend wanted to break-up with her that day. So, it is just logical that Evelyn returns from the beyond, hell-bent on restoring their relationship. And plans to make good on their promise to "always be together ... always and forever"—a promise Max is none too enthusiastic about as he has replaced her with Olivia.

In our liquid modernity, where identities are continually shifted, replaced, and commoditized, *Burying the Ex* foregrounds and contrasts concreteness and liquidity. Max and Olivia click together because both share love for common material possessions. Their longing for the vintage (and by the extension, the past and solid modernity), codifies them as foregrounded into a more tangible societal and cultural context, where the past is not something completely dead and obliterated, but living and attractive. On the other hand, Evelyn is depicted as a woman fulfilling and complying with the newest of the new trends: she is a vegan worried about the world's fate and is ecologically conscious. She follows any new development in ecological matters to the point of changing Max's apartment into a "100% green" habitat. It is important that her love for the environment is motivated by the fact that it is a "trendy" subject since she finds no value in "old" things, seeing them as passé and silly. At a pivotal point in the movie, Evelyn removes Max's favorite old movie posters from his walls. When he chastises her for rolling up the posters—thus ruining them—she cannot understand his anger. For Evelyn, these were only old, useless things. Only the "now" has value for the trendy Evelyn. However, after death, she will discard postmodernism and trends to embrace a value linked to fixity: eternal love. After showing up for the first time in Max's apartment, he demands to know how her resurrection was even possible. Her answer is a simple one, "I don't know. Love conquers all." She cannot let Max go and demands their relationship continue even though she is (un)dead. This contradictory movement could be read as symptomatic of our era where people are excited by the prospect of embracing constant change, albeit with an aching necessity to retain some of the concrete promise implicit in "eternal love."

In *Nina Forever*, Holly, a young, shy "vanilla" girl training to be a paramedic, believes that she has found the love of her life in Rob, a co-worker who is still haunted by the tragic and recent death of his girlfriend, Nina, whose name he wears tattooed on his skin as a mark of fixity. The film begins marking the contradictions of young romantic relationships; Holly is chatting with her friends about how "cool" it would be if a man killed himself for love. Holly's friends find the idea repulsive rather than romantic. In the next scene, Rob dumps Holly with the cliché "can we be friends?" Rob considers himself much too dark for such a "vanilla" girl, so the relationship must end.

Nina Forever illustrates identity as a fluid performance rather than a fixed performance through Holly and Rob's relationship; there is a possibility of them getting back together, so Holly changes her style, choosing darker hues in her makeup as well as wearing leather jackets. Clearly, she is trying to—borrowing from Bauman—"shop" for another identity that fits better in her boyfriend's world. While Holly dresses up for him in her "brand new identity," a voiceover of Holly's teacher instructs, ironically, about the meaning and power of a uniform. Holly uses her new clothes as a performative act, an essay about a new identity in a world and age where people can shop for identities as they shop for clothes. Fashion has always been "a mirror for social phenomena" where identity, class, and gender can be constructed and reconstructed (Tseëlon 134). There are not that many differences between the paramedic uniform and her new, "darker" clothes; both are superficial signposts of what she is trying to display as her identity.

Shortly after they both restart their relationship, a series of uncanny occurrences takes place. Rob's dead ex-girlfriend, Nina, materializes every time the new couple has sex. Thus, sex is simply impossible for the couple.

Rather than running away, Holly chooses instead to ignore the most fundamental lesson for paramedics: "some people you can not save." She looks for ways to rescue Rob (who has previously attempted suicide) from his attachment with the past, which haunts him in the form of a bloody, naked zombie.

Like the other films, *Life After Beth* revolves around a young man, Zach (Dane DeHaan), grieving over the death of his girlfriend. However, she soon comes back as a zombie, and, after the initial shock, the young man is happy to get his girlfriend back. At least, until she starts to rot, smells bad, and becomes increasingly erratic in her behavior. When Zach starts to date another girl, Beth becomes "disposable" since she is not the girl she used to be. The first thing that Zach appreciates about his new girl, Erica Wexler (Anna Kendrick), is her perfect, soft skin. Zach is clearly contrasting Erica's skin with that of the rugged flesh of his ex (dead) girlfriend, in what can be read as a very shallow and superficial interest, a trope associated with postmodernity and individualism. When Zach finally spills all the truth about Beth's nature to his ex—who was, until that point, totally oblivious to her zombified condition—Beth affirms, "you don't love me anymore," while denying her condition as zombie. What truly worries all these women is the fact that their men do not love them anymore, rather than their nature as rotting zombies. They are quick to contrast their rotten (liquid) nature with the fixity of eternal love that "conquers it all." In this sense, Beth, Evelyn, and Nina confront and exercise violence upon all the new girls as a form of negating reality. In the current era of liquid modernity, their zombified nature cannot endure and promises about eternal love are simply silly.

In a world where, as Zygmunt Bauman puts it, everything is less durable and in flux, social relations are constantly evolving (Bauman 19–20), and these situations especially affect young people. *Nina Forever* repeatedly addresses the young age of Rob's new girlfriend. "How old is she?" asks the resurrected Nina. Then, in another scene, "God, Rob, she is young. [To Holly] Naked, you could pass for 16." Even Nina's mother, who has been urging Rob to continue his life after meeting Holly, asks about her age. She also asks Holly if Rob is her first serious relationship with a man. Obviously, being young is a sure sign that the relationship will not last long. Nobody seems to take young love seriously. If liquid modernity is the figure of impermanence and change, where love has become fluctuating, youth, with their fleeting relationships and persistent mood swings, is the expression par excellence of current society.

However, Holly works hard to keep their relationship going, even accepting that she must share his bed with the battered and decaying Nina. In fact, in a last attempt to gain Nina's approval, Holly tattooes her skin with the same motto ("Nina forever") that Rob wears. Even if the attempt is unsuccessful, tattoos work as marks of fixity, a past inscribed in the skin. The tattoo, as a signifier of memory, becomes a subversive form of expression by reinstating fixity within social fluidity and ephemeral time. However, as Martin Butler argues, a tattoo "represents both fixity and fluidity" at the same time (158), since it can be imitated, emulated, and appropriated. In fact, the tattoo makes things worse. Nina comes back because Rob is unable to forget her, and Holly's new tattoo only works as a form of enhancement of the materiality of the "ex" lurking in the corners of their relationship. After her efforts at appeasing Nina are unsuccessful, Holly tries to wipe away any trace of Nina from Rob's apartment. However, Nina reappears over and over again, leaving a bloody trail of herself behind, a material reminder of her constant presence. In this narrative, playing with forms of fixity (the tattoo) only increases materiality.

The latter is clearly seen in the final scene. Rob visits Holly for the first time after a prolonged break-up. He is sure that Nina is now in the past, after Rob "breaks up" with Nina's parents, the last link to her. However, Nina still appears to Holly, even if she is sleeping with other men. Nina is under Holly's skin. There is no happy ending. It seems that Holly was aching for "solid modernity" from the beginning, when she desires a man ready to die for love. Also, Holly's stubbornness in continuing the relationship and her unbridled love for Rob could be read as an attraction to the dark, towards death. She seems fascinated by Rob and Nina's everlasting love (durability), their tragic love affair, his suicide attempt, and the mystery surrounding his gloomy person. Death and blood are always present in the story. Both Holly and Rob drive at high-speeds, risking their lives in a meaningless way, while pomegranate juice and pulp stands for blood and flesh, and dead dogs fill the streets. The fixity of death, heavily in contrast with the fluidity of life, seems erotic to both Holly and Rob. After all, we, human beings, "defend whatever gives us fixity—a sense of *being* grounded—over the dialectic of movement where freedom, truth and change lie" (Ragland 87, emphasis in the original).

All three female zombies seem indestructible: women who had come with renewed powers, thus increasing their material presence and persistence in the present. Nina shows up almost magically every time Rob and Holly have sex. She is a corpse. Her body still showing signs of her accident (crystal shards still deep into her flesh), but omnipresent all the same. Both Beth and Evelyn, on the other hand, have come back from the grave with super strength. A recurring gag in *Burying the Ex* is Evelyn's newfound super strength. She demonstrates a higher stamina as a zombie than when she was alive: she jogs without breaking a sweat, can have non-stop sex, and can crush metal with her bare hands. Their increase in strength highlights these women's decisions to keep the promises of eternal love enduring through the years. It should be noted that liquid modernity comes with a plethora of words and images related to frailty, such as volatile, ephemeral, and evasive (Bauman 74), which work in contrast with durability, fixity, and concreteness. These women's super strength anchors materiality in a world favoring disintegration.

As mentioned, these female zombies are rife with contradictions. They are both dead and alive, they are especially durable, if decaying, and they are creatures of liquid modernity but want everlasting commitment. Nina presents all the external features of a corpse. Beth and Evelyn, on the other hand, come back as beautiful and "fresh" as they were the day they died. However, their material presence—an allegory for the promises of everlasting love—cannot last. Liquid modernity is stronger and, with the exception of Nina (a presence sustained and later accepted by the two partners), they start to disappear. As *Life After Beth* and *Burying the Ex* progress, the zombies start to physically rot. It is interesting to observe that both Beth and Evelyn's processes of rotting seems to accelerate once their respective boyfriends meet or start to date new girls. It appears the process of liquid modernity begins after both Zach and Max start dating again, a signpost to the lack of durability of the promises of eternal love. The reality of an era dominated by the volatility of human relationships begins to destroy the bodies of these women who insist on getting attached to impossible promises. In fact, Beth's first manifestations of her new zombified nature (external rotting, increased strength, extreme feelings of coldness) manifest after Zach's first attempts to break-up with her. Before that, she was, at least physically, perfectly normal.

There is another issue that all three women share: all of them become increasingly irritating "exes." Nina impedes Rob's normal sex life. Both Beth and Evelyn get increasingly controlling about the whereabouts of their boyfriends. Beth gets temperamental if Zach is not around her and both she and Evelyn want sex even if their decaying bodies make them less sexually desirable. The situation can be read as their boyfriends exchanging their girls for "better" women, thus enhancing male shallowness.

Still, there is an important point to make. All three men, Zach, Rob and Max, react to their girlfriends' deaths with genuine sorrow. Even Max, who had wanted to break-up with Evelyn before her untimely death, falls into a deep depression. Rob attempts suicide to escape his pain and loneliness, while Zach insists on wearing Beth's scarf as a way to keep her somehow with him. These periods of mourning reveal genuine caring and love sustaining these young women and men rather than just shallow intimacy and the desire to "hook up" for a night. It is true that Zach, Rob, and Max forget their promises of eternal love, but they do so only when they fall in love again and only after a healthy process of mourning, in which they release the lost loved one in order to love again and move on. Thus, the zombies are doubly pathological because of their inability to accept postmodernity and volatility and because they could be framed as suffering from melancholia, a mental state linked to our liquid modernity.

Mourning, Melancholy and Zombies

Sigmund Freud wrote his famous essay "Mourning and Melancholy" in 1915 and published it in 1917. His purpose was to "cast some light on the nature of melancholia by comparing it with the normal effect of mourning" (Freud 267). Freud points to the fact that mourning and melancholy are similar since both conditions are answers to the loss of something beloved. The difference lies in a pathological condition. To Freud, it is important to point out that, even if both mourning and melancholy are departures from the normal attitude of life, the former does not require medical treatment and will, eventually, fade away. At some point, the suffering person will be able to resume some normalcy. On the other hand, melancholia works as a dark reverse of mourning: a melancholic person will experience a "profoundly painful depression, a loss of interest in the outside world, the loss of the ability to love, the inhibition of any kind of performance" and a general sense of depression of the Self (*ibid.*).

In mourning, the beloved object does not exist anymore, so all libido previously attached to that object must be withdrawn from it. At first, even in a healthy person, the task seems to be much too demanding, and the person experiences a phantasmagoric attachment to the lost object but, eventually, respect for reality wins the day (Freud 268), and the person resumes his or her common life, accepting the loss and moving on. But grievers do not simply detach libido from the lost object. According to Freud, they reinvest the freed libido in a new object, in so doing accepting consolation in the form of a substitute for what has been lost and bringing the work of mourning to a decisive end. In this sense, all the boyfriends meeting and dating new women are putting an end to their sense of mourning, thus moving on with their lives.

The melancholic state displays something which is lacking in mourning; the diminishing of the ego on a grand scale. Unlike mourning, libido completely identifies with the lost object in melancholia. So, when the object exists no more, the object-loss was transformed into an ego-loss (270). Thus, the person suffering melancholia cannot properly continue his or her daily life since what has been lost, in fact, was the ego, and with it, some sense of the Self. The person is trapped narcissistically in the past and is unable to continue properly with the normal rhythms of life. Between the aforementioned differences lie the aspects that formulate mourning as a normal state after some powerful loss, while mourning is a state of illness. In the melancholic state, the past is glued to the present, so the zombie is a fitting metaphor. It is in this way that the zombie might be thought as a melancholic figure due to their expressed goal of fidelity in the re-creation of a lost past.

It is worth mentioning that melancholia and clinging to the past is not merely zombie "business." There are other love triangles in the films, which are constituted with the torturous relationship that Rob shares with Nina's parents and Zach with Beth's parents, Maury (John C. Reilly) and Geenie (Molly Shannon). Zach continues visiting his ex-in-laws with the excuse of playing chess with Maury; Rob reads the chapters of the book that Dan (David Troughton) is slowly writing. Rob feels responsibilities towards his ex-father-in-law Dan and mother-in-law Sally (Elizabeth Elvin) and, therefore, maintains a close relationship with them although the link between them is gone. He visits them every Sunday, even after he has met Holly. While the three characters are paralyzed by Nina's tragic death, the relationship between them is framed by harmony (i.e., the three of them mutually feed their melancholic state). The Sunday visits shape a ritual of fixity where the loss is not addressed but reenacted. But when Rob decides to start his relationship with Holly and presents her to his former in-laws waiting for approval, some kind of rupture and uneasiness sits between them. That is the concrete moment in which Rob begins a process of mourning, which gives him closure.

The melancholic person sees his "Self" as unworthy, despicable and, therefore, expecting punishment (Freud 243–44). This manifests in the fact that Nina's parents live surrounded by their daughter's belongings (a painting of her hanging on the wall, her favorite songs saved in Dan's computer), thus torturing themselves with her absence. They are trapped in the past, unable to move on. The moral dimension of melancholy manifests in the scene where Rob sees his former in-laws in a restaurant to "break-up" with them. There, Dan tells Rob that he can choose any girl to replace Nina and move on, but they, on the contrary, cannot replace their daughter with another girl. It seems Sally and Dan are trapped in a melancholic (pre-modern) state.

Meanwhile, Beth's parents seem to be ready to move on. The first scene of them after the funeral depicts them boxing their daughter's belongings, a step toward healthy closure. However, they soon start to behave suspiciously, avoiding Zach's visits. The reality that both parents hide their zombified daughter, who has come back from the grave, spurs their sudden avoidance of Zach. Rather than manifest fear about this uncanny return, they choose to keep their daughter with them, living all together as a "happy family," to the point that they hide from Beth the fact that she is a zombie. For Beth's parents, her return is an example of biblical resurrection and nobody should question this fact. They do their best to avoid the "Z" word, an attitude that can be read as a negation of the death of their daughter. At first, Zach agrees with this attitude and together, with his (ex)in-laws, he decides to accept

Beth's return as if nothing happened, since issues such as life and death are just "relative" things. Zach is also unable to overcome Beth's death and chooses to live trapped within a state of melancholia. However, a rupture takes place after Zach meets Erica, replacing melancholy for mourning and proper closure.

The zombies, too, are trapped in the past, especially in relationships that were long dead. For example, when Nina visits Rob and Holly for the first time, he presents her as his "dead ..." while she finishes the uncompleted sentence with the word "girlfriend." We argue that Rob is desperately trying to put her behind as an "ex" underlining her dead condition, while she proclaims herself just as his girlfriend. Rather, she declares, "I'm not an ex!"

Now, why all this interest in melancholia? First, the context of 9/11, with the media imagery constantly oscillating "between trauma and melancholia" in eternal repetitions fosters a gloomy state and permeates the new millennium (Cavedon 170). Still, postmodernism and liquid modernity also sustain and channel melancholia. The engine of social progress and digital developments disrupts the sense of place and time for people (Blazer 142), thus working as sources of anxieties, while melancholy for the pre-modern world and for the failure of modernity sits within the general mood. Jean-Francois Lyotard claims that postmodernist aesthetics constitutes a discourse of melancholy: it fails to successfully mourn the metanarratives of emancipation so dear to modernism (81). The crisis of modernity and its goal of social progress mark an inexorable trauma in the social fabric of postmodernism (Moglen xiv), while melancholia remains a human reaction to unfilled promises. Liquid modernity is just the result of the debacle of the "betterment" of communities and citizens promised long ago. In this sense, melancholia is the postmodern affection par excellence (Gibson 77).

Interestingly, Martin Middeke and Christina Wald suggest that our present interest in melancholia follows a desire for the return of emotion into an emotionless (zombified) world. Further, they imply that present popularity of melancholia could be read as an indicator for postmodernism's waning (15). It is possible to argue that these zombies, returning for a promise of eternal love, and those young men, grieving for their lost objects of love, certainly sustain a potential waning of liquid modernity—an aching among youth for more material forms of relationships in our context of liquidity. It can be implied that, lurking in the dark corners of liquid modernity, exist the traces of "solid politics" of affection ready to come back from the grave and grab our legs.

Lastly, we must point out that ghosts, rather than zombies, may have worked well in these narratives. (In fact, Nina's implied haunting of Holly into the present codifies her more like a ghost from a long dead relationship rather than a zombie.) But the choice to use zombies in these stories, because of their tangible presence, clearly emphasizes material flesh and presence, which contrasts heavily with the ephemeral nature of liquid modernity. This highlights an uncomfortable duality present in these texts; the boys all long for permanence (demonstrated in the rituals of melancholia practiced by the ex-boyfriends such as wearing their ex girlfriends' clothes [signposts of fixity and desire of permanence]), but they want to accelerate the destruction of their undead girlfriends (liquid modern life-politics).

Current modernity is a meeting point of contradictions. The desire for eternal love is simultaneously desired and dreaded, a possibility and a utopia, a final destination in life and impossibility in life. The returning corpses of the three films here analyzed cheat death and remain, in a material way, in the present. But their materiality cannot escape rot. They become increasingly horrid, putrid, and fleshless as the days goes by, a reminder of our own future and a sign of the impossibility of lasting—in accordance with liquid modernity—while we melancholically and contradictorily ache for durability.

Beth, Nina, and Evelyn embody all these contradictions: they slowly rot and disappear, but not quickly enough, so their ex-boyfriends must accelerate things, formulating attempts to eliminate their undead girlfriends. The men must destroy all things solid to leave the past behind and fully embrace liquid modernity.

Conclusion

Robin Wood argues that the monsters of horror films are embodiments of our nightmares, creatures born from the repressed anxieties given in a concrete society and time. After our analysis, we could point out that these zombified girls allegorize the dread of an "ex" who is unable to understand that the relationship is over—that what once was, is there no more. They—zombies, ex partners—are "residues which go on past their endings" (Blackshaw 100), messy, untidy things that materially connects with the past, disrupting perfect liquidity and ephemerality.

These women, who are unable to overcome the end of a relationship, become material obstacles or symptoms within liquid modernity and its set of rules. These are times of flexibility and ephemeral relationships, of nightly "hook-ups" rather than serious commitment. Nothing is made to last anymore. Still, there could be people with passé ideas, zombies from other times, clawing for materiality in an immaterial world.

However, all the characters, parents and young people alike, want—within a melancholic state—to supplant ineffable loss with fixity. They are not happy to live in a world where promises of eternal love do not exist anymore. If melancholia is a side effect of the ever-changing nature of liquid modernity—melancholy for some durability—the zombies are embodiments of this melancholic state. These women are destroyed at the end; liquid modernity wins. However, they are destroyed because there is another object of love there to replace the lost one. Eternal love cannot exist within a scenario of liquid modernity, but some durability is saved at the end.

Current zombie films are obliged to engage with the politics of liquidity. Rotting corpses are material reminders of the past clinging to the present and act as signposts of our undeletable sins and actions, which still resonate in the present. Institutions based in interpersonal bonds, such as marriage, are increasingly becoming "zombies" within a world of radical lightness and mobility. Liquid modernity and new personal relationships (especially romantic relationships) create individuals who are incredibly anxious and incredibly desperate to find a source of certainty and, yet, incapable of achieving it. Consequently, there emerge paradoxical circumstances where individuals are progressively more aware of the dangers of too much liquidity and how impotent they are to stop this new form of sociability but find the forms of alleviation, i.e., materiality and serious commitment, equally dreadful, thus generating a new source of anxiety, which translates into rich paths for popular culture to explore, especially within horror cinema—a medium with social and individual fear at its core. The zombie film, which perfectly encapsulates and illustrates this contradiction (material flesh rotting away), is then the perfect vehicle to channel the new anxieties of our era of liquid modernity and melancholia for durability.

As the above analysis suggests, these zombies attempt to transcend the ideological, social, and cultural limitations of liquid modernity while constituting a significant movement towards the current melancholy for lost materiality, an issue shared by the living and the dead.

Works Cited

Bauman, Zygmunt. *Liquid Modernity*. Polity, 2000.

Blackshaw, Tony. *Zygmunt Bauman Textbook*. Routledge, 2005.

Blazer, Dan. *The Age of Melancholy: Major Depression and Its Social Origins*. Routledge, 2005.

Bramham, Peter, and Stephen Wagg. *An Introduction to Leisure Studies: Principles and Practice*. SAGE, 2014.

Burying the Ex. Directed by Joe Dante, Voltage Pictures, 2014.

Butler, Martin. "Tattoo Travels: On Mobilities and Mobilizations of American Skin Art." *Mobile and Entangled America(s)*, edited by Maryemma Graham and Wilfried Raussert, Routledge, 2016, pp. 155–66.

Caceres, Veronica. "Humanization in the Advertising Industry." *Organisations and Humanisation: Perspectives on Organising Humanisation and Humanising Organisations*, edited by Myrte van de Klundert and Robert van Boeschoten, Routledge, 2017, pp. 61–70.

Cavedon, Christina. *Cultural Melancholia: U.S. Trauma Discourses Before and After 9/11*. Brill, 2015.

Freud, Sigmund. "Mourning and Melancholia." *The Penguin Freud Reader*, edited by Adam Phillips. Penguin, 2006, pp. 201–18.

Gibson, Andrew. *Postmodernity, Ethics and the Novel: From Leavis to Levinas*. Routledge, 1999.
Kaklamanidou, Betty. *Genre, Gender and the Effects of Neoliberalism: The New Millennium Hollywood Rom Com*. Routledge, 2013.
Life After Beth. Directed by Jeff Baena, Abbolita Productions, 2014.
Lyotard, Jean-François. *The Postmodern Condition: A Report on Knowledge*. Translated by Geoff Bennington and Brian Massumi, U of Minnesota P, 1984.
Middeke, Martin, and Christina Wald. "Melancholia as a Sense of Loss: An Introduction." *The Literature of Melancholia: Early Modern to Postmodern*, edited by Martin Middeke and Christina Wald, Palgrave Macmillan, 2011, pp. 1–22.
Moglen, Seth. *Mourning Modernity: Literary Modernism and the Injuries of American Capitalism*. Stanford University Press, 2007.
Nayak, Anoop, and Mary Jane Kehily. *Gender, Youth and Culture: Young Masculinities and Femininities*, 2nd ed. Palgrave Macmillan, 2013.
Nina Forever. Directed by Ben and Chris Blaine, Jeva Films, 2015.
Ragland, Ellie. *Essays on the Pleasures of Death: From Freud to Lacan*. Routledge, 1995.
Round, Julia. *Gothic in Comics and Graphic Novels: A Critical Approach*. McFarland, 2014.
Schwartz, Pepper. "What Elicits Romance, Passion, and Attachment, and How Do They Affect Our Lives Throughout the Life Cycle?" *Romance and Sex in Adolescence and Emerging Adulthood: Risks and Opportunities*, edited by Ann Crouter and Alan Booth, Lawrence Erlbaum Associates, 2006, pp. 49–60.
Tseëlon, Efrat. "Fashion, Fantasy and Anxiety." *The Emotions and Cultural Analysis*, edited by Ana Marta González, Routledge, 2012, pp. 133–44.
Tester, Keith. *The Social Thought of Zygmunt Bauman*. Palgrave Macmillan, 2004.
Wood, Robin. "An Introduction to the American Horror Film." *Planks of Reason: Essays on the Horror Film*, edited by Barry Keith Grant and Christopher Sharrett, Scarecrow Press, 2004, pp. 107–41.

Braaaiiinnnsss
The Recipe for Love in iZombie

JENNIFER RACHEL DUTCH

The term "zombie" calls to mind the image of a reanimated, rotting corpse tearing chunks of flesh from a still-screaming victim. This scene of a mindless zombie engaging in thoughtless, violent, meaningless cannibalism reveals all of the traits that make this monster so terrifying for viewing audiences: inhuman appetites in a human-looking monster. From the slow-moving zombies in George A. Romero's 1960s classic film *Night of the Living Dead* (1968) to the wandering hordes of dead in the recent smash-hit television series *The Walking Dead* (2010–present), zombies instill horror for viewers because they break seemingly immutable rules: the dead stay dead and people do not eat people. Zombies are monstrous precisely because they violate society's norms, especially those related to food and eating. Since zombies do not plan their meals and feed exclusively on human flesh, any living person could become their next victim at any time. As out-of-control cannibals, zombies devour the raw flesh of their still-living human victims, without regard for anything resembling proper table manners. Finished with its feast, the zombie sets out to hunt for its next victim, with no sense of satiety. The zombie's futile existence focused on finding its next gruesome meal forces the audience to confront the idea that human existence may be just as empty as the monster's soulless, rotting eyes.

The CW series *iZombie* (2015–present) takes this trope of zombie cannibalism and flips it so that consuming human brains becomes the method that lead character Olivia "Liv" Moore (Rose McIver), the medical student turned zombie turned morgue-attendant, uses to preserve her humanity. By adhering to the social norms surrounding food and eating by planning and cooking meals, following elaborate recipes, and sharing meals with friends and family (including basic table manners like using silverware and sitting at a table), Liv leverages the "rules" of society to reaffirm her identity as a vibrant, productive person. For example, during the second season episode "Max Wager," Liv Moore sits down to a high-class meal of "Clams Casino." Instead of mindlessly gulping mouthfuls of fresh brains from the busted-open cranial cavity of a still-warm corpse like a typical zombie, Liv slurps finely chopped gambler brains skillfully combined with other delectable ingredients and baked atop a freshly opened clam. It is clear that Liv's meal violates all of the rules of a terrifying zombie feast. The recipe is carefully chosen and thoughtfully created, not mindlessly consumed; the food is cooked, not consumed raw; the meal is slow and savored, not rushed and meaningless. Step by step, as the audience watches Liv prepare and consume the meal—chopping brains, mixing ingredients, heating the prepared clam shells in the oven, and savoring the final dish—they are able to see a recognizably human experience in the delicious-looking meal. Instead of horror, the audience identifies with Liv's predicament. At this moment eating these brains does not signify a descent into inhumanity for Liv, but instead represents the opposite—her desire to cling to her human identity. For Liv, consuming human tissue is what keeps her human. Ignoring her need to feed and allowing the hunger to grow would mean that Liv risks descending into "full on zombie mode" and becoming the monster that she fears. Only by regularly eating human brains can she maintain some semblance of a real life, even while dead.

Moreover, the meals that Liv makes out of brains do more than just keep her alive—they become a powerful mechanism that Liv uses to forge connections with her closest friends and deepest loves. The individuals who accept zombified Liv for who—and what—she is represent the same people who watch as Liv cooks her brain-infused foods and sit at the table to eat with her. Her co-workers may eat sandwiches while she eats brains, but their calm acceptance of her dietary needs signals the growing trust in their relationships. Most important, Liv uses food to establish and stabilize in her romantic relationships with the men that she loves. Romance and food are inseparably interwoven as Liv connects over simple snacks with a man who shares her change in life status, cooks up a passionate dinner to woo an amorous zombie lover into a sexual liaison, or simply eats a meal filled with bits of brains in front of her still-human former fiancé. Far from finding Liv a repulsive monster, these friends and lovers see Liv as a crucial part of their own lives, not in spite of the fact that she is a zombie, but because of everything that goes into making Liv Moore herself.

In this essay, I argue that, in *iZombie,* Liv's elaborate recipes demonstrate that she has not transformed into a flesh-ripping beast but serves as the mechanism by which she maintains her tenuous hold on human culture. By connecting Liv's use of societal norms related to food and eating—cooking recipes, eating politely, sharing meals with friends and family—to her desire to live a fulfilling and complete life, even as a zombie, I demonstrate that brains are the most important ingredient in the recipe for Liv's life, loves, and hope for the future.

Eating Meat Makes Us Human

The aphorism "tell me what you eat and I shall tell you what you are," first published by French writer Jean Anthelme Brillat-Savarin in his groundbreaking work *The Physiology of Taste* (1825), has been quoted so often as to have become clichéd (Brillat-Savarin 15). The notion that the foods people consume communicate their identities has been the subject of research within and across disparate disciplines from anthropology to Women's studies and everything in between, coalescing in the emerging discipline of Food studies. As Jeff Miller and Jonathan Deutsch reveal in *Food Studies: An Introduction to Research Methods* (2009), Food studies "is not the study of food itself but rather the study of relationships between food and human experience" (3). Food studies researchers are interested in discovering how the whats, whens, wheres, whys, and with whoms of the foods people eat reveal individual, family, community, and societal identities.

For these experts, the rules that societies establish for cooking and eating "good" food are the cornerstones of civilization; it was not that being human enabled people to cook, but that cooking made people human. As Michael Pollan emphasizes in his ode to cooking, *Cooked: A Natural History of Transformation* (2013), applying fire to vegetables and meats enabled early humans the luxury of time. Pollan explains, "Freed from the necessity of spending our days gathering large quantities of raw food and chewing (and chewing) it, humans could now devote their time, and their metabolic resources, to other purposes, like creating a culture" (6). Cooked foods separate people from brutish animals who devour their prey uncooked on the spot of its demise (Visser 1). The tension between the oppositions of nature/culture and raw/cooked comes through in the "culinary triangle" proposed by French anthropologist Claude Levi-Strauss. This "culinary triangle" consists of raw, cooked, and rotted and draws a distinct binary opposition between nature and culture in which raw is associated with nature and "the cooked is a cultural transformation of the raw, whereas the rotted is a natural transformation" (41). Cooking led to the development of human culture which, in turn, supports and enhances people's ability to cook. In other words, without cooking there would be no culture, and without culture there would be no cooking.

While eating is a biological necessity, the meaning of food flows from culture; nature sets the need to eat, while nurture defines the rules. As E.N. Anderson explains in *Everyone Eats* (2005), food preferences are "a biocultural phenomenon. Biology sets the broad parameters; culture fine tunes the actual patterns of behavior" (73). Culture tells people not only what is considered "good" food, but what is considered food at all. Non-foods include products labeled "disgusting" or taboo, though these designations vary from group to group, and "for many people 'good food' is simply the food they are used to" (Anderson 99). Designations of "good" food and "bad" food, even taboo food and nonfood, serve as markers of identity. People who eat the same foods we do are like us, and people who eat weird, disgusting, or taboo foods are "Other" and therefore untrustworthy, unclean, and dangerous. As Prose declares, "Not only does the Other blithely and greedily consume what we know is unclean; they would like nothing better than to defile us by making us eat it, too" (225). Therefore, when seeing someone eat a food that is foreign or forbidden, people not only feel disgust but also fear. The meal is not only wrong because it consists of the consumption of nonfood, but it is disturbing because it challenges an individual's sense of identity. They must question if the eater of the strange or unusual food is even human at all.

Eating Humans Makes Us Monsters

The unease at the idea of a foreign or forbidden meal is even more distinct when the meal consists of human flesh. Cannibalism is the ultimate taboo (Visser 5). The threat of not only eating forbidden food, but being eaten as forbidden food, is so disturbing that the fear of cannibalism lurks unbidden below the surface of the human psyche. Margaret Visser declares in her book *The Rituals of Dinner* (1991), "Somewhere at the back of our minds, carefully walled off from ordinary consideration and discourse, lies the idea of cannibalism—that human beings might *become* food, and eaters of each other" (3). Perhaps that is why the most monstrous element of the zombie is not its dead, decaying, lumbering body, but its unrelenting, insatiable need to feed on human flesh. Zombies are the ultimate cannibals because they have no other reason for existing than to seek out their next meals.

Moreover, zombies not only engage in cannibalism but do so without any thought other than feeding. Even in human societies that engage in cannibalism, as Visser reveals, the eating of human flesh has been something steeped in culture: ritualized and rule-bound (15). The random attack of the individual zombie or feeding frenzy of the zombie horde violates all of the rules of polite society. No table manners guide the meal indicating that there is no meaning behind the consumption. Despite its often-ritualized reality, cannibalism has been used "for symbolic purposes as an embodiment of structureless confusion" (Visser 6). Zombies take cannibalistic confusion to new heights and layer the devouring of the human body with animalistic barbarism. Zombie feasting is the supreme example of cannibalism as "total confusion: a lack of morality, law, and structure; it stands for what is brutish, utterly inhuman" (Visser 6). The sight of a zombie's gaping maw dripping with blood chewing the skin of a still-living victim reaffirms the inhumanity of zombies. They are terrifying not only because they eat people but because, in so doing, they abandon all of the rules and regulations that govern civilization. The horror of their feasts is accentuated by a total lack of table manners.

Zombies are the nature/culture divide made flesh. The zombie's human-like body is a vessel for an insatiable appetite. They are borne by pure instinct and stripped of any connections to life, family, community, or culture. Zombies revert to the most basic of instincts: the need to feed. They are one with nature, stripped of culture. Shaka McGlotten and Steve Jones explain in their introduction to *Zombies and Sexuality* (2014), "The zombie—animated flesh evacuated of identity and agency—enlivens concepts of life or of humanity in which the human is unconstrained by social or cultural limits. Zombies are freed of any obligations, other than to their own hunger" (6). Although technically no longer human, zombies retain human form. They *look* human, though they no longer *act* human, especially during their ravenous, uncontrolled eating. This connection between human appearance and monstrous behavior enhances the horror for audiences as the corpse-like zombie devours human flesh and thereby reveals how thin the barrier is between civilization and barbarism. The audience comes face to face with an image of their own mortality and the fallacy of the power of their individual identity. They too could become zombies or the food for zombies.

Traditional zombie stories, from *Night of the Living Dead* to *The Walking Dead*, lend themselves to the binary opposition of monster versus human. As reanimated corpses bent on devouring the living, the horror in zombie behavior arises from just how *inhuman* they have become. Clasen supports this notion in "The Anatomy of a Zombie: A Bio-Psychological Look at the Undead Other," where he explains, "The zombie probably confirms the moral suspicion that most monsters are, or were, actually human. But simultaneously, the zombie in its utter repulsiveness panders to a more disturbing, base tendency to think in terms of us versus them, and it must be terminated with extreme prejudice. It might have been 'us' at some point, but certainly is no more" (19–20). Therefore, the plot of zombie stories often focuses on the human survivors, rather than the monsters themselves. Zombie stories, then, are human stories. The monsters are merely the means for the conflict.

What happens, then, when the zombie becomes the protagonist of the story? In many zombie stories, the dead rising is simply an excuse to focus on the plight of the human survivors. More recent zombie stories challenge this typical narrative, such as *Shaun of the Dead* (2004) and *Warm Bodies* (2013), where zombie characters are shown with recognizably human emotions and behaviors beyond a simple, animalistic need to feed. In his book *American Zombie Gothic*, Kyle William Bishop recognizes that these newer stories, with more human-like zombies, bring new demands for the audience as they are "being asked to relate to the zombies in a more direct way; instead of simply seeing their own potential death in the familiar visages of the walking dead foes, viewers are being encouraged to sympathize with the zombies, recognizing them as fully realized individual characters and even rooting for them in their narrative plights" (Bishop 167). This humanized zombie makes room for different ways for zombie stories to ask what it means to be human and to explore the anxieties and conflicts that infuse the society and the zombie stories that they produce (Bishop 207).

You Are Who You Eat

However, changing the rules of the zombie story also means renegotiating the relationship between the zombie and its human food source. For this new generation of humanized zombies, there is a need to grapple with the desire to devour people while attempting to live alongside them. Still fully aware of the taboo of cannibalism, self-aware zombies may be caught between the need to feed and the need to stay human. Instead of feeling horror at the idea of monsters mindlessly ripping at their victims, the audience is encouraged to identify with the struggle that these more sympathetic zombies must endure. Food and food source must live side-by-side and the result is a complex situation ripe for storytelling potential.

The CW television program *iZombie* tackles the question of a human-like zombie in its protagonist Olivia "Liv" Moore. At the beginning of the series, Liv has her life planned out. She will finish her residency, become a heart surgeon, marry the love of her life, Major Lilywhite (Robert Buckley), and live happily ever after. Instead, she attends a boat party where a scratch from a stranger turns her into a zombie. Only a few months later, she traded her hospital residency for a job at the morgue, dumped Major, spends most of her time avoiding her friends and family, and lives in terror of someone discovering her secret. Liv's struggle to remain human despite dining on human brains comes through in her struggle to find a food source and keep her need to feed a secret. The way in which *iZombie* presents this struggle is by transforming Liv's relationship to food so that eating brains no longer represents the loss of humanity but becomes the single route for holding onto the remnants of humanity without turning into a mindless monster. As a zombie, Olivia "Liv" Moore's access to a steady diet of human brains is the only defense against the destruction of her humanity.

For Liv, her transformation from human into zombie has been both physical and emotional. Her hair turned white, and her skin became intensely pale. Most importantly, she acquired what she calls "unique dietary needs"—an intense craving for and need to eat human brains. While eating brains is distasteful, she cannot go without. In the pilot episode, Liv explains her zombie diet to Ravi Chakrabarti (Rahul Kohli), her understanding boss at the morgue and unfailing ally, when he discovers her eating Insta-Noodles mixed with "Jane Doe" brain and hot sauce. Liv says, "If I don't eat I become dumber, meaner, and I'm afraid if I let it go too long I'll go all George Romero" ("Pilot"). In other words, Liv recognizes that she *must* eat human brains, even if she does not want to, otherwise she risks losing her humanity and turning into a mindless, brain-eating monster.

Liv's terror at the becoming a monster reveals the emotional side of the transformation. Everything that she wanted, and everything that made her who she was, ended when she became a zombie. Not only is Liv forced to eat brains, she is terrified of being discovered. Her fear has led her to isolate herself from her friends and family. She explains in "Pilot":

> I've tortured myself obsessing over every worst case scenario. Like my best friend catching me eating brains. Or my brother being consumed in a zombie apocalypse that I unwitting bring on. But it's not like I can talk it out or confide in my loved ones what's going on with me. I have no idea who I am anymore, what purpose, if any, I serve.

Her life as a doctor, daughter, sister, friend, and fiancée ended at the boat party. Now, her life must go on as a zombie. The question for Liv is how to continue to have a life, even while dead.

For Liv, the very food that reinforces her separation from the people who mean the most to her also represents a pathway back to a meaningful life. Eating brains establishes a relationship between Liv and the victim. As Liv explains in the pilot, it is one of the side-effects that, "When I eat a brain I get visions, flashes of memories or dreams." These visions allow Liv to share the past experiences of the people whose brain she consumed. Even more, after eating a person's brain, Liv takes on some of that person's personality traits. When she eats an artist's brain, Liv sees the world with a painter's eye and creates artwork of her own. When she eats the brains of a pathological liar, Liv cannot help but tell lies. Since the brains that Liv eats typically come from murder victims, she has the unique ability to help solve their murders. As Ravi exclaims in the pilot when Liv is reluctant to share information gleaned from a vision, "Liv, you ate the girl's temporal lobe. Going to the police with her potential murderer is the least you can do." However, helping police detective Clive Babineaux (Malcolm Goodwin) solve cases gives Liv a new sense of purpose. Pretending to be a psychic, Liv is able to parlay her visions into reliable clues that Babineaux can use to track down the culprit in each of the murders. As the pilot episode makes clear, for Liv, being "a zombie psychic who eats murder victim brains" becomes a way for her to reclaim her life and have "a way to contribute. A reason to be not alive." She may not be able to become a doctor since she cannot risk spreading the infection to her patients. She may not be able to marry Major since she does not want to "zombify" the love her life. She may not be able to confide in her best friend or her mom. But what she can do is help find justice for the people whose brains keep her alive and human, and that is a purpose in what would otherwise be a purposeless existence.

While some of Liv's meals are quick and easy, such as brain-infused pizza rolls, she also often takes time and effort to whip up elaborate recipes with many ingredients and multiple steps. For example, she blends freshly procured brain matter in a smooth batter and bakes brain scones. The time and effort that Liv puts into her recipes is especially noteworthy because zombie palates in this world are unrefined. They have a taste for brains while everything else, except for spicy hot sauce, is rendered thoroughly tasteless. Therefore, the fact that Liv denies herself the instant gratification of chowing down on fresh brains and instead takes the time to whip eggs, dice peppers, and chop brains to make an omelet reveals just how important maintaining her humanity is for Liv. After all, for Liv, there is very little difference in flavor between brains tartar or a brain "cheeseburger" complete with lettuce, tomato, and bacon on a fresh roll. Liv's choice to cook her meals (even when it is just adding brains on top of a frozen dinner) demonstrates that she has not transformed into a flesh-ripping beast, but instead maintains her tenuous hold on humanity. Liv's conformity to cultural norms—from preparing and cooking her food to eating her meals with a knife and fork—separates her identity from the image of an unruly, ravenous, flesh-ripping fiend. The rigid rules of the recipe and the structure of everyday table manners reassures Liv, and the audience, that she is more human than zombie—a fact that could change at any time if she were to lose access to a steady source of human brains.

Liv's grip on humanity is especially poignant in the moments when she is able to share her meals with friends and family. Her experience of feeding on brains just after her transformation is marked by isolation. She must hide her brain diet or risk being exposed as a zombie. However, over time, Liv surrounds herself with friends who know her secret, and she is able to share her struggles, and her meals, with them. She is no longer forced to eat alone. Sharing eating experiences becomes one of the most important ways that Liv is able to define the relationships with the people that she cares for the most. In fact, whether or not Liv can eat brains openly during a meal with another character indicates the status of their relationship. For example, Liv's engagement to Major ends because he is human and she is not; she cannot share her secret, her meals, or her life with him. At the other extreme, Ravi is her co-worker, friend, and confidante. He protects Liv and her secret while trying to find a cure for her affliction. Liv can not only eat her meals with Ravi, she can openly prepare fresh brains in front of him. In the second season episode "Real Dead Housewife of Seattle," Liv cracks open a murdered socialite's cranium, cuts the brain into bite size pieces, mixes them with tuna and mayo, scoops the mixture into a tomato half, and savors a delicate forkful of brains, tuna, and tomato all as Ravi looks on. While Liv carefully dabs the corners of her mouth with a napkin, Ravi munches on his own snack and comments simply "She looks as tasty as she was tasteful." Throughout the scene, it is clear that Ravi accepts Liv for who she is as a zombie. He recognizes that the victim's brain is the most important ingredient in Liv's "immediate dining plans" and does not shrink away from shoving handfuls of his own snack into his mouth while Liv consumes a person's brain. The closeness of their relationship is apparent in the way that they share space, and food, at the same time.

The ability to share food is even more poignant when Liv realizes that there are other zombies. First, she meets Blaine DeBeers (David Anders), the drug dealer turned zombie who scratched Liv at the boat party and turned her into a zombie. When they first meet, they are able to share a connection that no one else would understand since they both eat brains. In the episode "Brother Can You Spare a Brain," Blaine and Liv commiserate on how horrible it is to need to eat brains in order to survive. Liv had eaten brains that gave her a vision of a ravenous Blaine chasing the victim. Blaine explains that he did not kill the victim but had chased him after the man attacked him. Their conversation reveals the toll that becoming zombies has had on the two characters:

> BLAINE: "I'm about to crack this guy's head open for just the tiniest taste of brain, which is the single most disgusting thing a person can eat"
> LIV: "That it is"
> BLAINE: "It's the consistency that kills me"
> LIV: "I can't get around it and there's that weird metallic taste"
> BLAINE: "Is it metallic? I don't even know. I used to be a serious wine guy like *Sideways* crazy about it and now everything I drink is like iodine"
> LIV: "I saw a kid eating a peanut butter cup last week and I almost cried. I miss food so much"
> BLAINE: "I miss so many things. Who knew death would be this isolating, right?"

For the first time, Liv has found someone who understands what it is like to be forced to eat brains to survive. It is not surprising that Blaine and Liv are able to forge a connection based on the food that they eat. The fact that food serves as a conduit for creating and sustaining relationships is a well-recognized phenomenon. As Harris, Lyon, and McLauglin assert in *The Meaning of Food* (2005), "No matter who we are or where we live on this planet, all life revolves around food. Yet food is more than the sustenance we need to stay alive; it is part of our culture and tradition and can be the very thing that defines us as people" (vi). The same is true for zombies—they are defined by what they eat. By finding another individual who eats brains for survival, Liv and Blaine each affirm that they have a unique relationship that humans cannot understand.

However, Blaine and Liv differ substantially on what it means to survive as a zombie. They may eat the same food, but they share little else. For Liv, survival means maintaining her humanity and avoiding becoming a monster. For Blaine, survival means becoming rich and powerful. While Liv uses the visions caused by eating brains to find justice for the victims and maintain her humanity, Blaine loses his humanity by becoming a monster of a different kind: a serial killer. Blaine uses his ability to infect other people to create new zombies from among the most rich and powerful members of the community. Recognizing that these newly infected zombies will need a steady flow of brains, Blaine draws upon his expertise as a drug dealer to set up a brain smuggling syndicate out of the back of "Meat Cute," a butcher shop serving as the front for the illegal operation. While his clientele is rich and powerful, Blaine feeds their appetite for brains by murdering some of the most powerless members of society: homeless teenagers, junkies, and runaways. Blaine goes so far as to zombify a professional chef to whip up delicious recipes, such as "braised cerebellum a la Grenoble" and "medulla oblongata stuffed gnocchi in a fra diavlo sauce" for his gourmet clientele ("Live and Let Clive"). Blaine is even happy to take special orders, for the right price. In the episode "Patriot Brains," a newly turned zombie with an unlimited budget puts in a special order for astronaut brains and Blaine quickly sends out henchmen to harvest the brain of famous astronaut Alan York, hoping to reap a tidy profit from selling micro-meals of space-marinated memories to his wealthy customers. Blaine's single-minded devotion to profit and lack of concern for his victims, however, reveals that, while his outer demeanor appears human, his inner core is monstrous.

Don't Eat the Ones You Love; Eat with Them Instead

It is no secret that food intertwines with the ideas and experiences related to love, romance, and sex. Aphrodisiacs—from chocolate to oysters and everything in between—demonstrate the connections between the experience of eating and the sensuality of sex. It is no accident that the romantic dinner for two with soft candlelight, fancy food, and bubbly champagne is interchangeable with the notion of foreplay. All aspects of food—from preparing a meal to doing the dishes—offer opportunities for love and romance. "Sometimes cooking is foreplay," writes Buffy Crumpacker in her book *The Sex Life of Food* (2006), "eating is making love, and doing the dishes is the morning after" (xii). The visual nature of food on film has often leveraged the deep connections between food and love, food and romance, and food and sex to represent the relationships between characters. This representation was even more important in the days when any representation of physical intimacy between characters was strictly taboo. As Steve Zimmerman notes in *Food in the Movies* (2005), the rituals of courtship found in sharing food mirror the intimacy of sharing a bed. For Zimmerman, an "invitation to dine" often leads to an invitation to bed (182). "In the movies (as in real life)," writes Zimmerman, "when two people show an interest in each other, they often agree to dine together; and if one person offers to share 'a taste' of his or her food with the other, it's often a coded signal that he or she might be of a mind to share other pleasures that are not on the restaurant's menu" (182). These almost universally recognized signals—between the characters themselves and between the filmmaker and the audience—provide a romantic atmosphere and "sexually charged scenes" even when no sex appears on screen (182). Therefore, food becomes a powerful tool that can be "read" for the multitudes of meanings that are associated with the dishes and meals that appear on screen (Bower 6).

A relatively recent example of food that communicates more about the characters' relationships than their dialogue can be found in *Fried Green Tomatoes* (1991). The film adaptation of Fannie Flagg's novel, *Fried Green Tomatoes at the Whistle Stop Café* (1987), channels the same-sex attraction between Idgie Threadgoode (Mary Stuart Masterson) and Ruth Jamison (Mary-Louise Parker) into a "food fight" scene where the two women smear each other's bodies in a wide array of oozing, slippery, wet foods—from smooshed blackberries to thick, rich chocolate icing. Throughout the film, the possibility of a lesbian relationship between the two characters is hinted at, but never openly acknowledged. While Idgie and Ruth express their love for each other, live together, and even raise a child together, the reality of their physical relationship is barred from screen. As Laura Lindenfeld acknowledges in her assessment of the film, scenes such as Ruth's declaration of her love for Idgie while testifying during her trial, "insinuates the possibility of a sexual love and partnership between women, but it does so in a manner that is careful not to alienate a mainstream heterosexual viewing audience" (230). At the time of the film's release in 1991, even hinting at the possibility of a lifelong lesbian love affair was breaking long-standing taboos. In place of speaking this possible truth, the filmmakers instead rely on the "sexually charged and physical scene between the women" during the food fight to telegraph the possibility of the sexual nature of their relationship (Lindenfeld 234). As "Idgie feeding one of the fried green tomatoes she has prepared to Ruth in a flirtatious manner" to the ensuing "water fight" that devolves into a "food fight" where the "women proceed to rub ingredients necessary for making fruit pie all over each other's bodies, holding and stroking each other with the food as they fall to the floor" increases the "sexual tension" by employing the sensuality of the physical intimacy and the symbolism of love and sex associated with fruit and chocolate (Lindenfeld 235). The food reveals what remains silent in the film: the underlying sexual attraction and romantic connection between Ruth and Idgie. The ability for food to speak the language of love, romance, and sex gives filmmakers a powerful tool to communicate with the audience about the key features of the relationships between characters.

Just as other films and television series have exploited the deep connections between food and romance to communicate relationship status through cooking and meals, Liv's love life is also defined and displayed through the foods that she prepares, and shares, with the men that she loves. For example, Liv's first foray into the zombie dating pool is with Lowell Tracey (Bradley James), a musician who was transformed into a brain-eating zombie. In the first season episode "Virtual Reality Bites," their first date goes nowhere because Liv suffers from the after-effects of eating the brain of a man with agoraphobia. Since Liv cannot leave the house, Lowell comes to her rescue by bringing a bottle of anti-anxiety medication to her apartment. As a zombie, Lowell understands the personality swings that come with eating brains and, instead of judging Liv's reticence to enter a relationship he encourages her to share her feelings, frustrations, and food cravings with "probably the one guy who would understand" ("Virtual Reality Bites"). The remainder of their first date is spent sharing the stories of how they became zombies.

Because of these shared experiences, Liv is able to establish both an emotional and physical relationship with Lowell. The couple can share both a meal—super hot bloody Mary's and spicy cheese snacks—and intercourse because, as Liv reveals in the episode "Dead Air," "sex is back on the menu." In the scene of their intense, romantic date, Liv and Lowell eat from the same dish. Like lovemaking, this act of sharing food from the same dish is an intensely intimate act. These shared late night, date night snacks give Liv the opportunity to share her innermost thoughts and feelings while the fact that they are both zombies allows physical intimacy without fear of contagion. Love, sex, and food are all intermingled in Liv's new zombie romance.

The connection between food and intimacy is even more apparent in

Liv's second zombie relationship. After her liaison with Lowell ended and her relationship with Major became even more complicated, she met Drake Holloway (Greg Finley), a member of the drug syndicate that caused the zombie apocalypse. Liv and Drake share the ultimate zombie intimacy: she turned him into a zombie after she scratched him to save his life. After causing his transformation, Liv takes the responsibility of initiating Drake into the zombie lifestyle, including serving his first meal of human brains mixed with hot sauce. An almost immediate attraction between the couple grows into a relationship. The important connection between love, food, and sex in their zombie romance is clear the first time that Liv and Drake make love. In the episode "Lusty Liv," she invites Drake over to her apartment to share a romantic dinner. The key ingredient in the dish is brain from a murdered librarian who also happened to write erotic novels. With her libido racing from the librarian's erotic imagination, Liv confesses to Drake that "I roofied you with horny librarian brain" ("Lusty Liv"). Unwilling to "take advantage" of Drake, Liv sends him home until the after-effect of the brains wear off. At that moment, the line between Liv's own desire and the influence of the librarian's personality is unclear. While Liv and Drake do consummate their relationship, Liv realizes that there must be more to it than good food and good sex. Similar tastes may become the cornerstone of a relationship, but there is still more to life than the next brain fix. The complexity of Liv's love life—moving beyond romantic dinners and sweet-nothings about the zombie lifestyle—reaffirms her attempt to live life to the fullest: good, bad, and messy.

Just like the traditional zombie that spends the entirety of its existence looking for its next meal, Liv Moore's life revolves around food: craving food, finding food, and eating food. Unlike stereotypical zombies, Liv is also able to share food. With Ravi and her other friends, Liv can share her zombie secret and strengthen their relationship to the point where she feels comfortable eating brains in front of them. Her romantic relationships with zombie lovers revolve around sharing both food and zombie experiences. Most importantly, Liv's relationship with the victims whose brains she eats establishes a closeness that allows her to solve their murders while sustaining her own existence. Far from meaningless, Liv's consumption of human brains serves as the source of her attempts to reclaim her humanity. The significance of her relationship to food comes through in the care and concern that she takes in preparing elaborate recipes and formal meals. Following the rules of polite society—waiting for the food to cook, following table manners, sharing food with friends—allows Liv to establish and maintain her humanity. Moreover, she is able to transform the special abilities that eating brains gives her—seeing visions and taking on the personality traits of the victims—into a driving mission for justice that give her life new purpose. The visions of the victim's lives provide Liv with a vision of what her future can be like as she helps to solve the senseless crimes that now provide the food that sustains her life. Liv comes to know her food intimately and is able to pay them back by providing the justice they deserve. Liv's craving for brains may prevent her from pursuing the life she envisioned for herself, but they have provided her with a vision of a new future with a purpose worth dying—and living—for.

However, the fact that Liv uses cultural norms surrounding food and eating to affirm her humanity and define her relationships leads to an important question: should Liv continue to conform to human expectations? The life that she has created for herself revolves around holding onto her humanity. However, Liv is not human; she is a zombie. Eating instant ramen noodles with mixed in brains gives Liv a way to cling to her identity as a human just as she solves murders in order to give her life meaning. However, this drive to hold onto her humanity has also caused Liv to attempt to "pass" as human in her day-to-day life. She dreads the idea of her friends and family finding out about her secret and so Liv lives in hiding. Her reluctance to live openly as a zombie causes a rift with her family, alienates her friends, and turns Liv into a reluctant recluse. Only when she tells her friends and family the truth about her zombie status can Liv become her true self and eat openly. Is there a better life for Liv as a zombie? As Liv shares her secret with her human friends and family, *iZombie* hints that there might be a different option for finding happiness as a zombie other than just living hidden in the shadows. In the second season finale episode "Salivation Army," Liv sneaks into a party at Max Rager, the energy drink company whose owner Vaughn du Clark (Steven Weber) knowingly covered up the connection between his product and the zombie outbreak. At the party, Liv meets Vivian Stoll (Andrea Savage), the high-powered CEO of Filmore-Graves Enterprises who is considering acquiring Max Rager. Vivian Stoll's zombie-status is revealed when Liv finds her in the aftermath of the mini-zombie apocalypse that erupted and wiped out the party's attendees. As Vivian sits in the midst of the carnage, she calmly scoops handfuls of bloody brains from the musician Rob Thomas's (Himself) freshly killed corpse into her mouth. As she licks blood from her fingers, Vivian offers Liv a choice: "Are you ready for the new world order, Olivia Moore? Ready to do your part for your kind? Some day soon Seattle's going to be the capital of the zombie homeland and a lot of people aren't going to want to see that happen. So are you with us? Or are you against us?" ("Salvation Army"). From the way she eats brains in traditional zombie style, to the promise of a "zombie homeland," Vivian offers a different vision for Liv's future as a zombie. Instead of seeking to reclaim her humanity, Liv could embrace her zombie identity. Instead of hiding her true nature—cooking her food in elaborate recipes—Liv could eat raw brains openly for all to see. Instead of living within the norms of human society, Liv could embrace zombie culture.

Within the typical zombie story, the audience's visceral reaction against the sight of zombies eating flesh arises from the breaking of the taboo against cannibalism. An inhuman act, "engaging in cannibalism places characters squarely on one side of the divide between civilized and uncivilized behavior" (Baron, Carson, and Bernard 130). That divide—between humanity and inhumanity, civilized and uncivilized behavior—is exactly what Liv sought to cross by attempting to reclaim her humanity by employing the conventions of cooked meals and table manners. In contrast, the image of Vivian's brain meal—raw, bloody, and slowly savored—represents a different path for Liv and all zombies. While the show has made the idea that Liv Moore's morality will never allow her to murder people in order to live, the choice to break free from human cultural norms and embrace her zombie nature is a tantalizing promise for Liv's future. In fact, for those cultures that practiced cannibalism, the act of eating human flesh was often regarded not as a taboo, but as a meaningful ritual, bound by special circumstances and conveying important meanings for the community (Visser 13). This indicates that the choice to live a good life does not necessarily mean rejecting her zombie nature. Perhaps Liv, and other zombies, can find a new way of living that is neither fully human nor completely inhuman; perhaps zombies can find their own rules for civilization even while embracing the need to feed on human brains as part of their own experiences. By blurring the dividing line between humanity and inhumanity, as well as between civility and incivility, *iZombie* raises important questions related to the possibilities of counterculture, not only for Liv, but for the audience as well. Up to the end of Season 2, Liv focused only on reclaiming what she has lost when she became a zombie: her humanity. This entailed enacting the rules set by society surrounding food and eating: cooking her meals, following recipes, and eating with a knife and fork. She has never considered the potential of breaking free of society's definitions of "food" and "meal." When she does think of "full on zombie mode," it is only with the revulsion that has been part of Liv's indoctrination as a prerequisite for entering human society. The reality is, however, that Liv is *not human*; she now has the right to reject the rules that bind humanity and forge a new zombie future. Vivian's choice to eat brains directly from freshly opened skull with her bare hands in front of onlookers she barely knows offers a glimpse of the possibility of these new rules. Perhaps what is hiding beneath the surface of Liv's attempt to reclaim her humanity is the idea that the choice *not* to be human—not to live by someone else's rules—is just as much a possibility as getting her "life back." Perhaps it is not Liv and her fellow zombies who need to change. Perhaps, instead, it is the audience who needs to reject the disgust at the idea of zombie cannibalism and instead begin to see Liv in a new light. In a typical zombie story, the horror of the zombie arises from its familiarity. Seemingly alive, yet dead, seeking sustenance in human flesh, the zombie is a human gone terribly, terrifyingly wrong. In so doing, however, the zombie's existence reaffirms the status quo. As Roger Luckhurst notes in *Zombies: A Cultural History* (2015), "These creatures transgress but in the end uphold cultural categories of purity and pollution, the sacred and the profane, the living and the dead" (9). Viewing the dead and hungry zombies as they feed on human flesh reaffirms for the audience that these terrifying creatures are *not them*; In particular, their ravenous consumption of human flesh sets them apart as "other" (Brown 4). However, Liv Moore's experience as a zombie yearning to live as a human calls into question the opposition between human and zombie and opens the possibility that "human" does not belong in the privileged position. Yes, Liv is a zombie. Yes, she eats people's brains. However, the show raises the notion that simply returning to life as a human is not necessarily the right choice for Liv or other zombies. Instead of recoiling in horror from Liv's life as a brain-eating zombie, the affords the audience the opportunity to question their assumptions about what makes life worth living. Within the framework of the series, the audience can no longer simply reject Liv's zombie lifestyle in horror. Instead, Liv's experiences in *iZombie* provide the audience with the opportunity to look into themselves, recognize the socially-constructed revulsion against her character, and reject those prejudices. Yet, whether Liv continues to follow human customs or finds a new zombie equilibrium, what is clear is that Liv's identity is her choice and how she chooses to express that identity is irreversibly tied to the food she requires in order to live: brains.

Just like cooked food serves as the demarcation line between animal and human, nature and culture, barbarian and civilization, Liv uses brains to reaffirm her humanity. This choice breaks her free from the barbarism associated with traditional zombie cannibals but ties her to the cultural norms related to food and eating that are present in human society. Whether she chooses to hold onto her humanity or embrace her new zombie reality, food is a powerful medium through which Liv is able to negotiate her identity and relationships. Throughout the early episodes of the series, Liv rejects the monstrous drive to eat brains like an uncivilized zombie and embraces the food practices that allow her to grasp hold of her continued humanity and forge relationships with humans and zombies alike. Whether or not she continues to cook elaborate recipes, for Liv, eating brains is about more than just staying fed; it is about negotiating the line between zombie and human. For Liv Moore, brains will continue to be the most important ingredient in her recipe for life, love, and lasting happiness.

Works Cited

Anderson, E.N. *Everyone Eats: Understanding Food and Culture.* 2nd ed. NYU Press, 2014.

Baron, Cynthia, Diane Carson, and Mark Bernard. *Appetites and Anxieties: Food, Film, and the Politics of Representation.* Wayne State University Press, 2014.

Bishop, Kyle William. *American Zombie Gothic: The Rise and Fall (and Rise) of the Walking Dead in Popular Culture*. McFarland, 2010.
Bower, Anne L. "Watching Food: The Production of Food, Film, and Values." *Reel Food: Essays on Food and Film*, edited by Anne L. Bower. Routledge, 2004, pp. 1–13.
Brillat-Savarin, Jean Anthelme. *The Physiology of Taste or Meditations on Transcendental Gastronomy*. Translated by M.F.K Fischer. The Everyman's Library, 2009.
Brown, Jennifer. *Cannibalism in Literature and Film*. Palgrave Macmillan, 2013.
Buccini, Anthony. "Defining 'Cuisine': Communication, Culinary Grammar and the Typology of Cuisine." *Food and Communication: Proceedings of the Oxford Symposium on Food and Cookery 2015*, edited by Mark McWilliams. Prospect Books, 2016, pp. 105–21.
Clasen, Mathias. "The Anatomy of a Zombie: A Bio-Psychological Look at the Undead Other." *Otherness: Essays & Studies*, edited by Maria Beville and Matthias Stephan, vol. 1, no. 1, December 2010. www.otherness.dk/journal/vol-1/.
Crumpacker, Bunny. *The Sex Life of Food: When Body and Soul Meet to Eat*. Thomas Dunne Books, 2006.
Douglas, Mary. "Deciphering a Meal." *Daedalus*, vol. 101, iss. 1, 1972, pp. 61–81.
Harris, Patricia, David Lyon, and Sue McLaughlin. *The Meaning of Food*. The Globe Pequot Press, 2005.
iZombie. Co-created by Rob Thomas and Diane Ruggiero-Wright. The CW, 2015–present.
Jones, Steve and Shaka McGlotten. "Introduction: Zombie Sex." *From Zombies and Sexuality: Essays on Desire and the Living Dead*, edited by Shaka McGlotten and Steve Jones. McFarland, 2014, pp. 1–18.
Levi-Strauss, Claude. "The Culinary Triangle." *Food and Culture: A Reader*. Third Edition. Edited by Carole Counihan and Penny Van Esterik. Routledge, 2013, pp. 40–7.
Lindenfeld, Laura. "Women Who Eat Too Much: Femininity and Food in Fried Green Tomatoes." *Betty Crocker and Feminist Food Studies: Critical Perspectives on Women and Food*, edited by Arlene Voski Avakian and Barbara Haber. University of Massachusetts Press, 2005, pp. 221–45.
Luckhurst, Roger. *Zombies: A Cultural History*. Reaktion Books, 2015.
Miller, Jeff, and Jonathan Deutsch. *Food Studies: An Introduction to Research Methods*. Berg, 2009.
Pollan, Michael. *Cooked: A Natural History of Transformation*. Penguin, 2013.
Prose, Francine. "From Cocktail Hour at the Snake Blood Bar: On the Persistence of Taboo." *Eating Words: A Norton Anthology of Food Writing*, edited by Sandra M. Gilbert and Roger J. Porter. Norton, 2015, pp. 222–29.
Visser, Margaret. *The Rituals of Dinner*. Penguin, 1991.
Zimmerman, Steve. *Food in the Movies*. 2nd ed. McFarland, 2010.

The Zombie Apocalypse as Hospice Care

Maggie and the Zombie Turn as Cipher for Terminal Illness

William A. Lindenmuth

Traditionally, those bitten in a zombie story should expect to die gruesomely in short order. This "turn" from human to "other" is usually the most dreaded event in these sorts of stories, with many characters preferring suicide or asking their comrades to kill them. While there might be a protracted scene where your friends and family lament the appalling deed of shooting you in the head (e.g., *Shaun of the Dead* [2004]), rest assured, death will occur promptly. The turn from human to "other" can happen almost immediately (*28 Days Later* [2002]) or over some time (*The Walking Dead* [2010–present]). It is often one of the most interesting parts of the zombie genre: how will the protagonists deal with having to destroy what are often the very people keeping them going? It is usually shown that the ultimate act of love is to "do what must be done." When a character is unable to do this, everyone dies. The idea that you could "enjoy" the time you have left is anathema.

The underrated *Maggie* (2015), directed by Henry Hobson, rejects this idea, takes the turn, and makes it the entire film. Starring traditional blockbuster action star Arnold Schwarzenegger and *Zombieland* (2009) survivor Abigail Breslin, *Maggie* takes us on a patient and artful journey of just how unspectacular and sad it would be to have a zombie outbreak, presenting it as a society dealing with terminal illness. Contrary to the abject, numbing terror that *Night of the Living Dead* (1968) inspires, or the post-apocalyptic, glee-filled romp *Zombieland* offers us, *Maggie* presents a purposefully thoughtful and compassionate story of a father coming to terms with the loss of a daughter who meant the world to him. We see moments that in a typical genre film would be used to otherize, frighten, and alert. In this story, these moments are used to generate care and concern specifically about the afflicted and more generally about pain, human connection, and memory.

Focusing on *Maggie* and its rejection of the proposed simplicity of the zombie story, i.e., "the only thing we need to worry about now is headshots," this essay compares and contrasts zombie films, emphasizing the progression towards understanding and sympathizing with otherness over its destruction. I present *Maggie* as part of a new wave of the zombie tale, one that is more interested in preserving and expanding our idea of humanity, as opposed to contracting it.

Traditional Zombie Films and the Role of the Turn

White Zombie (1932) is held as the first film portrayal of the zombie, featuring an appropriation of the Haitian concept: a mindless worker who can be controlled. Most continued with the voodoo-inspired stories such as *I Walked with a Zombie* (1943). In all of these stories, the zombies are enchanted husks, not contagious flesh eaters. The turn to becoming a zombie is generally shown to be a magical switch and is usually immediate. American films in the 1950s often reflected apocalyptic/Cold War fears similar to many of today's zombie stories, that of either being alone and surrounded by enemies (1964's *The Last Man on Earth*), or being replaceable, e.g., the "pod people" of *Invasion of the Body Snatchers* (1956). Interestingly, the conversions are not depicted. Someone is a human being, then is suddenly replaced with something decidedly not human.

The sixties gave us the genre-defining classic of zombie films in George A. Romero's *Night of the Living Dead* (1968), which set a number of standards for the zombie monster: purposely violent, slow-moving, cannibalistic corpses that are resilient and can reproduce asexually.[1] Romero created a number of other zombie pictures and inspired probably every subsequent film of that type. How and why people become the undead generally shifted from their Haitian origins (*The Serpent and the Rainbow* [1988] is an exception), instead coming from supernatural evil in *The Evil Dead* (1981–present) series, or as a virus created by an evil corporation in the *Resident Evil* (2002–2016) series.

Zombies are at this point also usually shown as rotten, decaying, disgusting carcasses, rather than the pale, transfixed-eyes of voodoo creations. These films also all convey the zombie as something beyond our help, something uncontrollable that we have a duty to destroy. This holds up through the 1970s, where we distinctly begin the trend towards gore and camp, e.g.,

1979's *Zombi 2*, 1980s (1985's *Return of the Living Dead*, 1986's *Night of the Creeps*), and 1990s (Peter Jackson's 1992 *Dead Alive/Braindead*).[2] The undead must be made dead again. One cannot reason with them as their brains are lifeless. One cannot appeal to their emotions but it would seem that their heart is dead as well. Again, the turn is never the focus of the narrative. You are human, then you are not. Killing a human is murder, but once turned—no matter how rapidly—you must be eliminated. Or rather, you *were* you, and no longer are so. Of note is how *excited* the audiences of zombie films of this type are to kill zombies. The characters often most lauded in these films are the ones that show no mercy. They are not shown as vicious, but as smart.

"Man has only been around for a few blinks of an eye. So, if the infection wipes us all out ... that is a return to normality."[3]

The fantastic reboot of the zombie genre came with 2002's *28 Days Later*. While not exactly involving the undead, this film is every bit in tone a zombie film. As Andrea Wood, who taught a course at Georgia Tech entitled *Apocalyptic Nightmares of the Living Dead* says, "Since the zombie doesn't have the long literary tradition of the vampire or a number of other monsters, it allows artists a degree of autonomy to conceptualize the zombie any way they see fit."[4] *28 Days Later* involves dire straits, the risk that anyone can become a monster and quick thinking is a necessity. The experience of living in a zombie world, with the questions one would have to ask, e.g., "Am I the last person on Earth?" and "Will I survive this?" along with the concept of what it means to be human and whether or not we *deserve* to survive are all conveyed powerfully throughout the film.

Indeed, James Parker's "Our Zombies, Ourselves," from *The Atlantic*, explains the variety of zombie-types and symbols, "Much can be made of [a zombie], because he makes so little of himself."[5] The difference is that, in *28 Days Later*, the infected move very quickly, and they are not technically "dead," as they are infected with what is only described as "rage." It has all of the terror and existential dread of the Romero stories, but at a much faster pace. The turn in this film, from a normal human to a rage-filled, homicidal, uncontrollable one takes mere seconds. It is terrifying to witness, but not squandered by the storytellers. One of the most powerful and memorable moments of the film is when Brendan Gleeson's character Frank is infected. A drop of blood gets into his eye when he is trying to scare away a crow feeding on a corpse. He knows what is about to happen, and quickly says to his daughter

"Hannah, I love you very much. Keep away from me." In thirty-eight seconds after a speck of blood touches him he is convulsing and writhing like a ferocious beast. The group he is travelling with now have to deal with what was, a moment earlier, a loving, kind, and brave father-like guardian figure, that now has lost total control and will attack them, unless the protagonist beats him to death with a baseball bat. The film challenges the viewer whether mankind can endure these monstrous acts and still retain its humanity. It is a serious, alarming tale, where the greatest threat to ourselves is each other.

Two years later, *Shaun of the Dead* provides a new type of story, not in that it is the first to add humor—there is plenty in terms of campiness in other zombie films—but in how it manages to combine sharp satire and wit with sincere emotion and drama, and remain a horror movie all at the same time. While hardly the first movie ever to do this, it is arguably the first zombie film to do so. It is also the first to suggest that there might be something in keeping the undead around. Unlike *28 Days Later*, the turn is slow and happens over time. The touching drama of the film comes mostly from the infection and death of Shaun's parents, both of which he has to deal with in a single afternoon. His step-father uses his final moments before passing to say that he tried his best to be a good father and has always loved him. When his mother turns, Shaun is forced to shoot her just after watching her die.

Fido (2006) spends a lot of time on this idea, but in quite a different way. Some see the zombie as representative of slavery,[6] or at least historically connected to that brutal tradition.[7] This film explores this notion, presenting a re-imagined 1950s post-zombie apocalypse world where the humans either destroy zombies or use them as slaves. Either way, their labor and confinement translates to more freedom for the captors, who feel generally free to treat them as they please. Along with the young boy who "owns" him, the eponymous Fido of the film teaches the town that being human is a lot more about what you do than what you are.

"I don't like hurting people, but this is the world now"[8]

Subsequent zombie films have told a different story. While some renditions (*The Walking Dead* [2010] or *World War Z* [2013]) imply that all zombies are the same, i.e., single-minded monsters that can only focus on one thing at a time and will insistently pursue the possibility of eating humans above all else, other tales imply that there is a connection between the lives they lived and who they are now. *Fido* and 2014's *Life After Beth* both emphasize the personal past as remaining a deep connection to their humanity. *Shaun of the Dead* humorously shows Ed as remaining chained up in the garden shed to play video games with his best friend Shaun, seemingly in perpetuity.

In 2013's *Warm Bodies*, it is precisely one's memories and links to the past that prevent one from becoming a different kind of zombie, known as a "boney." The protagonist, simply known as "R," (Nicholas Hoult) himself a zombie ("corpse" in the film), distinguishes boneys as willing to "eat anything with a heartbeat. I mean, I will, too, but at least I'm conflicted about it." The cause of zombies in this film is less about the ills of mall culture and sameness (*Dawn of the Dead* [1978]) or a punishment for allowing science to go too far (*Re-animator* [1985]), but rather alienation and loneliness. Feeling a connection to people, ideas, and the material world grounds and humanizes zombies, and they stave off becoming boneys as long as they can maintain their ties. R claims that he does not want to feel disconnected and removed from people and meaning, but does not know what else to do. He ends up consuming the brain of a young man, and subsequently falls in love with that man's former girlfriend, Julie (Teresa Palmer).

The villains of this film are the boneys on the undead side *and* the leader of the remaining humans on the living side. What makes them both villainous is their inability (or refusal) to tell the difference between what is capable of consciousness and what is not. After meeting the zombie protagonist, we are given an uncompromising description of him from the human side in a warning from the leader of the survivors, Colonel Grigio (John Malkovich): "Corpses look human; they are not. They do not think, they do not bleed. Whether they were your mother or your best friend, they are beyond your help. They are uncaring, unfeeling, and incapable of remorse. Just picture them as this," a video of a boney follows this mandate. While there is the reality that this film's zombies do hunger for human brains, it is because they get to experience the victims' memories—it is the thing that makes them feel the most human. As R explains, "I don't want to hurt you, I just want to feel what you felt. To feel a little better. A little less dead."[9]

There is an interesting comparison here with a film outside the zombie genre, but bears mention: *Eternal Sunshine of the Spotless Mind* (2004). In that sci-fi imagining, we have a world where people can hire a service through which they can erase memories, and we follow a man going through the process of eradicating memories of a former lover after he learns she has gone through that process regarding him. An unscrupulous employee of the memory erasing service decides to take advantage of the couples' erased memories by using knowledge about the woman to earn her affections. When she becomes alerted to his machinations, they disgust her and, consequently, the audience. In *Warm Bodies*, R continually eats sections of his romantic interest's former lover, whom R has killed, in order to feel and learn more about her. It is interesting that while both of these contain willful manipulation of wrongfully commandeered memories, even if we do not approve of it in the latter film, we tolerate it and sympathize, yet abhor the act in the former film. Of course, R does not really know what he is doing, while the memory eraser does.[10] The memory eraser seeks to cheat in order to achieve intimacy, while R wants the real thing in a genuine way.

A major point of *Warm Bodies* is that people—even dead ones—can change. The boneys are indeed too far gone, but not all of the corpses are. It is a re-definition of the genre, and, much like the redeemable vampires in *True Blood* (2008–2014) or *Twilight* (2008), the point is that not everyone that is different is "gone." Most of us have the potential for change. Julie and R have the following exchange:

> JULIE: "Hey ... do you have to eat people?"
> R: "Yeah."
> JULIE: "Or you'll die."
> R: "Yeah."
> JULIE: "But you didn't eat me. You rescued me ... like, a bunch. It must be hard, being stuck in there. You know, I can see you trying. Maybe that's what people do, you know, we try to be better. Sometimes we kinda suck at it but when I look at you, and you ... you try so much harder than any human in my city. You're a good person, R."

It is R's desire to be something better, something more, and his sacrifice to attain that goal, along with Julie's ability and willingness to recognize this and attempt to convince others that unity leads to the redemption and salvation of that world. The turn in this film is the opposite from what we have been accustomed. We do not see anyone turn into a zombie, but back to human after being removed and alienated from it. Rather than the dehumanizing zombification of mankind, we get the life-affirming, reintegration of the walking dead.

"I can't begin to imagine how hard this must be for you. But we can't afford to fall apart."[11]

> ANA: "I'm sorry, what are we talking about here? Are.... Are we talking about killing him?"
> MICHAEL: "Would you rather we wait for him to die and then he tries to kill us?
> ANA: "Yes! No, no. You can't kill him. He's got a daughter."
> MICHAEL: "I'm sorry. I don't think there's any other choice.... You've been bitten. It's only a matter of time."

So goes the exchange between two people in 2004's *Dawn of the Dead* remake. Discussions such as this are abundant in the zombie genre: if you get bitten, you must die or everyone else is at risk. Often, these moments are the tensest and most revealing about our characters in these films. Shaun, in *Shaun of the Dead,* experiences powerful character development with his parents when they are bitten and it raises the stakes, for Shaun is a man who has a hard time getting in touch with himself and his feelings. Yet, the situation demands he immediately face having the deepest conversation he has ever had with his parents while facing their imminent demise.

If it is true that horror films are stories about our real-life fears played out in simplistic, obvious, relatively easy-to-resolve ways (e.g., *Godzilla* represents the fear of nuclear weapons, *Dracula* of the foreigner taking over our culture and women), then most modern horror films show our fears to be more nuanced. For example, in Elizabeth Neal's "The Significance of the Zombie," she shows how the zombie was a cultural response to racism and colonialism, then nuclear war, then capitalism, then 9/11.[12] Early monster stories are almost always a fear of otherness. If something is different from us, if something presents ideas contrary to the status quo, it is the enemy. It is not to be listened to, understood, or engaged with, other than contributing to its destruction, since the presence of zombies encourage a fear that mankind will become obsolete.

"You shouldn't have brought me back"[13]

The world of 2015's *Maggie* is a melancholic one, but with a light at the end of the tunnel. It takes place in a nondescript Midwestern part of the United States where a "necroambulist virus" has been spreading and people are struggling to deal with it. Contrary to most "living dead" depictions, however, the world has not turned into a lawless, sadistic apocalypse without feeling or meaning. Much to its credit, the film treats necroambulism as we would treat any type of outbreak, which is to say, with some paranoia, religious confusion, and moralizing (like we have seen with HIV, bird flu, or Zika), but not as an excuse to do whatever you want.

The eponymous Maggie of the film is played by Abigail Breslin, who in her younger years played a very different role in a very different zombie apocalypse: *Zombieland.* While that film was a light-hearted dark comedy that ultimately was about learning to trust others and learning to love again after trauma, a lot of it was simply devoted to how much fun it would be to kill zombies—there is even a "zombie kill of the week"—and live celebrating excess. In *Maggie,* we have another ordeal, but instead of focusing on the post-traumatic stress, it emphasizes the pre-traumatic experience of knowing one will eventually turn."[14] The trauma in *Maggie* is certainly in getting bitten, but the true injury of the film is the anticipated reality: a world without Maggie. The story rotates around a loving, protective father who does not feel much of either, because his daughter is going to become a zombie, and there is nothing he can do about it. The majority of the film is this father stubbornly holding on to the idea that Maggie is okay and not a threat to others, despite mounting evidence to the contrary. The film shifts between seemingly siding with him and his fierce love for Maggie—she connects him with his dead wife and her dead mother, she represents so much of what he sees as good and worthwhile in the world—and the idea that he is stubborn and will incur a violent death at the unwitting hands of his daughter. When there is no more Maggie, then meaning and purpose will depart as well. It is a profound reflection on death and loss, and it makes one wonder why there have not been more stories like this already. Does anyone actually think a zombie apocalypse would be enjoyable? Of course, there is an important distinction to be made between enjoying a story and wanting it to be true. Illness, especially terminal ones, are heartbreaking for those experiencing them and for the ones who love them and must suffer the ordeal of them going through it.

What Do We Owe a Zombie?

Perhaps the supernatural aspect of zombies is what has allowed us to treat them more without regard. From another perspective, perhaps we are simply having a harder time expressing violent tendencies without realizing the consequences. As we start to see that "the bad guys" almost always have a side/perspective/reason for what they do, it becomes less acceptable socially and personally to indiscriminately slaughter them.[15] It is interesting to look at forms of entertainment over the years and see which groups we are allowed to murder for pleasure. Certain video games now feature "Nazi zombies" as enemies (2009's *Dead Snow*[16] is another example); what is a more-deserving target than that?[17]

The supernatural element may also signal to some that the normal rules of morality that guide and shape our lives no longer apply. In some cases this has a religious motivation, in that we are only accountable to beings with souls, and if something does not have a soul, morality does not pertain. The "dead" in the "walking dead" means we do not owe it anything anymore. Yet, a distinct line can be drawn over history of an increasing concern and regard for what was previously regarded as the other or that which we have dominion over, namely animals and the environment. As many of us have come to see that they are not only limited and finite, but that our treatment of them has a significant effect on their future, as well as ours.

As we de-supernaturalize many of our myths and find the real, human reasons, needs, and fears behind them, we hopefully get closer to not only getting what we want, but understanding one another and making sure everyone gets what they deserve. So what do zombies deserve? If we are in *Zombieland*, it is a sharp blow to the head and a witty rejoinder. But for Wade Vogel, Maggie's father, the idea that he is going to have to kill his own daughter is unthinkable. Regardless, she is not dead yet.

"Let's enjoy the time we have with her"

Maggie begins with Wade finding his sick daughter and bringing her home, despite the warnings and prohibitions to do so. After becoming ill, she had initially run away to protect the rest of her family. We can immediately see some physical effects of the virus, with deteriorating skin and darkened veins, and these effects become more obvious and turn mental as time goes on. Those with the virus are supposed to be in quarantine, but Wade uses his connections and even threats of violence to keep her at home. When two neighbors with an advanced stage of the disease approach her, Wade feels forced to kill them, including a young girl. This is significant, because we see that he is capable and willing of using lethal force. When the sheriffs arrive, they encourage him to quarantine his daughter because of the danger she represents:

> WADE: Now Ray, you and I, we go back a long ways. You've always done us right, especially after Sarah's passing. But I swear to God … if you, him, or anyone else come out here for her.… She's my daughter, Ray.
>
> RAY: Trucks will be down here in the morning to pick up the remains. Wade, think about what you had to do today. What you might have to do in the future.

Wade may be in denial about what is happening and what will happen, but the movie consistently presents this refusal to give up on Maggie as love and something to be admired..

Arnold Schwarzenegger, who has previously single handedly taken on criminal gangs, monsters, wizards, aliens, and entire armies, and emerged victorious each time, now is shown bowed, bent, and broken—believing himself unable to help the person he most loves. This casting choice contributes a lot to the film, and his minimalist performance adds to the weight of the decisions the characters need to make. Wade's compassion and fierce love for his daughter are contrasted with the various ways the infected are treated throughout the story. Some, like the doctor who treats Maggie, are understanding and warm, others, like the younger sheriff, are callous and impatient. But the plot is still (slowly) barreling towards a choice: what will Wade do when Maggie's turn completes? Will he kill her? The doctor presents the dilemma in stark relief. He explains that "pretty soon," she will not want to eat anything but human flesh:

DR. KAPLAN: When it finally happens, you're going to have a few choices. One, take her to quarantine.
WADE: I'm not going to do that.
DR. KAPLAN: I wasn't suggesting it. My report will say that she's progressing slow, so it'll buy you some time. Option two, we give her the cocktail they'd give her in quarantine. At least this way she'll be with you when she takes it, not a bunch of strangers or other infected people. But, you know how she doesn't feel anything right now? She'll feel this. Reports say that it's painful. Extremely. All the way up to the end.
WADE: What's option three?
DR. KAPLAN: Make it quick.

Wade cannot go along with any of these options, yet the turn is coming. They drive back from the doctor's and Wade plays a song with "Maggie" in the lyrics, causing her to smile. Is he in denial of what must happen, or is he just a father with a deep, deep love for his daughter? It seems the answer is both, but the point is that regardless of what is ahead, she is still his daughter, and he wants to make her happy. He wants to make every moment with her count.

What should my dad do to me? Quarantine?"

A touching sequence in the film comes when Maggie goes out with some friends. One of them, Trent (Bryce Romero), had dated Maggie at some point in the past. He now has an advanced form of the virus, which has spread dark veins like ivy across his body and face. These marks of decomposing would repel most people. Julia Kristeva, in her *Powers of Horror*, writes on the concept of abjection, which is a sort of response to a lack of difference between subject and object, the ultimate example being that of our reaction to a corpse. "Refuse and corpses *show me* what I permanently thrust aside in order to live.... There, I am at the border of my condition as a living being.... The corpse, seen without God and outside of science, is the utmost of abjection. It is death infecting life."[18] Zombies are animated corpses, and, if Kristeva is correct, there would be nothing more frightening or abominable.

But Maggie does not feel repulsed, but rather compassion, and even attraction to Trent. He's not so different than she is. They bond as Trent recounts how he became infected, having shown sympathy towards a woman who then bit him. He describes the regret he saw in her eyes, and says that she probably did not even know she had done it. Then his father arrived and shot the woman in the chest and head. Maggie sympathizes, and they kiss.

The moment stands out because it conveys how while their infected status differentiates them from others, it makes them more alike. It, along with attraction, is something else that they share. It is often small similarities that draw people to one another in the first place. How much, then, must this necroambulatory condition exist as a shared experience? Without even verbalizing it they both know the stares and fear felt from others, the decreasing appetite for human food, the physical transformation, and the impending doom of the inevitable trudge toward death.

This evening with friends and romantic interests is one of the most grounding and establishing of Maggie's humanity. Despite all that she is going through, she is still just a girl with a crush. Similar to other forms of prejudice, for many it would be hard to see past the jet-black veins scattered across Trent's face, representing otherness and disease, but also a somber future for Maggie, who will progress in kind. Unlike some forms of prejudice (against the disabled, for instance), it must be pointed out that what these people have is contagious, and those infected eventually turn violent. To make an obvious point, unlike many forms of discrimination and perception of the other as different and therefore a threat, there is *good reason* for concern and quarantine regarding the infected. But what a movie like *Maggie* wants to suggest is that what happens to one of us happens to us all, in a way. The traditional zombie film portrays the arrival of zombies as "you against the world," showing us who is cunning, fast, and ruthless enough to survive.[19] *Maggie* shows us that even in the event of an outbreak, we still rely on the same things that make us human.

Until recently, zombie romance has been a little-explored concept, and yet it does not stop these two because of *course* sick people also feel desire and sexual feelings, and much as this is often marginalized in culture and media. Love, and especially sex, has been normalized as occurring only between the young, healthy, and beautiful. It is generally portrayed ideally, purporting to show us what we all want, and while not plainly expressed, arguably says that if we *do not* share the same characteristics of the budding, robust, and gorgeous, we should not be happy with ourselves. Shaka McGlotten and Steve Jones claim as much in their *Zombies and Sexuality: Essays on Desire and the Living Dead*:

> What is at once central and strangely absent from current debates about the zombie is any detailed consideration of sex and sexuality. This oversight is startling, not least since sex is arguably the most intimate for of social engagement, and is a profound aspect of human social identity. What makes the omission even more remarkable is how appositely the zombie reflects socio-sexual desires and fears.[20]

They go on to say that zombie reproduction is a challenge to the heteronormative fantasy of forever inheriting the earth. This supports the idea that zombie romance is not simply a new transgression for horror to push the envelope. There is a genuine story and experience to be had here, and in our particular case, Maggie and Trent can no longer participate in this fantasy as they are now both teenagers who will never get to grow up and become adults. They will never get to marry or raise children. Their beauty and youth have been violently stolen from them. They do have this moment, though, and each other.

Maggie is about the humanization of the zombie, and that allows the possibility of romancing it. We are not shown how far the intimacy goes, but it does not really matter. It encapsulates some of the last moments Maggie will get to feel normal. When her friend Allie drops her off, she makes Maggie promise to see her next weekend; unfortunately, as they share a tearful embrace, it is implied they will not see each other ever again. The weight of this last visit—of what will be their last encounter with another, is palpable.

"Promise me you'll make it stop"

Soon afterward, Maggie smells her step-mother Caroline's flesh, confusing it with food. The same thing happens with Trent, and Maggie goes to his house to see him dragged off to quarantine. While disturbing in its own right: a father and heavily armed police removing a boy from his room forcibly, it functions as a frightening precursor as to what Maggie might rapidly undergo herself. When she comes home covered in blood (she had inadvertently attacked a wild fox while returning [it is unaccounted for in the film, but perhaps the taking of Trent triggered a traumatic reaction]), Caroline says that they have to take Maggie to quarantine:

> CAROLINE: Wade, please, just call them. It's time now. She has to go in.
> WADE: What if it was Molly? Or Bobby? [Caroline's biological children]
> CAROLINE: After everything that we've been through, you still think it's about that? I've loved her like she was my own. But she's not "her" anymore. Wade, please.
> WADE: Don't.

Caroline leaves, and the film seems to suggest she is not unwise or uncaring to do so.[21] This is enforced by implying that Maggie might be starting to sense her father as something to be eaten.[22] She does not want food anymore, and Wade catches her watching over him at night. When the sheriffs arrive to check on her—it is past time for her to be quarantined—Wade gets into a physical fight with one of them. Fatal violence is only avoided when Maggie runs out and says that she is all right, even though she is not, and everyone—except Wade—can see that. The sheriffs agree to leave (actually, Ray orders the other one to), but tell Wade sternly that they will be back, and he has to decide what to do because "you and her ain't the only ones in this town." The film handles this well, as it portrays the lawmen as sympathetic humans doing their jobs, but also susceptible to anger and frustration. The sheriff is, after all, not wrong. Wade knows this, yet cannot bring himself to act. He knows this is the last time he will get away with his behavior and the fact that something must be done about Maggie.

Maggie finally asks her father to end it, and this is important, because it is the first time we hear that coming from her, the infected one. This is a key moment, as we see that in certain ways, Maggie is more "realistic" than her elder father, and this represents a mature arc for her character. Wade receives a visit from Dr. Kaplan and procures a dose of what they give the quarantined, but the doctor encourages Wade to use his shotgun instead. When we next see her she has an episode of sorts where she does not seem to recognize her father and struggles with him. She regains consciousness, and he puts her to bed, while he falls asleep in his chair next to pictures of Maggie.

Early the next morning, she walks down the stairs and hovers over her father. We are meant to be very concerned. In this climactic moment, we are all unsure if she will bite him. She sniffs him, tantalizingly, but ends up kissing his forehead as he slumbers. Contrary to his feelings about being a failure as a father, unable to keep his family safe, he retains his daughter's love through the final act. It is not a stretch to say that the intense bond they share allows her to maintain composure and not surrender to the recently developed instinctual desires to feed on human flesh.

"Dad, you've protected me all your life. Now it's my turn to protect you."

By this point, Maggie's entire body is grey, cracked, and flecked with deep black and purple. Her flesh has decayed and her eyes are milky and covered in film. Her breathing is heavy and labored, and her gait compromised. It is important to note the physical change that happens to Maggie, because the film wants us to confront two simultaneous truths: Maggie is a "zombie"; she is also human, a girl, Wade's daughter.

In almost every single other instance in film (with the notable recent exceptions of *Warm Bodies* [2013] and television's iZombie [2015–present]), the slightest turn towards becoming a zombie has been grounds for destruction. In fact, the mark of a villainous and/or selfish character is when they have been bitten/infected, but hide this fact from the group.[23] We have been taught to view the necrotic turn as equal to death, and are encouraged to view Maggie as a lost cause. Zombies, whether a metaphor for terminal illness or a sign that the end-times are upon us, have historically been coded as something we not only do not have to care about, but can eradicate with zeal.

It is essential that we continue to tell stores and re-arrange our art. As the world changes, we succeed when we are able to re-think and contextualize it so it more accurately represents the type of place we want it to be. When we are strong, we can bear more and better protect the marginalized, while simultaneously seeing that others don't become marginalized in the first place. *Maggie* shows us just how easy it is to stigmatize and otherize the weak and mentally ill. We forget that they do not *want* to be that way; they are *sick*, not evil. It is a condition thrust upon them. Roland Barthes has much to say about becoming accustomed to equating a picture or brand with a set of meanings, and that, as we forget so often, a picture is arranged: "A pseudo-truth is surreptitiously substituted for the simple validity of openly semantic systems; the absence of code disintellectualizes the message because it seems to find in nature the signs of culture."[24] *Maggie* re-arranges this traditional scenario and picture that has historically been presented to us, and forces us to see the humanity left in the turn. Elizabeth Neal, discussing Barthes and zombies, writes "If myth is a language and it is a type of speech that is chosen by history, then the myth (or type of speech) surrounding the zombie will of course change with societal and historical changes."[25] People like Trent and Maggie are zombies. They eventually will crave flesh. They eventually will lose control and become a threat. But they are still human and deserve to be regarded as such. The film's final move cinches this claim.

The film ends in the most human, selfless act of all, right at the moment you would expect it the least, when she is "too far gone," and at her most monstrous. Ironically, the turn in this film is rather than Maggie becoming more and more inhuman: amoral, only interested in satisfying her own desires, no care for clan or kin—her final act is the most selfless one she could perform. She realizes that he father can never let her go, or that at the very least, it would destroy him to have to do it.

Zombie films, like most horror stories, act as cultural touchstones, a way of expressing our current fears and social criticisms. The zombie in culture has almost become a cathexis of justifiable violence. Stories like *Maggie* challenge this mental and cultural investment as hollow and misguided. It seems that we are more afraid now of loss, and of being guilty of misunderstanding or misjudging, rather than the simplistic rejections of otherness in earlier renditions of the zombie tale. Finding a way to love what was previously held to be unlovable is undoubtedly progress. As Wade loads a shell into his shotgun, Maggie climbs to the roof of their house and throws herself off. In her last moments of agency, she makes what is an oft-considered immoral act, suicide, moral. Maggie does to herself what her father could not, and in her symbolic act at the point of her turn, shows us that love is indeed stronger than death.

Notes

1. While not film, the television show *The Twilight Zone* (1959–1964) focused on the strange and paranormal and had a 1964 return-from-the-dead episode, "Mr. Garrity and the Graves," that brought zombies to the living room.

2. Some notable exceptions are 1989's *Pet Sematary* and the cultural phenomenon that is Michael Jackson's 1983 video "Thriller."

3. *28 Days Later*, 2002.

4. Doug Gross "Why We Love Those Rotting, Hungry, Putrid Zombies," CNN.com, October 2009

5. James Parker, "Our Zombies, Ourselves," *The Atlantic*, April 2011

6. Amy Wilentz, "A Zombie Is a Slave Forever."

7. For more on the nature of zombies as objects for slavery and enslavement, refer to the essay "From Slavery to Sex: Commodifying Romance in the Zombie Film," by Jennifer Huss Basquiat, in this collection.

8. *Warm Bodies*, 2013.

9. *Warm Bodies*.

10. The book version of *Warm Bodies* says the following: "A question for the zombie philosophers. What does it mean that my past is a fog but my present is brilliant, bursting with sound and color? Since I became Dead I've recorded new memories with the fidelity of an old cassette deck, faint and muffled and ultimately forgettable. But I can recall every hour of the last few days in vivid detail, and the thought of losing a single one horrifies me. Where am I getting this focus? This clarity? I can trace a solid line from the moment I met Julie all the way to now, lying next to her in this sepulchral bedroom, and despite the millions of past moments I've lost or tossed away like highway trash, I know with a lockjawed certainty I'll remember this one for the rest of my life" (Marion 91).

11. *Shaun of the Dead*, 2004.

12. Elizabeth Neal, "The Signification of the Zombie."

13. *Maggie*, 2015. All subsequent title quotes are from this film.

14. This is not to ignore the trauma of the event when Maggie is attacked, bitten, and infected. She has repeated flashbacks and nightmares of the event throughout the film. At one point, she awakes from a nightmare of this kind to find maggots eating the infected necrotic flesh on her arm.

15. For more on this idea and an expansion on "the myth of pure evil," see Roy Baumeister's *Evil: Inside Human Violence and Cruelty*, Holt Paperbacks, 1999.

16. It bears mentioning that this may not be the only reason Nazi zombies have been imagined. In her essay "The Rise and Fall—and Rise—of the Nazi Zombie in Film," Cynthia J. Miller argues that "The brute physicality of the zombie—decomposing predators, 'the great unwashed' of horror cinema—combined with the highly stylized, controlled, precise archetype of the Nazi ... [robs] the Nazi image of those elements which give it cultural power, and endowing a classically mindless creature with history and intent."

17. *Call of Duty: World at War* (2008).

18. Julia Kristeva, *Powers of Horror* (Columbia University Press, 1982), 3–4.

19. Under-rated *Carriers* (2009) (presenting a disease-ridden world rather than a zombie apocalypse, yet dealing with similar issues) has the lead characters say after committing some atrocities, "How did we get here?" "I don't know." "You know. We both know."

20. Shaka McGlotten and Steve Jones, eds. *Zombies and Sexuality: Essays on Desire and the Living Dead* (McFarland, 2014), 8.

21. Maggie also keeps wearing a necklace that Caroline gave her earlier in the film, which arguably indicates that Maggie does not blame her.

22. A Freudian/Elektra Complex analysis could be fecund here, but the film does not appear to explore this notion.

23. An example of this is in 2004's *Dawn of the Dead*, where Andre hides his infected

and pregnant wife from the rest of the group so he can keep her alive. Another is the infected teenagers entering mainland Europe in *28 Weeks Later* (2007).

24. Roland Barthes, *Image-Music-Text* (Hill and Wang, 1978).

25. Elizabeth Neal, "The Signification of the Zombie."

Works Cited

Barthes, Roland. *Image-Music-Text*. Hill and Wang, 1978.

Carriers. Directed by Alex and David Pastor. Paramount, 2009.

Dawn of the Dead. Directed by Zac Snyder, Universal, 2004.

Gross, Doug "Why We Love Those Rotting, Hungry, Putrid Zombies," *CNN.com*, October 2009, cnn.com/2009/SHOWBIZ/10/02/zombie.love/index.html?iref=nextn.

Kristeva, Julia. *Powers of Horror*. Columbia University Press, 1982.

Marion, Isaac. *Warm Bodies*. Atria/Emily Bestler Books, 2011.

McGlotten, Shaka, and Steve Jones, eds. *Zombies and Sexuality: Essays on Desire and the Living Dead*. McFarland, 2014.

Moreman, Christopher M., and Corey James Rushton, eds. *Race, Oppression, and the Zombie*. McFarland, 2011.

Maggie. Directed by Henry Hobson, Lionsgate, 2015.

Neal, Elizabeth "The Signification of the Zombie," *Hawaii University International Conferences*. http://www.huichawaii.org/assets/neail,-elizabeth---the-signification-of-the-zombie.pdf.

Parker, James. "Our Zombies, Ourselves," *The Atlantic*. Apr. 2011, theatlantic.com/magazine/archive/2011/04/our-zombies-ourselves/308401/.

Shaun of the Dead. Directed by Edgar Wright, StudioCanal, 2004.

28 Days Later. Directed by Danny Boyle, DNA Films, 2002.

Warm Bodies. Directed by Jonathan Levine, Summit Entertainment, 2013.

Wilentz, Amy. "A Zombie Is a Slave Forever." *New York Times*. 30 Oct. 2012, nytimes.com/2012/10/31/opinion/a-zombie-is-a-slave-forever.html.

Disaster Utopia and Survival Euphoria

(A)Sexuality in the Zombie (Post)Apocalypse

George J. Sieg

> "It was a great fucking time, the short era of disaster euphoria, for nothing enhances pleasures and blocks guilt like a looming cataclysm."—Alexsandar Hemon, *The Book of My Lives*

A superficial consideration of the post-apocalyptic and disaster genres might suggest their popularity to be cathartic, given their distressing content and tendency toward apparent realism. Vivid portrayals of panicked flight, looting, mayhem, lawlessness, and chaos, usually in a devastated contemporary setting, would seem to strike a familiar chord with the fears and anxieties of the present. The plausibility of such catastrophes appears to loom ever greater, and such a confrontation with dreads (of which the zombie horde is the most polyvalent and evocative) waiting just ahead of the everyday would seem at first glance to offer little of the escapism provided by the more fantastic elements of the broader horror genre. Instead, such depictions of doom suggest intense catharsis, even as their monumental tragedy is foregrounded by classic romances exemplifying the cinematic formation of the couple, or the personalized drama of a conventional nuclear family triumphing against a hostile world.

Yet, the irony is otherwise: such grim depictions only seem realistic due to extensive popular misconceptions about human behavior during and after disasters. The broad appeal of disaster fantasies is actually consonant with the generally beneficial psychological and social consequences of disasters (although there are some notable exceptions to this benign pattern, which I will address). The zombie romance presents a particular intersection of disaster and apocalypse, and its increasingly broad appeal spans demographics and has entered the mainstream of popular culture. With the rising popularity of AMC's *The Walking Dead* (2010–present), boasting a fifth season premiere which was the most watched show in cable television history, the zombie horde has undeniably eaten its way into the hearts and brains of the average television viewer, adding unexpected irony to the dire adage concerning the effect of television on brains. *The Walking Dead* is remarkable not only for its breakout popularity which finally broke the barricades against zombies in the living room in prime time but also for its deviation from the established cinematic tropes concerning positive depictions of survivor sexual intimacy during the zombie apocalypse; specifically, the lack thereof. Not only does *The Walking Dead* deviate from tradition obviously and consistently, it centralizes the role of intimate survivor relationships, both positive and negative, as critical to the story. The differences in human behavior in this context are so radical as to comparatively diminish the otherwise seemingly extreme variations in zombie behavior among examples in the genre (despite that the difference between slow and fast zombies is a matter of survivor life and death). But why does *The Walking Dead* vary so markedly from the subgenre's conventional desexualization of zombie apocalypse survivors, or its horror-genre-like tendency to doom those who transgress this invisible barricade, and among whom some of the most common transgressors are post-apocalyptic rapists? For that matter, where and how do such conventions originate, and how do they relate to what is known (or believed) about general human behavior during catastrophic circumstances?

For decades, psychologists and sociologists have been aware that the immediate aftermath responses of disaster victims are not only generally adaptive but most often subjectively positive. In many cases, such responses approach a kind of "disaster euphoria," but even most moderate responses tend to be much more positive than the grief, confusion, outrage, and trauma expected by those removed from the actual disaster, all of which suggest that the enthusiasm with which Zombie Response Teams look toward the coming "zombie apocalypse" (hereafter for brevity, frequently rendered as "zombocalypse") is not altogether irrational. In "How I Learned to Stop Worrying and Love the Zombie Apocalypse," in *The Walking Dead Psychology* (2015), Frank Gaskill describes his own experience of bonding with his Philadelphia suburban apartment community while snowed in with his wife for over two days, concluding that "The blizzard of 1996 is the closest personal reference I have to a zombie apocalypse" (Gaskill 2015). Aside from the zombie reference, such reports are by no means unusual. Sociologist Rebecca Solnit presents numerous cases in which disaster victims report experiences of joy and social bonding, even later recalling the time of disaster fondly. In her introduction to *A Paradise Built in Hell: The Extraordinary Communities That Arise in Disaster* (2009), she writes about social bonding:

> In the wake of an earthquake, a bombing, or a major storm, most people are altruistic, urgently engaged in caring for themselves and those around them, strangers and neighbors as well as friends and loved ones. The image of the selfish, panicky, or regressively savage human being in times of disaster has little truth to it. Decades of meticulous sociological research on behavior in disasters ... have demonstrated this [Solnit 2].

She continues to recount that, following the earthquake in California on October 17, 1989, "most of the people ... in the Bay Area were ... enjoying immensely the disaster that shut down much of the region for several days, the Bay Bridge for months, and certain unloved elevated freeways forever—if *enjoyment* is the right word for that sense of immersion in the moment and solidarity with others caused by the rupture in everyday life, an emotion graver than happiness but deeply positive" (Solnit 5). Kai Erikson summarizes previous references to "post-disaster euphoria" in his *A New Species of Trouble: The Human Experience of Modern Disasters* (1995), citing Anthony F.C. Wallace referencing the "stage of euphoria," and also noting the classic *Disaster: A Psychological Essay* (1957) by Martha Wolfenstein, which emphasized the communitarian formation of the "post-disaster utopia." Erikson describes renowned disaster sociologist Charles Fritz as referring to such scenarios as "therapeutic communities," but he emphatically contrasts such previous research on natural disasters with his own findings on the traumatic responses characterizing personal and community reactions to disasters perceived as human-made, a point I revisit later in more detailed analysis of the sense in which the zombocalypse can be characterized as a "disaster." Such a distinction remains debated; Solnit describes "that strange pleasure in disaster ... emerged after September 11, 2001, when many Americans ... abhorred what had happened, but ... clearly relished who they briefly became" (Solnit 5), while the human-made disasters in Erikson's work involve perceived betrayal or oppression by institutions, organizations, and governments—not criminal outsiders. Recent circumstances in which both factors are the case, such as the social disasters consequent to refugee crises such as in Germany, are too close at hand to yield consistent data thus far.

Nevertheless, euphoric responses of the type generally described by sociologists and psychologists have also been observed to occur in scenarios similar to, but not identical with, "disasters" proper. Various formal definitions of disaster have been suggested by disaster sociologists, but the most popular remains the original 1961 definition of Charles Fritz:

> actual or threatened uncontrollable events that are concentrated in time and space, in which a society, or a relatively self-sufficient subdivision of a society undergoes

> severe danger, and incurs such losses to its members and physical appurtenances that the social structure is disrupted and the fulfillment of all or some of the essential functions of the society, or its subdivision, is prevented [655].

More recently, Henry W. Fischer emphasizes a more exclusively sociological focus when he asks in response, "What are the various circumstances under which communities and societies suddenly diverge from partially or totally adhering to their prescribed social structure and temporarily or permanently replace it with an alternative?" (Fischer 93). Fischer also contrasts the sociological responses to disasters with those that perpetuate riot or revolution:

> When social structure emerges in response to emergent norms that define the situation as demanding a riot or a revolution, there is a perceived adversary. When social structure emerges in response to a potential or actual tornado, flood, and hazardous materials spill, the emergent norms demand a social structure that meets the collective needs, an adversary is normally absent. In what has been commonly labeled a "disaster" (really the disruption resulting from the "disaster" agent), the emergent social structure universally prescribes altruistic norms and roles as well as an initial social bonding among victims and responders. In riots and revolutions the initial social bonding occurs within separate groups that are in opposition to one another [Fischer 94].

Note that, here, Fischer observes commonalities in responses to both natural and man-made disasters which distinguish them from the other categories of social conflict (riot and revolution) which he mentions. Nevertheless, other scholars have observed similar processes at work in human conflict. Barrington Moore, Jr., in his work *Injustice: The Social Bases of Obedience and Revolt* (1978), writes describing the aftermath of the Social Democratic Party's long-forestalled proclamation in support of war in Germany, 1914:

> The most striking feature ... was an almost drunken sense of belonging together with everybody else in one huge social body ... there was great relief at the apparently sudden disappearance of the daily demands of a rather boring existence. Such sense of relief and belongingness resembles closely the "disaster euphoria" that modern investigators have observed to be the result of the temporary suspension of social routines and obligations in the wake of sudden disasters like floods, tornadoes, and hurricanes [Moore 226].

Given the commonalities observed in this range of catastrophes, Fischer concludes his inquiry into the definition of the disaster by considering the merits of the general usage:

> Perhaps our ongoing struggle to come to grips with what is a disaster (see Quarantelli 1998) is resolvable after all. I have grown weary of fighting the vernacular. Lay people, as evidenced in any dictionary (for example, see *The American Heritage Dictionary of the English Language*, 1992, p. 529), define "disaster" as "an occurrence causing widespread destruction and distress." Why not graciously accept the common usage? Why not accept that a disaster, simply put, is the mess that results from a

precipitous event which itself is the disaster agent or cause of the big mess? [Fischer 94]

As we will see, when zombies are proposed as the disaster agent, the mess conceived is a consuming one, in all its variations. Based on the vernacular definition, the zombocalypse is definitely a disaster, but it differs from natural disasters in presenting zombies as a perpetual threat with a degree of agency, however limited. The zombocalypse is sometimes caused through human malfeasance, but it is just as likely to manifest as a virus, plague, pestilence, or seemingly supernatural affliction. The othering of the zombies makes it reminiscent of war; their destruction of the social order reminds one of revolution. Yet, the zombocalypse is none of these things, precisely, and has become established as a unique category of disaster on a global scale, varyingly described as metaphorical fears of infection, terrorism, communism, capitalism, post capitalism, and "the latest scientific or cultural development" (Bishop 17). It is so distinct as a category that it even has its own section on the official website of the Center for Disease Control ("Zombie Preparedness").

Predictable patterns of human behavior seem to emerge in most zombie-induced post-apocalyptic scenarios which are distinct from general post-apocalyptic survivor-responses in fiction. Many of these tropes recur sufficiently to contribute to the formation of conventions concerning how survivors act after a zombocalypse. In comparing these expectations to real findings about disaster survivors, and to expectations for survivor behavior in post-apocalyptic fiction generally (certainly a broader and looser category), we can gain further insight into one aspect of the continuing appeal and popularity of this subgenre, as well as its significance as an indicator of popular conceptions about how behavior in disasters might interact with fears and projections about world-ending catastrophe.

This article focuses on just one of these conventions: with the notable exception of *The Walking Dead* (in both its print [2003–present] and screen incarnations), which will be discussed later, film survivors of a zombie apocalypse, even those who last beyond the immediate aftermath, in general seem to display little interest in intimate/romantic relationships or consistent sexual gratification. The emphasis on the "formation of the couple" generally observable in the broader "disaster genre" (just about any contemporary "disaster movie" features this trope) and, to a lesser extent, in some examples of the post-apocalyptic genre (*Mad Max: Fury Road* [2015] comes to mind, in the case of Nux [Nicholas Hoult] and Capable [Riley Keough]; both *The Postman* [1997] and *Waterworld* [1995] include more conventional romantic tensions), is almost entirely absent throughout zombie post-apocalypses. When it does occur, it is quite frequently subverted in some way. The film version of

Autumn (2009) pointedly implies and then frustrates the expectation of a sexual liaison between two of its protagonists; Zac Snyder's *Dawn of the Dead* (2004) ensures the heroic sacrifice of the protagonist, the only one of the survivors to form a new, serious intimate relationship.

Snyder's *Dawn* also seems to punish two supporting characters for their casual sex in horror-film fashion. Steve (Ty Burrell) is presented as a jerk whom the surviving female protagonist is foreshadowed to shoot in the head after his later zombification, and his casual partner, Monica (Kim Poirier), is presented as something of a bimbo who is scripted as unworthy of being killed dramatically by zombies at all, instead being accidentally killed by another survivor in an epically horrific motor-vehicle-crash chainsaw accident. This horror-movie sex logic continues in the appalling Steve Miner remake of *Day of the Dead* (2008), which manages to similarly punish early supporting characters for their promiscuity, and—just like Snyder's *Dawn*—*deny* the heroine the partnership formed in the course of the film by zombifying her male companion, though unlike the heroine of Snyder's *Dawn*, she never has the opportunity to consummate the relationship. Instead, Miner adapts Romero's training-receptive zombie "Bub" into "Private Bud" (Stark Sands), zombified vegetarian love-interest of the film's protagonist. Zombie Bud comes to her defense in a strange *Day of the Dead*/*Warm Bodies* (2013) cross-over, ironically demonstrating a zombie-human romance to be more survival-enhancing in this film than human intimacy. Such an irony in *Warm Bodies* is compounded through its presentation of significant survivor intimacy in flashback, though it somehow implies this to be the exception rather than a rule, reinforced by reflections on the part of the protagonist Julie's (Teresa Palmer) friend, Nora (Annaleigh Tipton), about the difficulty of finding mates in the small pool of survivors.

That said, films (and, in the first case, literature) like *Warm Bodies*, *Shaun of the Dead* (2004), and *Zombieland* (2009) are otherwise excluded from this analysis, for the reason that their sub-subgenre status as romantic comedies (*Warm Bodies*, despite its seemingly serious tone, is a comedic refashioning of *Romeo and Juliet* with zombies) provides thematic and plot constraints which skew their representation of the zombocalypse or post-apocalypse. Similarly, other sub-subgenre or exploitation films that focus on intimate human-zombie interactions are also ignored, as is the comedically oriented *Return of the Living Dead* (1985–2005) film series, as well as *Pride and Prejudice and Zombies* (2016), due to its constraints as a concept-parody.

In summary, and again noting the exception of *The Walking Dead* to be considered later, film survivors of zombie (post) apocalypses seem to be significantly less interested in intimate relationships than survivors of comparable non-zombie calamities, and less successful at continuing them even when they are, or might become, interested. George A. Romero's entire film series lacks significant attention to this issue, foiling the possible romantic aspirations of a male protagonist in *Survival of the Dead* (2009) with the death of the woman he began to develop interest in, and avoiding the issue among the soldiers in the film by creating the female soldier in the group as lesbian.

Even John Wyndham's zombie-like, shambolic vegetal predators, the Triffids, dubbed by scholar Nicole LaRose as "ZnZs" ("zombies that are not zombies," a concept akin to zombie scholar Jamie Russell's "zombies-by-proxy" [Russell 2014]), along with the ZnZ survivors whom they threaten, stumbling about a post-apocalyptic world (in which Wyndham focuses on London and the surrounding countryside) blinded after a spectacular meteor shower which commences the *Day of the Triffids* (1962), do not seem to be as preventative of human intimacy as actual zombies, the formation-of-the-couple following reasonably predictable lines in the course of the *Day of the Triffids* in its various re-presentations, ranging through the original novel to radio, film, and television. LaRose situates both the *Day of the Triffids* and *28 Days Later* (2002) (its concept directly inspired by Wyndham's work [Kermode 2007], particularly the opening scenes, including the hospital scene itself resumed to commence *The Walking Dead*) in the context of modern British history in her contribution to the anthology *Generation Zombie* (La Rose). Her article is preceded by Terry Harpold's describing Wyndham's Triffid "cozy catastrophe" (a post-apocalyptic subgenre in 1950s–1970s British science fiction presenting an apocalyptic calamity), which Harpold defines as "global in its effects but guarded in terms of the damage it leaves behind" (Harpold 157) as a thematically and structurally equivalent precursor to the "zombie cozy," which Harpold suggests as a "strain" of the "classic cozy" which includes the now equally classic shambling hordes as "a stupid but implacable menace that threatens survivors and forces them to remain barricaded (though never for long) or in constant flight" after "the rupture of a sudden catastrophe" (Harpold 158–59). Yet despite the close similarity of Wyndham's cozy to the zombocalypse, survivor intimacy seems to be significantly less inhibited in the *Day of the Triffids*, a condition that is the case throughout the "cozy" subgenre.

28 Days Later considers post-apocalyptic sexual intimacy only in the context of brutality and coercion, presenting British soldiers as intending to justify systematic gang-rape as a method of repopulation. (A less systematic or justified expression of military sexual aggression against helpless survivors seems to be the sole reference to sexuality in the first two volumes of Manel Loureiro's *Apocalypse Z* series [Loureiro 57–58].) The subsequent British zombocalypse *The Zombie Diaries* (2007), its sequel *World of the Dead: The Zombie Diaries* (2011), and *Night of the Living Dead: Resurrection* (2012), which attempts to transport Romero's farmhouse to Wales, also feature survivor rape, as does Taiwanese *Z108* (2012). Sexual coercion and domination both appear in *The Walking Dead*, as well as in attempted form in the acclaimed PlayStation game *The Last of Us* (2013).

An expansion to *The Last of Us*, entitled *Left Behind* (2014), also features experimental adolescent lesbian sexuality. Lesbian intimacy is a major theme in the *As the World Dies* trilogy of Rhiannon Frater (2008–2012), which eventually culminates with the marriage of a bisexual protagonist to a male hero, followed by a pregnancy. Sexual violence is certainly present, however, in zombie literature. Brian Keene's *The Rising* (2003) is a particularly iconic example, featuring a "Meat Wagon" in which surviving U.S. National Guardsmen (exemplifying a classic institutional attempt to preserve control of survivor populations) imprison surviving women as sex slaves and features multiple rape scenes (Keene, 145–148; 239–240; 253; 281; 287–289; 293–294). No consensual survivor sex occurs anywhere in the 339-page novel. Nevertheless, intimate relationships do seem to fare somewhat better, generally, in zombie literature than in zombie film, although they tend to follow formation-of-the-couple conventions more rarely and appear more likely to emphasize less conventional relationships. Sophie Littlefield's *Aftertime* trilogy (2011–2012) presents a full spectrum of intimate behaviors conditioned by post-apocalyptic circumstances, ranging from "manic ... hookups" to those who remain "dead inside" (Littlefield, *Aftertime*, 75). The protagonist, Cass, is herself described as having "been with so many [men that] ... by Sunday, she couldn't remember the name of the one she'd brought home Friday." This is explained as "Not a hunger for the coupling itself, but a need to beat her pain and confusion into a thing that could be contained again" (Littlefield, *Aftertime*, 63). The second novel in the series almost immediately introduces a new focus to her erotic desires, Dor, an investor before the zombocalypse, who previous to his introduction in the story ran "the Box, a fenced-in pleasure mart" (Littlefield, *Rebirth: An Aftertime Novel*, 30). Despite the illicit nature of their lust-driven relationship, "neither of them had been able to stop. Not once" (Littlefield, *Rebirth: An Aftertime Novel*, 32). Dor's daughter, Sammi, reflects on the behavior of the adults, summarizing, "...evidently Aftertime meant that parents could just fuck around and do whatever they felt like" (Littlefield, *Rebirth: An Aftertime Novel*, 37). Disaster utopia indeed, with intermittent doses of illicit erotic survival euphoria. As a final example, Joe McKinney presents a single near-kiss in the second book of his *Deadworld* series, *Apocalypse of the Dead* (2010). The hero, Billy, saves a character named Kyra from imminent death, and "They were very close at that moment, their lips only inches apart. He could taste the wintergreen coolness of her breath. In a movie, he'd have kissed her then. But this was really happening" (McKinney 488). Based on the conventions of the subgenre, that movie would presumably not have been a zombocalypse film, however.

Data on human intimacy and sexual behavior in disasters is sparse. Aside from data suggesting that the rates of rape rose dramatically in the aftermath of Hurricane Katrina ("Hurricanes Katrina/Rita and Sexual Violence"), there has been little systematical sociological research on this subject. Aside from the *Deadworld* scenario which combines the zombocalypse with a Gulf Coast hurricane, the rising of the dead seems to have little in common with natural disasters. Yet, as we have seen in this brief survey of scenarios of intimacy in zombocalypse fiction, its comparatively frequent references to rape scenarios appear as accurate as its offering of "disaster/survival euphoria" through the formation of organic new communities. Solnit's model combined with the limited data from the Katrina studies seems to be broadly reflected throughout the subgenre, though the greatest emphasis on survivors forming new lives and communities appears in *The Walking Dead*, perhaps due to its longer timeline and its emphasis on human social interactions generally:

> The post-apocalyptic world is one in which it is hard to take anything for granted. Having lost their quotidian luxuries and possessions, survivors are forced to acknowledge and appreciate the simple pleasures of companionship.... The protagonists [of *The Walking Dead*] are visibly concerned about finding food, shelter, and weapons, as is characteristic of post-apocalyptic narratives. However, these details are mechanical rather than pivotal.... The primary concern ... is attaining and sustaining human contact ... to find a suitable home in which to settle down, begin anew, and very importantly, to fornicate [Vossen 90].

Yet, despite the distressingly high rates of sexual violence reported after Katrina, there is no evidence that natural disasters—especially those which present opportunities for survival euphoria—inhibit nonviolent intimacy. This article earlier considered Erikson's research that disaster euphoria is significantly mitigated when institutions and agencies are blamed for the disaster, but such a condition could only potentially apply to zombocalypses which occur due to human endeavors gone awry, such as *28 Days Later*.

Considering zombies as "the infected" or resulting from the spread of contagion suggests possible comparisons to human behavior during virulent plagues. Yet even the various influenza pandemics never approached sufficiently apocalyptic proportions to present a relevant analogy. Only consideration of the Black Death of medieval Europe might offer some insight. Gordon Taylor, citing Nohl (1926), refers to "the wave of frantic debauchery which followed in the wake of the Black Death," but despite the overwhelming prevalence of Christianity in Western societies, which are usually the prime focus of zombocalypse fiction, the comparison would seem to be confounded by the particularities of medieval Catholicism, and the significant differences between medieval and post-medieval society. Contemporary chroniclers of the plague were in any case more likely to take note of significant deviance such as the "pseudo-flagellants" who proceeded from city to city performing sexual acts instead of self-mortification, than to make systematic observations about more ordinary sexual responses and behaviors (Taylor).

Before offering new speculations on this peculiar feature of the zombocalypse subgenre, a brief consideration of potentially relevant scholarly analysis of different but related aspects may be helpful. One anthology on *Zombies and Sexuality* (2014) has been published by McFarland, edited by Shaka McGlotten and Steve Jones. While most of its articles focus on specialized readings of particular zombie media, particularly queer readings, Emma Vossen's article on *The Walking Dead* addresses survivor intimacy in a broader sense: "What makes this series such a distinct artifact in the saturated zombie subgenre is the prominent roles that sex and relationships play in sustaining the storyline" (Vossen 91). Vossen ties *The Walking Dead*'s focus on intimacy directly to what she terms its "apocalyptic expectation" for a scenario which clearly embodies a Solnitian "disaster utopia," in which the survivors themselves seek to find, create, and ultimately, to live, summarizing "in contrast to the difficulties we face in the real world, the apocalyptic world presents romantic fantasies of falling in love and building a family that seem worth pursuing. The apocalypse essentially offers utopian escapism" (Vossen 91). Considering what factors make *The Walking Dead* an exception to the general desexualization of zombie narratives, Vossen quotes Robert Kirkman, creator of *The Walking Dead*, as identifying himself as "the Stephenie Meyer of Zombies" and as having deliberately introduced romance into the mold of Romero's zombie apocalypse (Vossen 94).

Yet, unlike the zombedies and zom-rom-coms excluded earlier from this article's analysis, *The Walking Dead* remains an iconic representative of the standard zombie (post) apocalypse subgenre, due to its serious delivery and its refusal to adopt comedic, romantic, or parodic tropes. However, the question remains: is its realism *due to*, or *in spite of*, its depiction of post-apocalyptic life as a relationship oriented "soap opera" in a post-apocalyptic "disaster utopian" setting? Vossen's reading of the text is that *The Walking Dead* functions as a disaster utopia precisely because the confining institutions of postmodern late capitalism are abolished, offering Millennials and Generation Z a literally romantic fantasy of domestic and sexual fulfillment. Such an interpretation would also be supported by evolutionary psychological models suggesting that human beings remain most adapted to the lifestyle which prevailed for the vast majority of human evolutionary history: small hunter-gatherer tribes. Such a model, combined with both the sociological research on survivor behavior during natural disasters (and the "elite panic" which often opposes utopian and euphoric community responses, as embodied in *The Walking Dead* by the Governor of Woodbury [David Morrissey]), both adaptive and otherwise (in the cases of statistics concerning sexual violence, also depicted in *The Walking Dead*) implies that the post-apocalyptic world of *The Walking Dead* registers as realistic precisely because it accords with what is known, however little, about the spectrum of responses likely to occur in human survivors in the presented conditions. The popularity of the rest of the zombocalypse subgenre despite its more limited inclusion of human intimacy (often limited to aversive and frustrated expressions in the film genre) seems to demonstrate the "apocalyptic expectation" described by Vossen: audiences are attracted to the liberating possibility of an apocalyptic disaster even if it is presented as a pessimistic dystopia, and according to Solnit, it is common for those outside the immediate area of the disaster to presume its effects to be horrifically traumatic even when that is not the case for the survivors themselves.

That *The Walking Dead* seems to be an exception to the cinematic trend against survivor intimacy may be due to its origins as graphic novel, with this more literary form only later adapted for the screen; the earlier survey and analysis in this article included a number of examples of survivor intimacy being realistically addressed in literature, but demonstrated that its introduction in Romero remakes has been generally limited to horror tropes or pessimistic frustrations. Vossen emphasizes that *The Walking Dead* depicts characters dispensing with the rituals of courtship and mating tropes generally enshrined by "formation of the couple" narratives, such as those that appear more persistently in disaster and post-apocalyptic fiction generally. This seems to be a clue to the absence of such narratives generally in the zombie apocalypse subgenre beyond *The Walking Dead*: the zombie post-apocalypse almost uniformly rejects these tropes, and their inclusion seems to automatically segregate the zomedy and zom-rom-com from the rest of the genre as a whole. *The Walking Dead* reintroduces intimacy, sexuality, and romance without resorting to those tropes, and therefore retains its kinship with the broader genre, despite that it superficially appears more comparable with the zombedies in its level of emphasis on relationships.

The Walking Dead is clearly exceptional, but why does the zombie subgenre in general so depend on rejecting "formation of the couple" tropes, which do not seem out of place in the context of natural disasters or post-apocalypses generally? Following Vossen's observations that those characters in *The Walking Dead* who cling to pre-apocalyptic life seem to be the worst adapted to new circumstances (and therefore likely to perish), it could be the case that the utopian possibilities offered by the zombocalypse are only utopian when accompanied by the abandonment of the norms of the vanquished status quo. The formation of the couple in other fictional disasters and apocalypses serves to illustrate a restoration of the lost social order: the euphoria of these disasters and apocalypses is more akin to the carnival, which by definition is a temporarily liminal circumstance which can produce a revitalizing effect on the social body. Ironically, Kyle William Bishop interprets the (Anne) Ricification of the zombie into a romanticized, or at least popularized, monstrous identity to be adopted as well as dreaded (not only in the increasingly sympathetic zombies of *Warm Bodies* and *iZombie* [2015–present], but also in the phenomena of zombie walks and crawls) as also having a carnivalesque function (Bishop 26–38). Bishop's theory supports the model developed here by providing a striking contrast. *Temporarily* becoming a zombie is in a sense quite similar to *temporarily* being stripped of conventional social roles and thrust into a scenario of communitas. As such, the permanent "zombocalypse" which confronts survivors and forces them to distinguish themselves from the zombie horde in order to live renders a return to the pre-zombocalyptic social order untenable. While the carnival of a zombie crawl ends, the perpetual revolt and permanent anarchy of the actual zombocalypse never ends. The old order has been overthrown, and survival is only achievable when this is recognized.

Romero's continual indictment of various aspects of American culture through the course of his original zombocalypse repeatedly emphasizes the unsustainability and unsuitability of the vanquished social order. This would seem to indicate the unsustainability and unsuitability of the "formation of the couple" as well. The Romero remakes go further and illustrate not only the absence, but the direct destruction, of pre-zombocalyptic modes of intimacy. LuAnne Roth and Kate Shoults also note that "Romero's films typically require females to assume typically masculine traits, such as firing weapons or becoming ruthless, but the supposed shucking of binary norms rarely works the other way (forcing men to cook, clean, or assume caretaking roles). Performing masculinity is assumed to be enough to ensure survival" (Roth and Shoults 229). In this interpretation, Romero presents the zombocalypse as invalidating the gender binary which is a significant feature of romantic couple formation in the pre-apocalyptic setting, implying the question of what, if any, mode of relationship might replace it. That *The Walking Dead* attempts to present one possible answer to Romero's implicit question illustrates its central importance to the subgenre and further demonstrates the incompatibility of the conventional formation of the couple with its attendant standard courtship, with the disaster utopia offered (or even, required for survival) in the zombocalypse. Yet, as clearly demonstrated by Cathy Hannabach in her article "Queering and Cripping the End of the World: Disability, Sexuality and Race in *The Walking Dead*," the "hetero-normative nuclear family" is very much central to its disaster utopia (Hannabach 106–19). It seems, then, that the zombocalypse revolts against and overthrows not only traditional socially constructed modes of romantic courtship, but also against contemporary expectations about their applicability to less conventional relationships as well. Survivors in *The Walking Dead* concern themselves neither with the established patterns of heteronormative courtship nor with establishing similarly contrived recognition of "queer" relationships. Neither have they simply reverted to primordial, tribal social structure, or attempted to restore the features of the vanished society. While Roth and Shoults argue that *The Walking Dead* is blatantly and persistently patriarchal, they also consider the possibility that a patriarchal society would continue to be so after an apocalypse. While the latter speculation seems to be plausible, insofar as basic cultural norms tend to remain stable even in disastrous circumstances, Roth and Shoults' critique seems determined to blur the distinction between the series' own message concerning patriarchy, or lack of such a message, and its attempt to realistically depict the behavior of the characters. Their conclusion cites research "that, as a group, women are likely to respond, experience, and be affected by disasters in ways that are qualitatively different" (Roth and Shoults citing Morrow and Phillips), and that women frequently under rate their own performance and thereby contribute to their own subordination. However, Roth and Shoults criticize fiction that aspires to realism for not addressing this problem by presenting female characters that vary from these patterns, somewhat paradoxically concluding that "Women need art to start mimicking real life by proving that reliance on patriarchy will only decrease the chance for survival." Yet, in the same article, Roth and Shoults previously establish that Romero's originally realistic but pessimistic portrayal of Barbra (Judith O'Dea) depicted her demise with that very intention. Further, they seem to largely ignore the difference between some characters' deliberate, self-conscious attempts to restore or retain pre-apocalyptic social norms, and the tendency for habitual attitudes and expectations to persist in individual characters, and this Roth and Shoults analysis blurs the distinction between description and prescription. Survivors in *The Walking Dead* continually define themselves against the unending undifferentiated homogeneity of the walkers, tying their performance of intimacy directly to both their own survival and the survival of their community. Andrea's (Laurie Holden) relationship with Rick (Andrew Lincoln) returns him to life after Lori's (Sarah Wayne Callies) death, restoring him fully to the community after his zombicidal rampage through the prison, in which he is depicted as so gory as to resemble the walkers themselves; in the graphic novel, it also allows Andrea to resume the vitality and maturity that she experienced through her intimacy with Dale. Glenn (Steven Yeun) and Maggie (Lauren Cohan), in each other, gain a focus and purpose which enhances their dedication to the community. Until Rick's return, Shane (Jon Bernthal) and Lori establish their relationship in the context of survival in the newly hostile world. All of these examples depict characters enacting their own pre-apocalyptic inclinations unfiltered through social contrivance.

In summary, the zombocalypse offers the complete abolition of large-scale, institutionalized social engineering (including the type of deliberate contrivance Roth and Shoults recommend as an antidote to chauvinism), and this is part of its appeal. This condition seems to be a prevailing feature of every zombocalypse: the community of survivors, in whatever form it takes, is automatically contrasted with the mass of undead, whose loss of individuality and identity is a constant reminder of what happens to those who lose themselves to unconsciousness, whether in the form of carelessness or misfortune, or in the form of identification with some non-sustainable mode of life. Instead of the familiar opposition of the individual to the community, the individual in synergy with the community is opposed to the anti-communitas of the zombie, which has no relationship with the other zombies in the horde and yet has no individuality either. The presence of the walking dead/living dead/undead ensures that the group of survivors has an external reminder of the consequences of allowing individuality or community to overwhelm or negate each other and provides the necessary environment for a unique kind of disaster utopia: one which has the opportunity to establish itself as self-renewing, in contrast to the many "failed states" of the zombocalypse, particularly well-represented by Romero's Fiddler's Green in *Land of the Dead* (2004). Whether or not he is to be regarded as a good leader, or described as filling the role of a "patriarch," Rick Grimes does not embody or represent an "institution" in the same way that the Governor does. The realistic presentation of sexual violence by the Governor exemplifies the subgenre's frequent condemnation of elite attempts to retain control in the midst of disaster, and it presents a strong contrast to the organic expression of individual mating preferences (without regard to their social desirability) in the protagonists' community of survivors.

That *The Walking Dead* is presently unique in its near-total focus on survivor intimacy suggests that its outstanding popularity may inspire responses featuring very different interpretations of intimate behavior on the part of zombocalypse survivors. All of the examples considered in this article serve to demonstrate that the popularity of the subgenre is due, at least in part, to its largely accurate portrayal of (and direct appeal to) the yearning for a "disaster utopia" and attendant "survival euphoria," both of which fulfill apocalyptic anticipation and expectation. Colson Whitehead's novel *Zone One* (2011), set during three days of the post-zombocalyptic cleanup of New York City, even illustrates this concept with the same term; when the barricades against the remaining undead finally, climactically fall, Whitehead says of his protagonist's return to disaster-survival-mode that "he'd entered a state of tremulous euphoria" (312).

The utopia and euphoria of the zombocalypse are distinct in that they present the possibility of their post-historical persistence, in perpetual contrast to the walking/living dead as shambling signifiers of the historical reality overcome and then trapped, fixed in a carnivalesque condition of necrotic liminality. Since the zombies are necessarily *our own remains*, never to be completely buried or forgotten, they offer the opportunity for social convention, particularly concerning sexual behavior, intimacy, mate selection, and romance, to be revealed—and rejected—as equivalent to an unconscious state of indiscriminate reproduction-through-consumption. Whatever intimacies are ultimately embraced by the survivors of any zombie apocalypse, they are initially enabled by the negation of the social norms and conventions of their predecessors in history who progressed from forming units of the unliving, standardized, conventional couple to forming the mass of the undead, undifferentiated, devouring horde.

Works Cited

Autumn. Directed by Steven Rumbelow, Renegade Motion Pictures, 2009.

Bishop, Kyle William. *How Zombies Conquered Popular Culture: The Multifarious Walking Dead in the 21st Century*. McFarland, 2015.

Darabont, Frank, creator. *The Walking Dead*. AMC, 2010–present.

Dawn of the Dead. Directed by Zac Snyder, Strike Entertainment, 2004.

Day of the Dead. Directed by Steve Miner, Millennium Films, 2008.

Erikson, Kai. *A New Species of Trouble: The Human Experience of Modern Disasters*. Norton, 1995.

Fischer, Henry W. "The Sociology of Disaster: Definitions, Research Questions, & Measurements; Continuation of the Discussion in a Post-September 11 Environment." *International Journal of Mass Emergencies and Disasters*, vol. 21, no. 1, March 2003, pp. 91–107.

Frater, Rhiannon. *As the World Dies* series. Tor, 2008–2012.

Fritz, Charles. *Disasters and Mental Health: Therapeutic Principles Drawn from Disaster Studies*. University of Delaware, 1961.

Gaskill, Frank. "How I Learned to Stop Worrying and Love the Zombie Apocalypse." *The Walking Dead Psychology: Psych of the Living Dead*, edited by Travis Langley, Sterling, 2015, pp. 9–19.

Hannabach, Cathy. "Queering and Cripping the End of the World: Disability, Sexuality, and Race in *The Walking Dead*." *Zombies and Sexuality: Essays on Desire and the Living Dead*, edited by Shaka McGlotten and Steve Jones. McFarland, 2014, pp. 106–122.

Harpold, Terry. "The End Begins: John Wyndham's Zombie Cozy." *Generation Zombie: Essays on the Living Dead in Modern Culture*, edited by Stephanie Boluk and Wylie Lenz. McFarland, 2011, pp. 156–64.

Hemon, Alexsandar. *The Book of My Lives*. Picador, 2013.

"Hurricanes Katrina/Rita and Sexual Violence: Report on Database of Sexual Violence Prevalence and Incidence Related to Hurricanes Katrina and Rita." *National Sexual Violence Resource Center*. Jul. 2006. www.nsvrc.org/sites/default/files/Publications_NSVRC_Reports_Report-on-Database-of-Sexual-Violence-Prevalence-and-Incidence-Related-to-Hurricane-Katrina-and-Rita.pdf.

Keene, Brian. *The Rising*. Deadite Press, 2013.

Kermode, Alan. "A Capital Place for Panic Attacks." *The Guardian*. 6 May 2007. www.theguardian.com/film/2007/may/06/features.review.

Kirkman, Robert. *The Walking Dead*, Compendiums 1–3. Image, 2012–2016.

Land of the Dead. Directed by George A. Romero, Atmosphere Entertainment, 2005.

LaRose, Nicole. "Zombies in a 'Deep, Dark Ocean of History': Danny Boyle's Infected and John Wyndham's Triffids as Metaphors of Postwar Britain." *Generation Zombie: Essays on the Living Dead in Modern Culture*, edited by Stephanie Boluk and Wylie Lenz. McFarland, 2011, pp. 165–81.

Littlefield, Sophie. *Aftertime*. Luna, 2011.

Littlefield, Sophie. *Rebirth: An Aftertime Novel.* Luna, 2012.
Loureiro, Manel. *The Beginning of the End: Apocalypse Z.* AmazonCrossing, 2012.
Mad Max: Fury Road. Directed by George Miller, Village Roadshow Pictures, 2015.
McKinney, Joe. *Apocalypse of the Dead.* Pinnacle, 2012.
Moore, Barrington, Jr. *Injustice: The Social Bases of Obedience and Revolt.* Sharpe, 1978.
Night of the Living Dead: Resurrection. Directed by James Plumb, North Bank Entertainment, 2012.
Nohl, Johannes. *The Black Death: A Chronicle of the Plague.* Unwin, 1926.
The Postman. Directed by Kevin Costner, Warner Bros., 1997.
Pride and Prejudice and Zombies. Directed by Burr Steers, Lionsgate, 2016.
Roth, LuAnne and Kate Shoults. "'Three men, and the place is surrounded': Reel Women in the Zombie Apocalypse." *...But If a Zombie Apocalypse Did Occur: Essays on Medical, Military, Governmental, Ethical, Economic, and Other Implications*, edited by Amy L. Thompson and Antonio S. Thompson. McFarland, 2015, pp. 227–45.
Russell, Jamie. *Book of the Dead: The Complete History of Zombie Cinema* (Updated and Fully Revised Edition). Titan, 2014.
Shaun of the Dead. Directed by Edgar Wright, StudioCanal, 2004.
Solnit, Rebecca. *A Paradise Built in Hell: The Extraordinary Communities That Arise in Disaster.* Penguin, 2009.
Survival of the Dead. Directed by George A. Romero, Artfire Films, 2009.
Taylor, Gordon Rattray. *Sex in History.* Vanguard, 1954.
Vossen, Emma. "Laid to Rest: Romance, End of the World Sexuality, and Apocalyptic Anticipation in Robert Kirkman's *The Walking Dead*." *Zombies and Sexuality: Essays on Desire and the Living Dead*, edited by Shaka McGlotten and Steve Jones. McFarland, 2014, pp. 88–105.
Warm Bodies. Directed by Jonathan Levine, Mandeville Films, 2013.
Waterworld. Directed by Kevin Reynolds, Gordon Company, 1995.
Whitehead, Colson. *Zone One.* Anchor, 2012. First printing Doubleday, 2011.
Wolfenstein, Martha. *Disaster: A Psychological Essay.* Free Press, 1957.
World of the Dead: The Zombie Diaries. Directed by Michael Bartlett and Kevin Gates, Dimension Films, 2011.
Wyndham, John. *The Day of the Triffids.* Crest, 1951.
The Zombie Diaries. Directed by Kevin Gates and Michael Bartlett, Offworld Films and Bleeding Edge Films, 2006.
"Zombie Preparedness." *Centers for Disease Control and Prevention.* 10 Apr. 2015. www.cdc.gov/phpr/zombies.htm.
Zombieland. Directed by Ruben Fleischer, Relativity Media, 2009.

About the Contributors

Jack D. **Arnal** is a cognitive psychologist and associate professor of psychology at McDaniel College in Westminster, Maryland. He specializes in human memory, research methods, and statistics. You can find his work in various psychology journals. He also teaches courses about the science of zombies and *Doctor Who*.

Simon **Bacon** is an independent scholar based in Poznan, Poland. He has contributed articles to many publications on vampires, monstrosity, science fiction, and media studies and has authored or coedited *Undead Memory* (2014), *Seductive Concepts* (2014), *Little Horrors* (2016) and *Becoming Vampire* (2016).

Jennifer Huss **Basquiat** is a professor of anthropology at the College of Southern Nevada in Las Vegas. She earned her Ph.D. in cultural studies from Claremont Graduate University and an M.A. in communication studies from California State University, Los Angeles. She is working on an ethnographic study on polygamous communities in northern Arizona.

Kyle William **Bishop** is a professor at Southern Utah University, where he directs the Honors Program and teaches courses in film and screen studies, American literature and culture, and fantasy/horror literature. He has published articles on popular culture and cinematic adaptation, two monographs on zombies, and a collection of essays on literary zombies, coedited with Angela Tenga.

Whitney **Cox** is an adjunct professor in the religious studies and women's, gender, and sexuality studies departments at the University of Houston. She earned her Ph.D. from Temple University. Her work focuses on Christianity, sexuality, and AIDS, though she likes fictional epidemics better than real ones.

Jennifer Rachel **Dutch** has a Ph.D. in American studies from the Pennsylvania State University, Harrisburg. Her dissertation explored the shifting practices and meanings of home cooking traditions in American culture. She teaches a variety of writing and literature courses at York College.

Connor **Jackson** is an M.A. film and media graduate from Edge Hill University, UK. His thesis explores the influence of widespread terrorist-related paranoia on digital depictions of the undead as well as their surrounding iconographies. His research interests include representations of gender, sexuality, and zombies.

Ashley Ruth **Lierman** is the instructional design librarian at the University of Houston. She received her Ph.D. in American religious history from Drew University. Her dissertation focused on interactions between gay and lesbian activist organizations and Christian right organizations during the AIDS epidemic of the 1980s and early 1990s.

William A. **Lindenmuth** is an associate professor of philosophy at Shoreline College. He received his M.A. in philosophy from the New School for Social Research. He specializes in normative ethics and moral psychology and has contributed to numerous anthologies on philosophy and culture.

Paul **Muhlhauser** is an assistant professor of English at McDaniel College in Westminster, Maryland. He received his M.A. and Ph.D. in English, rhetoric, and composition from Washington State University. His work has appeared in *Harlot*, *Women and Language*, and *Computers and Composition Online*.

Fernando Gabriel **Pagnoni Berns** is a Ph.D. student who works as a professor at the Universidad de Buenos Aires (UBA)—Facultad de Filosofía y Letras (Argentina). He teaches seminars on horror film and has published essays in *To See the Saw Movies* and *Reading Richard Matheson*, among others.

Amy Carol **Reeves** has a Ph.D. in nineteenth-century British literature from the University of South Carolina. She is an independent scholar as well as the associate editor for *Girls Studies*. Apart from publishing academic articles, she also writes young adult novels including paranormal historical fiction.

Jessica K. **Richards** has an M.A. in English with an emphasis in literature from Weber State University in Ogden, Utah, where she also works as an adjunct instructor. Her studies deal with gothic/sensation fiction in the late Victorian period. She has presented at national and regional conferences on contemporary culture.

Canela Ailen **Rodriguez Fontao** is an M.A. student at the Facultad de Filosofía y Letras, Universidad de Buenos Aires (UBA), Argentina. She has published essays in *Cine y Revolución en America Latina*, *Bullying in Popular Culture*, *Deconstructing Dads* and *Representations of Cruel Children in Popular Texts*.

Scott **Rogers** is a professor of English at Weber State University. He earned his Ph.D. in English from Oklahoma State University in 18th and 19th-century British literature. He teaches and publishes on popular culture, including articles in *The Journal of the Fantastic in the Arts* and *Victorian Transformations*, among others.

George J. **Sieg** has a Ph.D. in Western esotericism from the Exeter Centre for the Study of Esotericism. His research interests include the (post)-apocalyptic genre, New Religious Movements, occultism and occulture, deviance, alternative worldviews, radicalism, extremism, and dualism.

Ashley **Szanter** is an adjunct instructor teaching college composition at Weber State University. Her research deals with cultural monsters and monstrosity and 19th-century monster fiction. She is the chair of the Monster Studies and Pedagogy panel at the Rocky Mountain Modern Language Association regional conference and a regular attendee and presenter in the SWPACA Zombie Culture area.

Amanda **Taylor** has an M.A. in English composition and rhetoric and is a lecturer at California State University, San Bernardino. In addition to zombies and other monsters, her research interests include *Supernatural, Doctor Who, Firefly,* and *Futurama* as well as John Keats, science fiction, the cultural studies of science, and posthuman theory.

Patricia **Vazquez** has an M.A. from the Universidad de Buenos Aires (UBA)—Facultad de Filosofía y Letras (Argentina). She is a lecturer in horror cinema and popular culture. She integrates the research group on horror cinema "Grite." Her work has appeared in *Lindes, Gothic and Racism*, and *Projecting the World.*

Index